Thomas Hughes

Loyola

and the educational system of the Jesuits

Thomas Hughes

Loyola
and the educational system of the Jesuits

ISBN/EAN: 9783744648493

Printed in Europe, USA, Canada, Australia, Japan

Cover: Foto ©Lupo / pixelio.de

More available books at **www.hansebooks.com**

LOYOLA.

The Great Educators

Edited by NICHOLAS MURRAY BUTLER

LOYOLA

AND

THE EDUCATIONAL SYSTEM OF THE JESUITS

BY

THE REVEREND THOMAS HUGHES
OF THE SOCIETY OF JESUS

NEW YORK
CHARLES SCRIBNER'S SONS
1892

PREFACE.

In the following work on the Educational System of the Jesuits, I have endeavored to present a critical statement of the principles and method adopted in the Society of Jesus. The effort to explain the sources, process of development, and present influence of the system within and without the Order, has made of the first part a biographical and historical sketch, having for its chief subject the person of the Founder; while the details and the pedagogical significance of the various elements in the method appear, in the second part, as a critical analysis of the *Ratio Studiorum.*

The educational literature which treats of this system is very extensive. Various estimates and conclusions have been arrived at, on the merits of documents frequently referred to, for an exposition of the meaning and philosophy of the system. Hence, with the view of facilitating a clear and comprehensive judgment on the subject, I have thought it not inadvisable to quote accurately from such documents, omitting none which bore upon the matter, if only they were within reach. It so happens that, at present, a large number of the sources, regulations, and commentaries, heretofore rare and altogether out of reach, have been rendered easy of access, being embodied in the great work, *Monumenta Germaniæ Pædagogica,* which is already beyond its tenth volume. Three of the volumes so far issued are upon the Jesuit System; they have been compiled by the late Rev. G. M. Pachtler, S.J. If the three or four volumes, which still remain to be issued by the Rev. Bernard Duhr, S.J., had been available, they too could have been laid under contribution for examples and illustrations. But perhaps the theme will appear sufficiently illustrated as it is.

Besides the original documents, I have used no less authentic an exponent than that which the maxim of law approves: *Consuetudo, optima legis interpres,* "Custom, which is the best interpreter of law."

While all that is oldest and most authentic has thus been made use of in explaining the *Ratio Studiorum,* the actual condition of pedagogics to-day is new, and so is the state of the question involved. Hence, to satisfy the requirements of the present, reference has been made not exclusively either to the customs or the learned documents of a former age.

In a word, the object aimed at has been to indicate the chief traits which are characteristic of the system, and which may be suggestive in the development of pedagogical science. Whether such an object has been attained, so as to meet many questions which may possibly arise, and to satisfy the desire which actually exists, it will be for others to decide.

THOMAS HUGHES, S.J.

St. Louis University.

CONTENTS.

	PAGE
PREFACE	v

PART I.

EDUCATIONAL HISTORY OF THE ORDER.

CHAPTER I.
INTRODUCTION 3

CHAPTER II.
KNIGHT, PILGRIM, AND SCHOLAR 19

CHAPTER III.
THE UNIVERSITY OF PARIS. ROME 30

CHAPTER IV.
COLLEGES AS PROPOSED IN THE JESUIT CONSTITUTION . 52

CHAPTER V.
COLLEGES FOUNDED AND ENDOWED 68

CHAPTER VI.
THE INTELLECTUAL SCOPE AND METHOD PROPOSED . 82

CONTENTS.

CHAPTER VII.
THE MORAL SCOPE PROPOSED 98

CHAPTER VIII.
IGNATIUS ADMINISTERING THE COLLEGIATE SYSTEM. HIS DEATH 109

CHAPTER IX.
SUBSEQUENT ADMINISTRATIONS 124

PART II.

ANALYSIS OF THE SYSTEM OF STUDIES.

CHAPTER X.
AQUAVIVA. THE RATIO STUDIORUM 141

CHAPTER XI.
Formation of the Master. HIS COURSES OF LITERATURE AND PHILOSOPHY 156

CHAPTER XII.
YOUTHFUL MASTERS 175

CHAPTER XIII.
THE COURSES OF DIVINITY AND ALLIED SCIENCES. PRIVATE STUDY. REPETITION 191

CHAPTER XIV.
DISPUTATION. DICTATION 208

CHAPTER XV.

Formation of the Scholar. SYMMETRY OF THE COURSES. THE PRELECTION. BOOKS 225

CHAPTER XVI.

THE CLASSICAL LITERATURES. SCHOOL MANAGEMENT AND CONTROL 248

CHAPTER XVII.

EXAMINATIONS AND GRADUATION. SCHEDULE OF GRADES AND COURSES 259

CHAPTER XVIII.

CONCLUSION 285

BIBLIOGRAPHICAL APPENDIX 297

Part I.

EDUCATIONAL HISTORY OF THE ORDER

LOYOLA;

OR,

THE EDUCATIONAL SYSTEM OF THE JESUITS.

CHAPTER I.

INTRODUCTION.

A LEARNED and elegant work, which narrates the rise and progress of Christian Schools, from the sixtieth year of the Christian era onwards, ends its long journey at the date of the Reformation, and takes leave of its varied subject, and of its lines of Christian Scholars, in these words: "We leave them at the moment when the episcopacy was recovering its ancient jurisdiction over the ecclesiastical seminaries, and when a vast majority of the secular schools of Catholic Christendom were passing into the hands of a great Religious Order, raised up, as it would seem, with the special design of consolidating anew a system of Christian education."[1]

Two centuries and a half later, when the Society of Jesus had run a long course, from the date of the Reformation which had seen it rise, up to the eve of the Revolution which beheld it extinct, a General of the Order, Ignatius Visconti, addressing the Provincial

[1] Christian Schools and Scholars, by A. T. Drane; 1881; last chapter.

Superiors over the world, takes note of a new stage in the process of educational development: "The taste for letters now," he says, "is more keen and exquisite, and the number of literary schools has increased so much, that ours may no longer appear so necessary. For I may mention the fact that, besides our schools of polite letters, there were, for a long while, either none or very few. So that parents were forced to send their children to us, even if otherwise they did not want it."[1]

This refers in a quiet way to what Leopold von Ranke states with more emphasis. Speaking of Grammar classes, the German historian says: "Here also the Jesuits succeeded to admiration. It was found that young people gained more with them in six months, than with other teachers in two years. Even Protestants removed their children from distant gymnasia to confide them to the care of the Jesuits."[2] Ranke narrates in the same place how it was "toward the universities above all that the efforts of the Jesuits were directed." And he describes what the results were in Germany.

D'Alembert writes of their progress in France: "Hardly had the Company of Jesus begun to show itself in France, than it met with difficulties without number, in the endeavor to establish itself. The universities especially made the greatest efforts to keep the new-comers out. It is difficult to decide whether

---

[1] On the Furthering of Humane Studies; Monumenta Germaniæ Pædagogica, vol. ix, p. 129.

[2] History of the Papacy, vol. i, book v, § 3; Jesuit Schools in Germany.

this opposition is a praise or a condemnation of the Jesuits who stood it. They announced gratuitous teaching; they counted among their number celebrated and learned men, superior perhaps to those whom the universities could boast of," etc.[1]

Speaking of the Protestants in the Netherlands, a chronicle, which reviews the first century of the Order's existence, records that "the Jesuit schools were expressly interdicted, under severe penalties, to all members of the Protestant communities. Even in a twelve-year truce which the Order partially enjoyed, a monthly fine of one hundred florins was still imposed upon all delinquents, or on their parents, who persisted in patronizing the Jesuit schools. To escape the fine, parents sent their children under an assumed name.[2]

In every country, the same drama of struggle and contest evolved itself through two and a half centuries, till a momentous scene was witnessed. It was a scene of such a kind as seldom has occurred in history; and never certainly was any similar event thrown into such relief by the sequel. The event which I refer to was a universal and instantaneous suppression of the Order; with consequences following thereupon which were exceptional, both in the world that witnessed it, and in the subject-body that suffered it.

The sequel in the world at large was that, a few

---

[1] Sur la destruction des Jésuites, par un auteur désintéressé, p. 19.

[2] Imago Primi Sæculi, lib. vi, Societas Flandro-Belgica, cap. iii, § 1, p. 772.

years later, at the close of the eighteenth century, there broke out the great Revolution under the leadership of men, of whom scarcely one had been more than seven years of age at the date of the Jesuits' expulsion.[1] They represented in France the first generation which had not been educated by the Society. The remote causes which overwhelmed the Order were the same that ushered in the Revolution. But, among the immediate causes, assigned by historians to account for the precise form which the great convulsion assumed, and for the date at which it occurred, is placed the dissolution of this Order. According to the Count de Maistre, who speaks of the political sentiment of his own times, all observers agreed that the revolution of Europe, still called the French Revolution, was impossible without the preliminary destruction of the Jesuits. And, in keeping with this, it was equally a subject of observation, as being a palpable historical fact, that during two centuries the Jesuits had formed in their College at Paris, the élite of the French nobility; and that, only a few years after the expulsion of the Jesuit Masters, the same college turned out the Robespierres, Camille Desmoulins, Tallien, Noël, Fréron, Chénier, and other such demagogues. This College of Clermont, or Louis-le-Grand, from which the Jesuits were expelled in 1762, had been immediately occupied by the University of Paris. The Revolution broke out twenty-seven years later.

Another sequel, not heard of before in history,

[1] Crétineau-Joly, Histoire de la Compagnie de Jésus, tom. iv, ch. 3, p. 210; 3me edit. 1851.

affected the Society itself. Europe, having gone through the violent commotions which changed the old order of things into the new, reached the beginning of this nineteenth century, and found the Society alive again. This was in defiance of a political maxim, which we may admit with Baron von Hübner, that in politics, in the affairs of states, in the life of all great social institutions, when once death supervenes, there is no resurrection.

And now, at the end of the nineteenth century, the same forces of repulsion and attraction, of devoted love on the part of friends, of intense hatred on the part of enemies, have been seen operating as always before. It has become a commonplace in the philosophy of history, — this hatred which has been sworn against the Order of Jesus, and the multitude of enemies whom it has made. One explanation suggests itself to the Viscount de Bonald, — the presence in it, he thinks, of something good; of that good which, as it alone is the object of the most ardent love, can alone become the object of the intensest hate; and therefore has always made persecutors and martyrs.

The purpose of this book is to give an historical sketch, with a proportionate analysis, of the educational development effected through the Society of Jesus. Others have taken different fields of Jesuit history to survey, either general and comprehending all the paths of external and internal activity, or particular and comprising only parts of the history. Some of these particular views, especially in later years, are in the line of studies, and are most valuable contributions to the history of pedagogic development. None of them, however, happens to coincide with the scope, purpose, and form which have been designated for this; as the Series to which it belongs, the Editor in charge, and the country for which it is intended, sufficiently indicate.

The subject then is the educational system of the Jesuits, that system which technically is called the *Ratio Studiorum*. It requires no literary nor historical ingenuity to centre all that has to be said about it in the personality and character of St. Ignatius of Loyola. I shall draw upon Jesuit sources of information, except when it will be necessary to state results, or give estimates, which imply commendation. Then I shall quote freely from sources outside of the Order. Otherwise, for the purpose of explaining and analyzing domestic matters, these extraneous references would be imperfect indeed.

The situation, which met the military view of the cavalier, lately the knightly captain of Loyola, was a new one, on an old field of battle. The demand, which it seemed to make upon tactical resources, was as intense as the political and religious crisis which created the situation. From the year 1522 till 1540, while Ignatius was prospecting the scene in Europe, and preparing to take an active part in it, he had time and the opportunities for observing, what precisely, at that epoch, were the accumulated results of all the Christian ages gone before; and why the results just then were only what they were. The issue appeared fatally determined by social conditions around, which more than neutralized the Christianity visible. Education, in particular, was laboring under the action of causes, which had begun to operate several centuries earlier, and which were then evidently working themselves out to one final effort. That was the undermining of Christian education.

In this respect, it was the same question which had confronted the Augustines, the Basils, and Jeromes, of one thousand years before. But it was a different state of the question. Augustine, the brilliant youth of Hippo Regius in Africa, will serve as an instance of what the issue then had been. He had made himself master of the very best results, which the public schools of the time were able to accomplish in the most gifted of minds. But he had lost his virtue. He lived to complain with bitterness, that it was accounted a grievous error to pronounce *homo* "a man," without the " h," but it was no error at all to hate a man, signified by the word, *homo*. The consequence with him was that, when he became a Bishop of the Church, he met the need of providing a Christain education, by instituting in his own house a kind of school, for the moral and spiritual education of his clergy.

Thus arose the cathedral or canonical school. So too, the cloistral schools came to flourish in the abbeys and the monasteries. And, even if these two kinds of educational centres had not also been, as they really were, in the Middle Ages, the preordained means for the salvation of learning in Europe, they would still have had reason enough for their existence, in the paramount necessity of continuing, for the tender age of youth, the ministry of a virtuous education.

Events took a new turn with the rise and progress of the university system. At first, the universities were mostly annexed to cathedral churches. As they developed, the cloistral influence waned. And again, as they developed still more, they presented phenomena which originated the subsequent system of the Jesuits.

From the twelfth to the sixteenth centuries, as many as sixty-six of these universities were in existence; sixteen of them are credited to Germany; about as many to France; and the rest to Italy, Spain, and other nations. It is not within my province to describe their formation, or the order of their foundation. They received their charters from the Popes, who used their power thus, and showed it under a form, which no age will be apt to depreciate; least of all, our own. Addressing these habitations of "General Studies" with the appellative, *Universitas Vestra*, the Sovereign Pontiffs sent them on their course, and encouraged them in every line of Theology, Law, or Medicine; whether all these lines were followed in each centre, or respectively some here, some there. Orleans, Bourges, Bologna, Modena professed Law, either as their specialty, or as their distinguishing faculty; Montpellier, Salerno, Medicine; Padua, the Liberal Arts; Toledo, Mathematics; Salamanca, and, above all, Paris, general culture, Philosophy, and Theology.

These universities became such well-springs of learning, that for Theology the Bishops' seminaries practically ceased to exist; and, to acquire the general culture of the times, the children of the faithful no longer turned to the monastic schools. Nay, in quite a contrary sense, the clergy and the monks themselves, in pursuit of the best learning that the age could give, left their cloisters for a while, and betook themselves to the universities. They followed up that step by settling down there. Paris beheld the great old orders of Augustinians, Benedictines, Carthusians, the Carmelites, the Bernardines, all establishing monasteries or colleges; no otherwise than the newest order of Trinitarians, which was chiefly made up of university men. Two institutes arose, those of the Dominicans and Franciscans; who with men at their head, like St. Thomas Aquinas and St. Bonaventure, placed themselves right in the heart of these intellectual centres; and they became bulwarks of sound learning, as opposed to the inanities of a false scholasticism. They kept the leaven of religion and virtue in the midst of what was not quite a perverse generation, but was most certainly, from whatever side we view it, a very dubious multitude, belonging, it is true, to a Christian generation. Consider the 10,000 at Bologna, which was the centre for Law studies; the 30,000 at Oxford; or the 40,000, all at one time studying, or reckoned to be studying, in Paris, the acknowledged centre for Theology.

An indiscriminate mass of humanity like this, pressed, thronged, and crowded together, stimulated with all the ardor, and alive with all the passions of youth, could not fail to be little better than a nursery for indiscriminate license. Whatever might be the vigilance of the Church, or however strenuous the exercise of legitimate authority, nothing in the usual course of human society could prevent its becoming a prolific soil for the propagation of every species of error. And, as during three hundred years the intellectual and educational powers of Europe followed this course, the law of evolution asserted itself in many directions.

On the one side, those tens of thousands of Christian youths, who were aiming at all the posts of influence in Church and State, and who, entering their native university, or journeying to foreign ones, began life there at as early an age as twelve or fourteen years, to remain in this environment some nine or twelve years more, became, as was natural, the living, swarming members of a state of society so dissolute, that successive occupants of the Papal See depicted the condition of things as one of moral contagion. In the manner of thought and mind which prevailed, no form of theoretic error was wanting. In philosophy, there was scepticism; in theology, heresy; while, in politics, Cæsarism and absolutism became rife. Then, at the end of the fifteenth century, the Renaissance came; and one of the first things, which it expressly and formally did, was to renew in life, art, and politics, the same old paganism, upon the ruins of which, so many centuries before, Christianity had begun its upward and laborious ascent. Newly fashioning then much of what was old, Christianity had augmented all this with so much which was new, that in a thousand years it had made a Renaissance possible. And now the form of this Renaissance threatened its own ascendancy in morals and in life.

On the other hand, the old spirit of conservatism in

religion, and of preservation in the matter of morals, maintained itself for a time, through those bodies of religious men and clergymen, who had left the cloister or the seminary, to take up their abode in the secular seats of learning. It was this spirit which originated the latest and best development of the universities, that of the "college" system, established in their midst. Salamanca had twenty colleges; Louvain, forty; Paris, fifty. Still, in the final issue, there was now scarcely any reserve force of cloistral or episcopal learning behind the universities, and outside of them. And the religious and the clergy themselves, who at best were not a little out of their element from the moment they migrated into the secular environment, conformed insensibly to the conditions in which they found themselves, and so far ceased to be the power they had been.

Witness, in the time of Ignatius, the Paris University, as described by contemporary records. "It was fallen from its ancient splendor. The bonds of discipline had been gradually relaxed; studies were abandoned; and with masters, as with scholars, all love of letters, and respect for the rule, had given place to sombre passions, to political hate, to religious fanaticism and dissolute habits."[1]

Here then we have two elements in the educational condition of Europe, which explain the rise of the

---

[1] Histoire de l'Université de Paris, par Charles Jourdain, liv. i, ch. 1; quoted with other testimonies, in the learned work, Un Collège de Jésuites aux xvii and xviii siècles, Le Collège Henri iv de la Flèche, par le P. Camille de Rochemonteix, 1889; tom. i, ch. 1, p. 3.

Jesuit system. One was the positive, concrete fact, embodied in that great developed system of university learning. The other was a negative element, the decline therein of the essential moral life. These two factors are not mere antecedents in the order of time, as being only prior to the method of Loyola. One of them, the university system, supplied the very material out of which his method and matter were taken; yes, and the men themselves, the Jesuits who applied the principles of reform to education. The other factor, which I have called negative, that decline of the essential moral life, was the adequate occasion, which prompted Ignatius to approach the question of education at all. For we may say with confidence that, if the universities of the sixteenth century were still doing the work which originally they had been chartered to do, the founder of the Society of Jesus would not only have omitted to draw out his system as a substitute for them, and as an improvement upon them, but he would have done, what he always did with anything good in existence; he would have used what he found, and have turned his attention to other things more urgent. He did use these university centres for his own young men, until he had better educational institutions, and a better method of his own in progress.

Hence the educational problem, when it falls under the notice of Ignatius, presents itself as the identical one of old, that of moral regeneration. But it is a different state of the same question. In circumstances rendered acutely critical by the agitations of the epoch, social, moral, and religious, it was a favorite contemplation of his to look with compassion on men living like the blind, dying, and sinking into eternal depths; on men talking, blaspheming, reviling one another; on their assaulting, wounding, slaying one another; and all together going to eternal perdition.[1] It was from this moral point of view that he descended into the arena of education.

But before he can teach men, or mould teachers of men, or even conceive the first idea of legislating for the intellectual world, he must himself first learn. There are two fundamental lessons which he does learn, and they go to form him. One is that, among all pursuits, the study of virtue is supreme; the other, that, supreme as virtue is, yet, without secular learning, the highest virtue goes unarmed, and at best is profitable to oneself alone. He learns these two lessons, not only in theory, but in practice. To accomplish the purpose of the latter, he takes his seat upon the scholars' bench, and begins to learn with little children. Though he may not meet with brilliant success in the art of learning, still in the art of understanding what learning is, and in the lessons of experience, he becomes a finished scholar. He remains even then too much of a chevalier to give up a cherished idea of his about a spiritual crusade in the East. And it is only when thwarted in this project that, like a true knight, he simply turns to another side of the field. He stays in the West. He is still the Captain of a Company. But he becomes also a legislator among doctors; and, amid his other works, he effects an educational reform.

[1] **Exercitia Spiritualia.**

In his whole campaign, we may discern two characteristics in the spirit of his movements. One is that of defence, the other that of advance. His method of defence showed itself in the reassertion of old principles, in the conservatism of morals, — a plan of campaign, which determines the whole frame of mind, and the social construction of the Company. It rests on the principle of upholding what is, and not moving the ancient landmarks. On the other hand, his advance is towards the solution of the highest questions which can interest mankind. These formed part of the very object and direction of the Order's march. And so it came to pass, that his Company drew to itself that class of minds which are most powerfully arrested by the prospect of solving such questions, especially when times are agitated. His times were agitated, if any ever were, more so than our own, when the same questions still must dominate. His were times of wars with Turks in the East, and with Christians at home; of battles lost and won, with their effects reaching into every household; of royal and imperial administrations confused and overthrown; of new opinions without number; of the Church losing ground along the whole line of the frontier, and withal new worlds looming over an horizon, where from the beginning of time the unknown had brooded in absolute darkness. At such a moment, "Defence and Advance," or as the Papal authority expressed it in the solemn instrument which chartered his Institute, *Defensio ac propagatio fidei*, were stirring watchwords to men of parts, who felt restive under the inactivity and inefficiency of older methods, on older lines.

I will not pause to say, that the personal poverty and exact obedience, required in the new service, presented no obstacles to the minds and characters which were otherwise attracted to his standard. The antecedents of all antiquity seem to show that such conditions, to such minds, are rather an inducement than a check. And if one takes notice that to this was added, in the Order of Jesus, an absolute equality, whereby every formed member binds himself to accept no dignity within or without, or, at least, to affect no dignity at home or abroad, which will prejudice his full franchise as a member, then, perhaps, the attractiveness of such a life, the conservatism and intense concentration of the Order, as well as the alacrity and endurance manifested in the service, will not appear inexplicable to the minds of this age, in which, under a very different form, the same equality is called liberty, is made to construct republics, to bring down monarchies, and develop some of the most potent agencies for unfolding the energies of men. Yet the liberty of this latter equality reflects but faintly, and as from a broken surface, the freedom of him, who having liberated himself from the shackles of the world, and from all solicitude as to his movements, office, and place, finds in turn, as the German historian expresses it, "his own personal development imposed upon him";[1] and, in the firm companionship of one aim, formation, and life, enjoys the manifold support and ready sympathy of individualities as developed as his own.

I shall narrate, in the first part, the facts of Igna-

[1] Ranke, History of the Papacy, vol. i, book ii, § 7.

tius' career, so far as to indicate the stages of that magisterial art, by which he himself was formed, and which then he reformed in the Jesuit *Ratio Studiorum*. In the second part, I shall sketch briefly the history of the *Ratio* itself, and analyze the System as a theory and practice of education.

CHAPTER II.

KNIGHT, PILGRIM, AND SCHOLAR.

THE story of the cavalier wounded on the ramparts of Pampeluna has often been told. Loyola was not at the moment governor of the city, nor in any responsible charge. But official responsibility was not necessary for him to see the path of duty and follow it. As one bound to the service of his sovereign by the title of honor and nobility, he retired to the citadel, when the town surrendered; and then, when the ramparts began to give way under the cannonading, he stood in the breach. A ball shattering the rock laid him low, maimed in both his limbs. At once the defence collapsed. Cared for chivalrously by those whose arms had struck him down in battle, he was transported with every delicate attention to his castle of Loyola. It was found that one of his limbs had been ill set. He had it broken again, to be set aright. Meanwhile, instinct with all the ambition of a knight, belonging to a chivalrous nation in an age of chivalry, he was not insensible to the charms of society and affection. And, out of a sensitive care for his personal appearance, he must needs have a protruding bone, which still threatened to mar his figure, sawed off while he looked on. In the loneliness and tedium of a sick-room, he whiled away the hours by dreaming of his ambitions and his aspirations, and he sought to feed them with suitable nourishment. He wanted a romance to read. There was none to be had. So, instead of the novel which was not forthcoming, he took what they gave him, the Life of Christ, and the Lives of some who had served Christ faithfully. The soldier of the field and of blood felt the objects of his ambition change; he became a soldier of the spirit and eternal life. And, after the experiences of his bed of pain, and the protracted communings with another world, he arose another man; he went forth a knight as ever, but not on an expedition terminating as before. An evening and night spent in the sanctuary of Montserrat, as once before he had passed a vigil of arms, when dubbed a chevalier by the King of Navarre; a morning begun with the Holy Sacrifice attended and Holy Communion received, opened to him a new era; and he went forth, bound now by a new oath of fealty to the service of the King of Heaven.

At the side of the altar in this sanctuary of Montserrat, the Abbot of the monastery, eighty-one years later, committed to a marble tablet the record of this event, for the perpetual memory of the future: "Blessed Ignatius of Loyola here, with many prayers and tears, devoted himself to God and the Virgin. Here, as with spiritual arms, he fortified himself in sack-cloth, and spent the vigil of the night. Hence he went forth to found the Society of Jesus, in the year MDXXII."

He first looked about him to find a retreat, and immerse himself in the contemplation of time and eternity. It was a Saturday. John Sacrista Pascual tells us that his mother, a devout lady of Manresa, was in the church that morning; and, accompanied by two young men and three women, she was at her devotions in the chapel of the Apostles. A young stranger came up and accosted them. His clothing was of very common serge; for Ignatius had given away his knightly robes to a poor man. The youth looked like a pilgrim. He was not tall; he was fair in complexion and ruddy in cheek. His bare head was somewhat bald. Altogether he was of a fine and grave presence, and most reserved in look. He scarcely raised his eyes from the ground. Coming up, he asked if there were a hospital anywhere which might serve him for shelter. Regarding his noble and fair features, the lady, as became a Christian woman, offered her services; if he would follow her company, she would provide for him, in the best way possible. Courteously and thankfully he accepted her offer, and followed the party as they left the sanctuary. They proceeded slowly; for they noticed that he was lame. However much they urged him, they could not induce him to ride upon the ass. Three leagues away from Montserrat, they arrived at the little town of Manresa; and he took up his residence in the common hospital for the poor and pilgrims. Whatever alms or food was henceforth sent him first went to others, whom, in these matters, up to the end of his life, he always considered to be more in need than himself.

He now entered on his probation of Christian virtue. In the mind of the Catholic Church, the degree of virtue which he practised is that accounted heroic. As it is not for me to dwell on it here, I will pass it over with one remark. That which is accounted ordinary Christian virtue, resting as it does on faith and hope, on principles not barely natural but supernatural, is not very intelligible to the world at large. Still less the heroic degree of the same. Both however claim to be estimated by their own proper motives and principles. When they enter into the very subject, which the biographer means to treat, it appertains to his art not to ignore the objective motives and reasons of things, as they operated in his subject. In the shortest monograph, like the present, we cannot separate from the work, which he did, the man who did it. And the man is made by his motives. It were bad literary art to describe feats, which are confessedly great, and not to find motives which are proportionate.

Ignatius, after a year more or less spent at Manresa, took his pilgrim's staff and journeyed on foot to Italy, and thence to the Holy Land. It was in the spirit of the old Crusaders, whose chivalry had a charm for him up to the day many years later, when, with his first associates of the Company, he endeavored once more to cross over from Italy to Palestine. Had he succeeded on this later occasion, he would most probably never have known the others who attached themselves to him; nor might history have busied itself with him or with them.

At the date of his return from the Holy Land, we find that he has advanced already to the second lesson in the development of his future. It is, that mature in years as he is, and full of desires for doing good to his neighbors, yet neither does mere piety place in his hands the instruments for such work; nor, if study alone can give the means of apostolic zeal, can he consider himself exempt from the law, that he must labor to acquire what are only the results of labor. He was thirty-one years of age, when he betook himself, after his night's vigil, to the cave of Manresa. He is two years older now. So, at the age of thirty-three, he sits down on the school-bench at Barcelona, and begins his Latin declensions.

Begrudging his studies the time which they demand exclusively, he mistakes the situation, and allows himself the exercises of an apostolic life. At his age, even supposing his earlier pursuits to have been more in harmony with his present life of letters, he is not an apt pupil. However, he labors conscientiously. After two years spent at Grammar, he is judged by his teacher, who takes a lenient view of the case, to be competent for approaching his higher studies.

He himself was dubious. His friends recommended him to ascend. He still hesitated. But, receiving the same favorable opinion from a theologian whom he consulted, Ignatius acquiesced, in accordance with his unvarying rule, to follow competent direction. How unfortunate this step was for the happy progress of his studies, but how advantageous for his experience as a future legislator, I shall proceed to show.

Leaving Barcelona for Alcalà, he meant to enjoy the best advantages which a great university could afford. He lived on alms as ever; and others lived on the alms which he received. It was the year 1626.

He entered upon the study of Logic, using the Summa of Di Soto; also the Physics of Aristotle; and he pursued besides the Master of Sentences.

He had stayed only a year and a half in this rich variety of pursuits, scholastic as well as apostolic, when the novelties apparent in his manner of life ended by making him a suspected character to the ecclesiastical authorities. To a few, among the population of the city, his fruitful zeal made him distinctly odious. The result was a juridical process against him, which issued in a complimentary verdict, the Vicar of the diocese pronouncing him and his companions quite blameless. But restrictions were imposed regarding his future ministrations, since Ignatius was not yet in holy orders. During a term of four years he was not to preach. After that time, his progress in studies would enable him to honor that important ministry, without giving offence. This was a deathblow to the aspirations of the student. He made up his mind to go elsewhere, to the famous university of Salamanca; and he turned his back on Alcalà.

The time was soon to come for a pleasant revenge; and apparently he knew of it long before it came. Just six years after the foundation of his Order, when he sent Francis Villanova to open a house at Alcalà, not only did he find men of the university embracing his Institute, but, two years after that, the whilom persecuted pilgrim received, in a single twelvemonth, thirty-four Doctors into the Society, all from that one seat of learning. The mere passing by of Francis Borgia, Duke of Gandia, who had become an humble follower of Ignatius, made the choicest spirits flock to his standard; and, all over Spain, colleges sprang up as if from the soil.

In Salamanca, where likewise he and his were to figure in the future, the personal history of Ignatius is briefly told. In ten or twelve days after his arrival, he was thrown into chains. He spent twenty-two days in prison. When released, with the same commendation for himself and his doctrine as he had received at Alcalà, but with a similar restriction on his action, he thought it was not worth his while to repeat the same experiences at the same cost. So, in spite of all the eloquence of dissuasion brought to bear on him by friends, he took a new departure, which seemed plausible to him, and therefore feasible. He would try his fortunes in another land, and continue his studies in the greatest philosophical and theological centre of the world, the University of Paris.

To any one who judged of things by an ordinary standard, the project was not feasible. War was raging between Spain and France; the roads were infested with hostile soldiery; many murders and robberies, committed on the persons of travellers, were recently reported. But these and other considerations of the kind had no weight with Loyola, to stay him in a course once deliberately adopted. Accepting some alms from friends at Barcelona, to obtain on the way the necessaries of life, he accomplished on foot the whole journey from Barcelona to the French capital; where he arrived at the beginning of February, A.D. 1528.

He has now had experience of prisons and chains, on the charge of teaching error, or of being a dangerous enthusiast. One of the calmest and coolest of men, who never acted, but he first calculated, and who never allowed himself to approach a conclusion, without first freeing himself from all bias and impulse, he had suffered repeated arrest for setting people beside themselves, for moving them to give up all they had in behalf of piety, or charity, and inducing them to go and live on alms themselves; nay, perhaps throw in their lives, talents and acquirements, to serve others gratis. The founder of the Jesuits, himself the first of an Order which has the reputation of being the staunchest upholder, as well of authority in every rank of society, as of the truths taught by the Catholic Church, was put in chains, or arraigned by the ecclesiastical authorities almost wherever he appeared, though always acquitted as blameless.

In a letter written at a subsequent period of his life to King John III of Portugal, Ignatius sums up his experiences, as including two imprisonments, at Alcalà and Salamanca; three judicial investigations, at Alcalà, Salamanca, and Paris; later on, another process at Paris; then one at Venice; finally another at Rome; — eight investigations about this one man in Spain, France, and Italy.[1] Wherever he came, in after life, it passed as a proverb among the Fathers, that his appearance was the sure harbinger of a storm, soon to break out against them somewhere, in the social or religious world. He braved all this fury in his own manner, weighing as deliberately every word

[1] Genelli, Life of St. Ignatius Loyola, p. 351.

he spoke, and measuring every step he took, as when he had stood in the breach of the ramparts at Pampeluna. But his personal experience made him commit to the sacred keeping of the "Spiritual Exercises" an important principle of liberal and humane prudence. It is couched in the first words of his little book, to guide teacher and learner alike. He says: —

"In the first place, it is to be supposed that every pious Christian man should be more ready to interpret any obscure proposition of another in a good rather than a bad sense. If, however, he cannot defend the proposition in any way, let him inquire of the speaker himself; and, if then the speaker is found to be mistaken in sentiment or understanding, let him correct the same kindly. If this is not enough, let him employ all available means to render him sound in principle and secure from error."

How far the personal experiences of its founder attached by a law of heritage to his Order, I can hardly undertake to describe. But, just for the sake of completing the family picture, I will mention the heads of a doleful list, which an historian of the Society catalogues. He enumerates, as objects of attack and misrepresentation, the founder himself, the name of the Society of Jesus, the dress, rules, manners, books, doctrine, schools, sermons; the poverty, obedience, gratuitous service of the Jesuits; that they affected a kind of literary empire, under the spur of an intolerable ambition; that they were lightly tinctured, and had just sipped of many things, of which they had nothing solid to offer; yes, that they wanted to have it believed there was no sanctuary of the

Muses, no shrine of sacred or human wisdom in existence, outside of their own colleges; that, from these offices of theirs, all arts and sciences came forth, done up in the best style. "In fine, whatever they do or don't do, granted that there are many false charges which their enemies concoct against them, — things too extreme to be believed, — granted that they are acquitted of many vices laid to their account, never certainly will they escape the suspicion, at least, which these charges excite."[1] We believe it. There is a good homely English proverb which expresses the very same idea — about the happy adhesiveness of a clayey compound when cleverly thrown.

This retrospect of history was taken, exactly one hundred years after the foundation of the Order. The story had begun some thirteen years before it was founded. When Ignatius became a responsible leader with associates, he had recourse more than once to the process of justice, to clear his reputation in full form. But, beyond the cases which rendered such defence prudent and necessary, his practical policy was expressed in a practical maxim, which after him his successor, James Laynez, had often in his mouth: *Deus faxit ne unquam male loquantur et vera dicant!* "God grant they never talk ill of me and be saying the truth!" Indeed, as there is no use in trying to change men, for they will never be born anew, Ignatius looked rather in another direction for the solution of difficulties; expecting that troubles, which defied other treatment, might still not survive their authors. Speaking of a powerful adversary, who was

---

[1] Imago Primi Sæculi, lib. iv, cap. ix, pp. 521-2; De Calumniis.

raising a great storm at Toledo and Alcalá, and whom it took the royal council and then a brief from the Pope to quell, Ignatius said of him to Ribadeneira: "He is old, the Society is young; naturally the Society will live longer than he will." The same dignitary, suppressed though he was, rose again in violent opposition. Whereupon Jouvancy makes the apt remark: "So difficult is it for even the most eminent men, and so rare a thing, when once they have conceived a notion, to get it out of their heads again!"[1] No, men are not born anew.

It is time now to contemplate Ignatius of Loyola at Paris, where some of the most precious elements in his educational experience are to be acquired.

[1] Jouvancy, Epitome Hist. S. J., p. 168, ad annum 1551.

CHAPTER III.

THE UNIVERSITY OF PARIS. ROME.

VOLUNTARY poverty, the austerest manner of life, the ungrateful labor of studies, and the perpetual self-discipline of a mind like his, ever bent on lofty thoughts and endeavoring to dominate the very first movements of his soul, all these conditions, added to the climate and the nature of the situation in which Ignatius found himself at Paris, brought such a strain to bear on his broken-down constitution, that, to keep up his course at all, he had to interrupt it awhile, and give some relief to his overtaxed body, or, as he held it to be, his "beast of burden."

And what about the studies themselves? If they had been a brilliant success thus far, they could scarcely have outlived such conditions of existence. As it was, they were as good as if they had never begun; or somewhat worse. He had gone about them the wrong way. Whatever solidity of learning he had kept objectively in view, something else, equally important with solidity, had been unwittingly omitted. That was a good method. Logic, Philosophy, and Theology, all taken up together, and with such compendious haste, now went together in his mind like a machine out of joint; and his speed was *nil!* The Latin language itself, the indispensable vehicle of all learning, was just so far possessed by him as to show him that, to be of any real use, it had better be commenced all over again.

Here his character asserted itself. And in no particular of his life is he more like himself, more thorough, more of a brave cavalier, "governing himself, in great things and small, by reasons most high," than when, having little facility for such pursuits, and less inclination, he makes up his mind, after a short breathing spell, to sit down again at the age of thirty-seven years, and resume his Latin declensions! In the college of Montague, he spends about two years acquiring this tongue. Meanwhile, he tries various plans to find wherewithal to live.

I need not dwell on the nature of this great centre into which Ignatius had penetrated, an unknown stranger, just one of its tens of thousands of scholars. It had more than two scores of colleges. To this, the queen of universities, though she was going to be no kind alma mater to him and his Order, still the recollections of Loyola in his future legislation would always turn back with reverence. His first Professors for the Roman College, the typical institution of the Society, would be taken from those of his men who were Doctors of this university. And, whatever might be the moral condition and the religious lassitude of the university men, as compared with this penniless stranger, in 1529, occasions were to come in after times, when they showed themselves not unworthy of the enemy whom they fought to the death. When the plague of 1580 made a desert about them, the university men and the Jesuits, otherwise never seen together, save in the lists and face to face, now were everywhere, and fell fast, side by side on the field of Christian charity.

For the understanding of the Jesuit system, in its origin and its form, attention must always be paid, in the first place, to the kinship subsisting between it and the Paris University. There are, besides, many other degrees of relationship, which do not go unacknowledged, in the formation of the *Ratio Studiorum*. The system of the English universities may be recognized in the line of ancestry. Whatever was best anywhere enters the pedigree; as Lord Bacon takes note, when delivering himself like a good philosopher, but also like a good Protestant, he eulogizes and stigmatizes in the same breath: "The ancient wisdom of the best times," he says, "did always make a just complaint, that states were too busy with their laws, and too negligent in point of education; which excellent part of the ancient discipline hath been in some sort revived, of late times, by the colleges of the Jesuits; of whom, although in regard of their superstition I may say, '*quo meliores, eo deteriores*'; yet in regard of this, and some other points concerning human learning and moral matters, I may say, as Agesilaus said to his enemy Pharnabaus, '*Talis quum sis, utinam noster esses.*'"[1]

In the University of Paris, then, as his real alma mater, Ignatius commenced his course of Philosophy in the year 1529. He finished it by standing successfully the severe examination, called *examen lapideum*,

---

[1] Advancement of Learning, book i; Philadelphia edit. 1841, vol. i, p. 167.

"the rocky test," considered the most searching of all in the Paris Academy. He thus became a Master of Arts, after Easter, A.D. 1534; having become Licentiate in the previous year. Particulars about his four examiners in the "rocky test," his graduation, the degrees of his companions, with the dates, as found in the Paris records, are given by the Bollandists.[1]

He now entered on his theological studies. It was evident that the obstructions, which had thwarted so many of his efforts heretofore, were disappearing one by one. And more than that; the means were being placed in his hands for the great work before him. These means were a company of men. He was in the midst of a devoted little band, each one of whom he had won individually. They were Peter Lefèvre and Francis Xavier; James Lainez and Alphonsus Salmeron, both of them mere youths; there were Claude Le Jay, John Coduri, Nicholas Bobadilla, Simon Rodriguez; and lastly, the only one who at this time was a Priest among their number, Pasquier Brouet. Among these, never at their head though considered a father by all, never leading the way, though on that account showing himself the more effectively a leader, Ignatius was all in all to each one of them. He had previously acquired some valuable experience in selecting and forming companions. But such as had gathered round him in Spain were no longer with him. Each one of his present party was a picked man.

When six of them were sufficiently advanced, he and they held a solemnity, which was the real birthday of the Society of Jesus. On the fifteenth day of

---

[1] Month of July, tom. vii; auct. J. P., § xviii, pp. 443-4.

August, 1534, they took a vow, in the church of the Blessed Virgin, at Montmartre in Paris. They bound themselves to renounce all their goods by a given date, and betake themselves to the Holy Land; failing in that, they would throw themselves at the feet of the Sovereign Pontiff, and offer him their absolute service. Meanwhile they pursued their studies; and, as each of the two following years brought round the fifteenth day of August, it found them in the same place, and with the same solemnity, and with an enlarged number, renewing this vow. The legal birthday of the Order came only with the Papal charter on September 27, 1540.

I shall pass over the movements of Loyola, when bidden to go and recuperate in his native climate. He returned to Spain, in 1535, leaving his companions to study till 1537; and he settled the affairs of his young Spanish associates at their homes. All, when the time came, disposed of their goods in a summary way. They gave to the poor, reserving nothing, except what would pay their way to Venice, and thence to the East. Their principle was, *Dispersit, dedit pauperibus,* "He hath distributed, he hath given to the poor." Besides this, Xavier, at the date appointed, gave up the last stage of his theological studies, and resigned the glory of receiving the Doctor's cap in Paris; the brilliant young Professor sacrificed the one thing which had appealed most powerfully to his ambition and imagination. Laynez was recuperating from a severe illness, and could do scarcely more than move. Nevertheless they are all in Venice, when the early spring of 1537 arrives.

Ignatius himself, meeting them there, has accomplished the work which faced him thirteen years before, and which he had taken in hand with his Latin grammar. He is now forty-six years of age.

There are three lines of activity, in which the ability and energy of Ignatius Loyola stand out before the world. One is the capacity he showed as a governor or leader of men; another is a similar competency to direct souls in the spiritual life; the third is that, which we are considering at present, his legislative genius in the intellectual order. Admitting the innate talent which must have been the basis and foundation of his gift for governing, we may affirm of all the rest, that the best part of his sagacity and tact had been acquired by personal experience. He learnt how to act by suffering. He perfected his natural gift of guiding and commanding by first submitting to all the contingencies of human life.

We may develop the meaning of this in the present matter, pedagogy; and the meaning of it will help to unfold the subject. In quest of the necessaries of life, he spent intervals of his studious career in travelling from Paris to a great distance. He found himself returning each year to Belgium, always on foot: he visited Rouen, and even reached London, to address the Spanish merchants there. It does not seem to have been parsimony on their side that kept him in such straitened circumstances. It was his principles which were not all in keeping with his conditions of life. He was endeavoring to combine the life of a student with absolute poverty; and he aggravated the inconveniences of such a state of dependence by placing no limits to the exercise of his charity. It was his deliberate choice; for he fed his mind continuously upon the life and example of the King, to whom he had sworn his service, Christ poor and in labor from his youth. He spoke afterwards from the wisdom of experience, when he said, that in absolute penury the pursuit of science cannot easily subsist, and the culture of the mind is impeded by the duties of providing for the body. Hence he legislated that, though poverty was to be the basis of his Institute, still the members, as long as they were engaged in studies, should be set free from all care of seeking the means of subsistence.

He had endeavored to combine a life of apostolic ministrations, though not yet a Priest, with that requisite absorption of mind, which alone can warrant scholastic success. And he saw what it had come to. The very esteem and love, which he entertained for the exercises of the higher spiritual life, interrupted with intrusive thoughts that application to study, which was the duty in hand. In order that no such intrusion of even the most sacred pursuits should obstruct the onward progress of the members in learning, he defined by rule the measure of such occupations, as long as study was the main duty.

Diseases weakened him. Therefore he took the greatest pains to protect the health of the members. While he lived, he did this with a personal and paternal solicitude. In his Institute, he provided the same for the future.

On commencing his studies, he embraced many

branches at the same time; and he had suffered all the consequences of disorder. Grasping at too many things, he lost all; and he had then to retrieve all with loss of time. To obviate any recurrence of such costly experiences, he provided that the courses followed in the Society should have nothing disordered in them, nothing mutilated or curtailed; everything was to be in method and system; until, system and method having been carried out in every line, and the special good of each department having been secured sufficiently for the general plan, specialized perfection should be consulted, after all that; and this was to be the appointed life of individuals, while a rounded and complete education remained the culture of all.

Once in later years he let fall these words, relative to his early experience: "He would very much question whether another but himself, having to struggle with so many difficulties and obstacles in the course of his studies, would have given so long a time to the acquisition of the sciences."[1] Thus then was he oppressed with poverty, without the satisfaction of acting under orders; suffering so many diseases, and yet looking neither to honor, dignity, nor other human reward, such as is wont to draw men on, and animate them under fatigue; finding no pleasure nor satisfaction in the life of studies, an inducement which is so great an alleviation to mortals in the work before them. And, in all these respects, he was quite unlike the very men whom he singled out, and enlisted in the new service of devotion; unlike Francis Xavier, who had seen with perfect indifference all his brothers take

[1] Genelli, Life of St. Ignatius Loyola, part i, ch. 8.

to their ancestral profession of arms, or to a courtier's life, while he himself, with the whole force of an ambitious soul, ran on successfully and brilliantly in his chosen career, as a Professor; unlike Laynez and Salmeron, whose extraordinary gifts had made them Doctors of Philosophy and Divinity, while still, in age, little more than mere youths; very unlike by nature to the gentle make of Lefèvre, who began life as a shepherd boy, and ever retained a pastoral sweetness of character. Unlike all of them, Loyola, a soldier born and bred, and still true to his profession, discarded every consideration of taste, comfort, and convenience, in view of one objective point to be reached: through thirteen years he struggled towards it; and, when that time of probation was over, he was a marked man. According to the law, that like attracts like, and like begets like, he was surrounded by a company of marked men, few if you count their number, many if you consider the type. His name was widely known, and favorably so. When he had been paying five times over the price of his daily bread, by travelling to Belgium, to Rouen, and London, and collecting there some Spanish florins, the event seemed to show that he had been but opening the door, here and there and everywhere, for his colleges and universities in the future; albeit, if they came, adversaries came too, in proportion. But clouds and storms purify the air. When they come again, they will still leave the air the clearer for their coming. If the laws of human conduct are consistent in one way, they are consistent in another. The disturbance comes, but it does its work and goes.

M. Cretineau-Joly, the popular French historian in our own times, speaking of events at a later juncture in the life of Loyola, makes the following observation: "Loyola," he says, "could apply to himself admirably well that proverb which says, 'When a Spaniard is driving a nail into the wall, and his hammer breaks, the Spaniard will drive the nail in with his head!'" Loyola would have his idea go through at any cost.

We shall now follow him to Italy and Rome.

In the year 1537, Rome was not quite the luxurious capital which had fallen under the sword of the Constable of Bourbon. The eternal city, whose Papal Sovereigns have left it on record from time immemorial, that in no part of the world were they less recognized as lords than in their own city, had undergone a purification, which differed, not substantially, but only in its consequences, from what was called for, over half the countries of Europe. The riches, the luxury, the idleness, which elsewhere resulted in a complete change of religious history for many of the northern nations, had here brought about a catastrophe which sobered minds. And no longer an exclusive absorption in elaborate sloth prevented a large portion of the influential element here from doing honor to the Queen of European civilization, by doing good to the world.

All roads still led to Rome. Thence too all roads diverged. It was still true, that whatever commanded this centre could reach out, if only by the force of prestige, to the uttermost limits of the civilized domain. Whatever this venerable source of authority chartered to go on its way, in strength and benediction, had reason to behold, in the privilege so bestowed, the auspicious opening of a useful career, intellectual or moral. It is so to-day, though not in a temporal sense. The charter, or confirmation, or bull, which conveys the recognition of the Church's Head to a project, a cause, or an institute, bestows thereupon a moral power which naturally transcends every franchise in the gift of the most powerful governments. Compared with it, they are local. And, standing no comparison with it, under a moral aspect, they do not pretend to such a power as touches the inner conscience of nations.

When therefore Ignatius turned to the great Rome, he was like the skilful commander whom he describes in a certain place; he was possessing himself of the vantage-ground, taking the citadel. It would be more correct to say, as all history avers, that he meant to defend that citadel, the See of Rome. He had waited nearly a year at Venice, to carry out his project of voyaging to Jerusalem. War made that impossible. Now, in accordance with the express proviso in their vow, he and his companions repaired to Rome, and offered their services to the spiritual head of Christendom.

To win approbation for a new religious institute was no easy matter; then less than ever. The recent occurrences in the North had been due to this, among other moral causes, that the later history of certain religious orders, which centuries before had begun one way, latterly had taken a novel and fatal turn. Still, in spite of criticism and hostility, chiefly in the high places, Ignatius received at length the approving word of the Pope; and his Institute was chartered with a bull of confirmation. Henceforth, the evolution of events belongs to general history. What concerns us, in this chartering of the plan and Institute of Ignatius Loyola, is the new character it gave to education, and the epoch it made in the intellectual history of the world. To explain this matter, we may follow briefly the deliberations which the Fathers held, and in the course of which, among other conclusions, they came to decide upon reëstablishing education.

It was the fourth of May, 1539, a year and a half before their services were finally accepted by the Pope. Such of the ten members as were then in Rome occupied themselves, after the labors of the day, in nightly deliberations, which were protracted during three months. They decreed, among other things, that they should teach boys and uncultured persons the necessary points of Christian doctrine, at least once a year, and for a definite time. This decree obviously is not about that secondary and superior education of youth, which is our subject; neither does it concern primary education, of which there is nowhere question in the Institute of the Jesuits. But, as the Constitution subsequently drawn up says, "this work of charity, in the Divine service, is more likely to be consigned to oblivion, and to pass into disuse, than other duties more specious in their character, as preaching," etc.[1]

Teaching Christian doctrine pertains to the duty of

[1] Bollandists, as above, nn. 313-4; ibid., Suarez, Nigronius, and others.

those who have the ordinary care of souls. No duty of this kind, as belonging to the ordinary sphere of the Church's clergy, would Ignatius assume as characteristic of his own Institute, except this one. He was, indeed, more than ready to throw in his contribution of personal zeal and charity, for the furtherance of all kinds of benevolence and beneficence. Personally, at the cost of untiring activity, he sowed, as Genelli well observes, the first seeds of those ameliorations in social life, and of those humane institutions, which are so marked a feature of later ages.[1] He was an original benefactor of humanity at the turning-point of modern history, which has since become an era of social organized beneficence. Urban VIII solemnly testifies, that Ignatius organized homes for orphans, for catechumens, for unprovided women; that the poor and the sick, that children and the ignorant and prisoners, were all objects of his personal solicitude.[2] These works of zeal and charity became, in subsequent years, the specific reasons of existence for various other communities, which rose in order and in number. But he did not adopt them as specific in his Institute; nor did he assume as characteristic anything within the province of the ordinary parochial clergy, except the teaching of Christian doctrine to boys and uncultured persons. The rest he attended to, while not provided for; ready to drop them, when provision should be made for them.

But he did assume five works, which were outside of the ordinary lines; and, among them, is the subject

---

[1] Genelli, Life of St. Ignatius Loyola, part ii, ch. 13.
[2] Bulla canoniz. S. Ign. de Loyola, § 22.

of our study, the Education of Youth.¹ As the selection of all these specialties for his Institute reveal the commander's eye resting on a field, where many issues were being fought out, so, in particular, his selection of education as a specialty betrayed the same masterly thought, in the institutions he projected, in the scope he proposed, and, above all, in the formation of his teachers.

There had been, among the Fathers deliberating, a difference of opinion, with respect to Christian doctrine. Bobadilla had dissented from making that work the subject of a special vow; and the others deferred to him. But there was unanimity with regard to every other topic of deliberation, including this one, "the education of youth, having colleges in universities."²

As defined by Jesuit authors, the education of youth means the gratuitous teaching of Letters and Science, from almost the first beginnings of Grammar up to the culminating science of Sacred Theology, and that for boys and students of every kind, in schools open to all.³ Evidently these university men, who were engaged in drawing up the Institute, considered that, if the greatest Professor's talents are well spent in the exposition of the gravest doctrines in Theology, Philosophy, and Science, neither he, nor any one else, is too great to be a schoolmaster, a tutor, and a father, to the boy passing from childhood on to the state of manhood, — that boyhood which, as Clement of Alex-

¹ Bollandists, nn. 313-4; 317.
² Bollandists, July, tom. vii, auct. J. P., §§ xxvii, xxviii.
³ N'gronius; Bollandists, n. 317.

andria says, furnishes the very milk of age, and from which the constitution of the man receives its temper and complexion.

It is requisite here to observe, that there was no such thing in existence, as State Education. Two reasons may briefly be mentioned for this, one of them intrinsic to the question, the other an historical fact. The intrinsic and essential reason was the sacred character of education, as being an original function, belonging to the primary relations of parents and child. States, or organized commonwealths, come only in the third or fourth degree of human society. It was much later, in that short interval between the extinction of the Society of Jesus and the outburst of the French Revolution, that new theories came to be proclaimed, as La Chalotais did openly proclaim them, of a bald and blank deism in social life, and therefore of secularizing education. Between deism and secularization the connection was reasonable. For, if the rights of God went by the board, there was no reason why the rights of parents and children should remain. All alike, the persons and "souls of men,"[1] fell back into the condition in which Christianity had found them; they became chattels of the state, mannikins of a bureau in peace, "food for powder" in war.

The other reason was an historical fact. For all the purposes of charity, mercy, and philanthropy, there were powers in existence, as part of the normal religious life of general Christian society. They were the same powers that had made Christendom, and had carried it on so far as the Christian world, the same

[1] Apocalypse, ch. xviii, 13.

to which we owe the civilization of to-day. More than that. As there is not a single work of charity or mercy, say St. Thomas Aquinas, which may not be made the object of an institution, religious men or women devoting their lives as a service to God, in a special service towards their neighbors; so, in point of fact, there were very few such objects which had not originated some service of religious self-consecration in their behalf.

Now, as operating on education in particular, the powers in the world were, as they had been, almost entirely clerical or religious. In the universities, there were clergymen and Religious. All the great institutions had the religious cast about them. The old ones have it still. Traces of it hang about Oxford and Cambridge. The Church founded them and supervised them. Kings protected them. And the highest outcome of their schools was Divinity in its widest sense; that is to say, the triple knowledge of God, and of man as signed with the light of God's countenance, and of nature as bearing the impress of God's footstep. As it was in the universities, so, outside too, all pedagogic influence had rested with religious men.

But no one of all these religious powers was bound by its constitution to this labor of education, which Loyola now, formally and expressly, assumed as part of his work. It is at this stage of history, that education enters into the fundamental plan of a Religious Order. This is a fact, and an epoch, of prime importance in Pedagogics.

For, inasmuch as education entered thus into the plan of a Religious Order, it became the vocation of a moral body, which, while incorporated like other bodies, did not confine itself, like single universities, to limited circumstances of place; it was a body diffusive. And so with regard to conditions of time; though all corporations give an assurance of perpetuity, a diffusive body like this does more; it multiplies the assurance, in proportion to its own diffusiveness.

And again, inasmuch as the body which undertook the work of education was a religious one, bound to poverty, it guaranteed that the members would endow the work, at their own cost, with that which is the first, the essential, and most expensive endowment, among all others, — the labors, the attainments, and the lives of competent men, all gratuitously given. This endowment, which is so substantial, is besides so far-reaching, that no other temporal foundation would be needed, were it not that the necessaries of life, and the apparatus for their work, are still necessary to living men, even though they live in personal poverty.

Thus then it was that Ignatius took in charge the secondary and superior education of the Christian world, as far as his services should be called for: he threw into the work the endowment of a Religious Order. This, as the sequel proved, meant the whole revival of learning. Lord Bacon bears witness to it in a few words, when he says, that the Jesuits "partly in themselves, and partly by the emulation and provocation of their example, have much quickened and strengthened the state of learning."[1] Father Daniel

[1] Advancement of Learning, book i, p. 176; Phila. edit.

gives some of the details in a summary way. He says: "The exclusively University régime of the late centuries replaced, for a notable portion of students, by a scholastic discipline much more complete; Scholastic Philosophy and Theology renovated, through the care applied to prevent young men from throwing themselves too early into the disputes of the schools; in fine, Literature and Grammar resuming the place they had lost in the twelfth century, and, over and above that, enjoying the new resources created for their use by the Renaissance; all this I call a capital fact in the history of the human mind, and even in the history of the Church."[1]

After the time of Ignatius, other religious congregations, fortified with their own special means for respective departments of activity, entered upon the same general field of work. They were the Oratorians, the Barnabites, the Fathers of the Pious Schools, the Brothers of the Christian Schools, and others whose names may occur in the course of this essay. And, for the education of women, inferior and superior alike, congregations of devoted religious women came into being, and opened their convents to supply the best and highest culture.

For fear that, in the execution of this plan, and in their other enterprises of devotion and zeal, any secondary intentions or results, with regard to power and office, might mar the purity of the work and defeat the main object, the same men, whose future under the generalship of such a leader was about to

---

[1] Père Charles Daniel S. J., Des Études Classiques dans la Société Chrétienne, ch. 8, La Concile de Trente; 1853.

open as one of transcendent influence in the civilized world, bound themselves by vow never to accept any dignity or office in the Church. Naturally they should keep aloof from affairs of state. In fact, it would be incompatible with their own purposes of literary and scientific competence, to leave themselves at the mercy of other men's views, and be drafted into posts outside of the Institute, and be placed in an impossible situation for working out the specific end intended. It would be suicidal too. Just when a man was capable of continuing his kind, he would be lost to the body, and be rendered incapable thereby of propagating his own type of eminence. Besides, without touching upon the inner reasons of the spiritual life, which made this resignation of all honors desirable, it is a fact standing out in clear relief, as history sketches the marvellous fecundity of an Order requiring such a high level of attainments, that many of the choicest souls have felt specially attracted to a kind of life, which at one and the same time satisfied their ideas of Christian perfection, and cut them off from all the paths of worldly glory.

And now, to mention in the last place another point, which is equally important for understanding the educational history of the Order, and to the general mind is equally obscure with some of those mentioned already, there was introduced the principle of religious obedience. It was sanctioned by a unanimous vote.[1] The Fathers had concluded the first deliberation, whether they should form a society at

[1] Bollandists, auct. J. P., nn. 293–7.

all; and they had decided in the affirmative sense.[1] Then the question took this phase. If they were to found a closely-knitted society, they could do so only by assuming a strict bond. That was none other than a strict obedience.

On this head, as on all others that came in order, they began the deliberation by reasoning, one day, in an adverse sense, all having prepared their minds to emphasize every objection which they could find against it. The day following, they argued in a positive sense. The motives in favor of strict obedience won their unanimous assent. They were such as these: —

If this congregation undertook the charge of affairs, and the members were not under orders, no one could be held responsible for an exact administration of the charge. If the body were not bound together by obedience, it could not long persevere; yet this was their first intention, to remain associated in a permanent body. Whence they concluded that scattered as they would be, and already had been, in assiduous and diverse labors, they must be united by a strict principle of subordination, if they were to remain such a body. Another argued thus: Obedience begets heroism of virtue; since the truly obedient man is most prompt to execute whatever duty is assigned him by one, whom, as by a religious act, he regards as being in the place of God, and signifying to him God's will: wherefore obedience and heroism go together.

This reasoning seems to be enforced by the history

[1] Bollandists, n. 292.

of all great nations, in the crises of their military and other public affairs. But, as is clear, the principles of religious obedience are of a different order; they are on a higher plane; and they reach much farther in time and eternity, than those of obedience elsewhere.

Here then we discern, sufficiently for present purposes, the meaning and historical location of this Institute. The members have cut themselves off from the possession of all private property, by the voluntary engagement to poverty, and thereby they have prepared the endowment, on which education will chiefly rest, — that is to say, the endowment consisting of the men to teach, and their services tendered gratis. Position and dignity are alike rendered inaccessible by an express vow of the members professed. Obedience keeps the organization mobile as a company of trained soldiers. And, if any observant mind, well acquainted with the course of human affairs, detects in these principles some reasons for success, normal, habitual, and regular, in the face of unnumbered obstacles, and of unremitting hostility, his view will be singularly corroborated when he rises to a plane higher, and regards the same principles as "religious," carrying with them the sanction of divine worship; which I should be loath to call "enthusiasm," much less "fanaticism." These sentiments are never very prudent, nor enlightened, nor cool; they are either very natural or are short-lived. A mild fever of fanaticism can scarcely produce high results; and a high fever of the same can scarcely last three hundred and fifty years, with perpetuity still threatening. But I would call this phenomenon, in its origin, religious devotion; in its consequences, a supernatural efficiency; and, taking it all in all, that which is called a grace of vocation.

On the 27th day of September, 1540, the Society of Jesus received from the See of Rome its bull of confirmation, by which it became a chartered body of the Church. While these pages were being penned, the 27th day of September came by, 1890. It was the anniversary of that foundation, three hundred and fifty years ago.

CHAPTER IV.

COLLEGES AS PROPOSED IN THE JESUIT CONSTITUTION.

The written rule about the system of education is found in a double stage of development. The first is that in which Loyola left it: it gives us the outline. The second is that in which Aquaviva completed it: this presents us with the finished picture. Likewise in the historical course of administration out in the world, the development is twofold. It runs its first course from Loyola to Aquaviva, while experience was still tentative. Its second course was subsequent to Aquaviva, when experience, having gathered in its results, had only to apply the approved form. This was subject thenceforth to none but incidental changes, as times and places change. And, for these contingencies, the application remained expressly and always pliable.

Hence, whatever was embodied in the *Ratio Studiorum*, as completed, had been the result of the most varied experience before legislating, an experience in the life of the Order extending over fifty-nine years. Whatever this universal experience had not yielded as a positive result, or as applicable to all places, was not embodied. Teachers are different; national customs vary; vernacular tongues are not the same. With regard to these mutable elements, the maxim of the Order in studies, in teaching, in conducting colleges, was the same as that which it proposed to itself in the various other functions of practical life. An exponent of the Institute states the maxim thus: "One should have a most exact knowledge of the country, nation, city, manner of government, manners of the people, states of life, inclinations, etc.; and this from histories, from intercourse, etc."[1] General indications alone are given with regard to these variable factors. The same is done with respect to new sciences, which from the time of the Renaissance were felt to be approaching and developing. Subsequent legislation arises to meet them as they come.

While the Fathers were carrying on the same deliberations to which I referred in the preceding chapter, a resolution was taken to leave the drafting of a Constitution in the hands of those who should remain in Italy. Circumscribing the task still more, they decided to appoint a committee of two, who should address themselves to this work, and report to the rest. The general assembly when convened would issue the final decree. Whatever that should be, such of those present as might then be absent hereby endorsed it beforehand.

Their small number of ten was already reduced to six members present, the other four being scattered in divers countries. They designated as a commission Fathers Ignatius and John Coduri. Soon afterwards Coduri died, and the rest were distributed through the countries of Europe, Africa, and the far East.

[1] Gagliardi.

During the following years, Laynez, who was for some time Provincial of Italy, remained more regularly than the rest within the reach of Ignatius. For this reason, therefore, besides several others, we may understand why Ignatius paid such a high tribute to this eminent man, when he said, as Ribadeneira tells us, that "to no one of the first Fathers did the Society owe more than to Laynez." Whereupon the historian Sacchini observes: "This, I believe, he said of Laynez, not only on account of the other eminent merits of so great a man, and, in particular, for devising or arranging the system of Colleges; but most especially because the foundations, on which this Order largely rests, were new, and therefore likely to excite astonishment; and Laynez, having at command the resources of a vast erudition, was the person to confirm and commend them to public opinion. And that this praise was deserved by Laynez will appear less dubious to any one who considers that other period also, during which he was himself General; if one reckons how many points, as yet unshaped and inceptive, in the management of the Society, were reduced to form and perfected by Laynez; how widely it was propagated and defended by him."[1]

But to return to Ignatius. After ten years of government, he gathered together in Rome such of the first Fathers as could be had, besides representatives from all the Provinces. Forty-seven members were present. He submitted to them, in general assembly, the Constitution as now drawn up, and as acted upon in practical life, during those ten years. The Jesuits

[1] Hist. S. J., 2da pars, Lainius; ad annum 1564, n. 220, p. 340.

present did not exhaust the number of those whose express opinions were desired. That not a single one of the principal Fathers might be omitted in the deliberation, he sent copies of the proposed code of laws to such as were absent. With the suggestions and approbations received from all these representative men he was not yet content. Two more years had elapsed when, having embodied the practical results of an ever-widening experience, he undertook to promulgate the Constitution, by virtue of the authority vested in him for that purpose. But he only promulgated the rule; he did not yet exercise his authority to the full, and impose it as binding. He desired that daily use might bring out still farther, how it felt under the test of being tried, amid so many races and nations. Thus 1553 came and went; and he waited, until the whole matter should be revised and approved once more by the entire Society in conclave. His death intervened in 1556.

Two years later, representatives from the twelve provinces of the Order met together, and elected James Laynez as successor to Father Ignatius. Examining once more this Constitution in all its parts, receiving the whole of it just as it stood with absolute unanimity, and with a degree of veneration, they exercised the supreme authority of the Order, and confirmed this as the written Constitution of the Society of Jesus. By this act nothing was wanting to it, even from the side of Papal authority. Yet, that every plenitude of solemnity might be added to it, they presented it to the Sovereign Pontiff, Paul IV, who committed the code to four Cardinals for accurate revision. The commission returned it, without having altered a word. From that time, whatever general legislation has been added, has entered into the *corpus juris*, or "Institute" at large, as supplementing or explaining the "Constitution," which remains the fundamental instrument of the Institute.

In the Constitution there are ten parts. The fourth is on studies. In length, this fourth part alone fills up some twenty-eight out of one hundred and eleven quarto pages in all, as it stands printed in the latest Roman edition. The legislation about studies is thus seen to be one-fourth of the whole. It has seventeen chapters. In one of them, on the Method and Order to be observed in treating the Sciences, the founder observes that a number of points "will be treated of separately, in some document approved by the General Superior." This is the express warrant, contained in the Constitution, for the future *Ratio Studiorum*, or System of Studies in the Society of Jesus. In the meantime, he legislates in a more general way. And he begins with a subject pre-eminently dear to him, the duty of gratitude. Since corporations are notoriously forgetful, and therefore ungrateful, he lays down in the first place the permanent duty of the Order towards benefactors: then he continues with other topics. They stand thus:—

The Founders of Colleges; and Benefactors. The Temporalities of Colleges. The Students or Scholastics, belonging to the Society. The Care to be taken of them, during the time of their Studies. The Learning they are to acquire. The Assistance to be rendered them in various ways, to ensure their success in studies. The Schools attached to the Colleges of the Society, *i.e.* for external Students not belonging to the Order. The Advancement of Scholastics, belonging to the Order, in the Various Arts which can make them useful to their Neighbor. The Withdrawal of them from Studies. The Government of Colleges. On Admitting the Control of Universities into the Society. The Sciences to be taught in Universities of the Society. The Method and Order to be observed in treating the foregoing Sciences. The Books to be selected as Standards. Courses and Degrees. What concerns Good Morals. The Officials and Assistants in Universities.

Reserving the pedagogic explanation for the next part of this essay, I shall here sketch some of the more general ideas running through the whole legislation of Ignatius of Loyola; and, first, in the present chapter, I shall begin with his idea of Colleges.

Choosing personal poverty as the basis on which to rest this vast enterprise of education, he did not therefore mean to carry on expensive works of zeal, without the means of meeting the expense. Obviously, it is one thing not to have means, as a personal property, and therefore not to consume them on self; it is quite another, to have them and to use them for the good of others. The most self-denying men can use funds for the benefit of others; and can do so the better, the more they deny themselves. It was in this sense that, later on in the century, Cardinal Allen recognized the labors and needs of the English Jesuit, Robert Parsons, who was the superior and companion of Edmund Campian, the former a leading star of Oxford, the latter, also an

Oxford man, and, as Lord Burghley called him, "a diamond" of England. Since Queen Elizabeth was not benign enough to lend the Jesuits a little building-room on English soil, but preferred to lend them a halter at Tyburn, Parsons was engaged in founding English houses of higher studies in France and Spain, at Valladolid, Seville, Lisbon, Eu, and St. Omer. Cardinal Allen sent a contribution to the constructive Jesuit, writing, as he did so: "Apostolic men should not only despise money; they should also have it." And just in this sense was Ignatius himself a philosopher of no utopian school. So we may examine, with profit, the material and temporal conditions required in his Institute, for the establishment of public schools and universities. I shall endeavor to put these principles together and in order.[1]

First, there should be a location provided with buildings and revenues, not merely sufficient for the present, but having reference to needful development.

Secondly, these material conditions include a reference to the maintenance of the faculty. The means must be provided to meet the daily necessities of the actual Professors, with adequate assistance of lay brothers belonging to the Order; also to support several substitute Professors; besides, to carry on the formation of men, who will take the places of the present Professors, and so maintain the faculty as perpetual; moreover, to "provide for some more Scholastic Students of the Order, seeing that there are so many occupied in the service and promotion of the

---

[1] Chiefly from P. Enrico Vasco, S. J., Il Ratio Studiorum Addattato ecc, vol. i, cap. vii, n. 33; a private memoir, 1851.

common weal." These conditions also include "a church for conducting spiritual ministrations in the service of others."[1]

Carrying out this idea, Laynez, in 1564, promulgated a rule or "Form regarding the acceptance of Colleges." He laid down the conditions, on which alone the Society would take in charge either a Latin School, requiring a foundation for twenty Jesuits; or a Lyceum, with fifty persons; or a University, with seventy.[2] Twenty-four years later, Father Aquaviva drew up a more complete and a final "Form," distributing colleges into the three classes, the lowest, the medium, and the highest. The lowest must have provision made for professing in the departments of Grammar, Humanities, Rhetoric, Languages, and a course of Moral Theology; — fifty Jesuits to be supported. The medium class of colleges consists of those whose founders desire, in addition to all the foregoing departments, a triennial course of Philosophy, which begins each year anew; eighty persons to be supported. The highest class is that of the *Studium Generale*, or University, in which, besides the above, there are professed Scholastic Theology, Sacred Scripture, Hebrew; one hundred and twenty persons to be provided for. However, the countries of the Indies, as well as the northern countries of Europe, were not, for the present, brought under this ordinance.[3]

---

[1] Monumenta Germaniæ Pædagogica, ii, p. 71; Ratio Studiorum, etc., by G. M. Pachtler, S. J.; Berlin, 1887.

[2] Ibid. Pachtler, p. 334 *seq.*

[3] Ibid. Pachtler, p. 337 *seq.*

Thirdly, the locality is to be such that, in the ordinary course of events, there should be no prospective likelihood of a deficiency in the concourse of students, and those of the right kind. As, on the side of the Jesuit Province, its educational forces are kept at least equal to the posts which it has undertaken to fill, so, on the side of the population, the prospect should correspond to this undertaking, and give assurance of filling the courses. Hence it was only in larger cities or towns that Ignatius contemplated the foundation of colleges; as the distich has it, contrasting the different fields of activity chosen by different orders in the Church: —

> Bernardus valles, montes Benedictus amabat,
> Oppida Franciscus, magnas Ignatius urbes.

That is to say, "The monks of Clairvaux loved their valleys; the Benedictines their mountain-tops; the Franciscans the rural towns; Ignatius the great cities."

This was the more obviously his idea, as we find him reluctantly granting permission for ministerial excursions through a country, if thereby the Fathers' influence in a great city be likely to suffer. He writes to Father Kessel, the Rector at Cologne, where as yet the Society had no college of its own, that "under the circumstances he approves of Kessel's making a short excursion through the province, provided he and his companions are not long absent from the city, and do not sacrifice the main thing to what is accessory; but he does not give them permission to fix their abode out of the town, because places of less importance afford fewer occasions of gathering the desired fruit: and, besides, they must not leave so famous a university; their exertions will be more useful for the good of religion, in forming scholars to become priests and officers of the State, than all the pains they may bestow on the small towns and villages."[1] Again, when in 1547 he had accepted the donation of a church, buildings, and gardens at Tivoli from Louis Mendosa, he found the place not suited to the convenience of scholars; it was too near Rome, and yet too far; subsequently, the institution had to be transferred within the city."[2]

Fourthly, in addition to these material and local conditions for the normal conduct of colleges, it is supposed that the external relations of political society are so far favorable, as at least to tolerate freedom of action on the part of this educational Institute. Such toleration was, as a general rule, not only the least that could be asked for, but the most that was enjoyed.

These are the chief conditions, material and temporal, which Ignatius requires. They give him a footing to commence his work, and allow the animating principles of his Institute to come into play. The animating principles, to which I refer, may be reduced to three brief heads: First, an intellectual and moral scope, clearly defined, as I shall explain in the following chapters. Secondly, the distinct intention to promote rather the interests of public and universal order and enlightenment, than a mere local good of any city, country, province. Thirdly, a tendency in the intellectual institution itself to become rather a great one

[1] Genelli, part ii, ch. 8.
[2] Jouvancy, Epitome Hist. S. J., Anno Christi, 1547.

than a small one, with more degrees of instruction, more and more eminent Professors, a greater number of the right kind of scholars.[1]

As to the forces available for all this, and the proportion of colleges to be manned in perpetuity, the mind of Ignatius was most express, and became more fixed from day to day. "Cut your cloak according to your cloth," he said to Oliver Manare, when the latter, on going to establish a college at Loretto, asked how he should distribute his men. Ignatius preferred to refuse Princes and Bishops their requests, excusing himself on the score of limited resources, than compromise the reputation of the Society, by an ill-advised assent.[2] And he said, as Polanco his secretary tells us, that "if anything ought to make him wish to live a longer time, it was that he might be severe in admitting men into the Order."[3] He did not want to have many members in the Society; still less, too many engagements.

Having stated thus briefly the material conditions required by Ignatius, and the animating principles or motives which determined him, we are in a position to discern more distinctly the central object of his attention, that for which the material conditions were provided, that by which the ultimate objects were to be attained. It was the teaching body, the faculty, the "College," properly so called. The "College" was the body of educators who were sent to a place. For them the material conditions did but

---

[1] Vasco, vol. i, cap. vii, n. 33 *seq.*
[2] Orlandini; Bollandists, n. 843.
[3] Bollandists, n. 839.

supply a local habitation, subsistence, books, apparatus. The very first decree quoted by Pachtler, from the first general assembly, uses the term "College" in this sense: "No college is to be *sent* to any place," etc.[1]

It is only by derivation from this meaning that the term is applied to the buildings and appointments. It is the body of men that makes the institution. It is this also which makes the institution perpetual; and therefore must itself be so; and must have the material conditions provided for continuing itself, by means of a constant stream of younger men under formation, who will perpetuate the same work.

Now it would be an ideal conception of practical life to be looking for virtuous and erudite men, *viri boni simul et eruditi*, as Ignatius calls them, ever pouring into the Order, straight from the chairs of universities, from benefices, and posts of leisured ease; and, armed already with the full equipment of intellectual and moral endowments, presenting themselves and their services thenceforth, under the title of absolute poverty, to cities, provinces, and countries, which never had anything to do with their formation. "These men," says Ignatius, "are found to be few in number, and of these few the majority would prefer to rest, after so many labors already undergone. We apprehend that it will be difficult for this Society to grow, on the mere strength of those who are already both good and accomplished, *boni simul ac literati;* and this for two reasons, the great labors which this manner of life imposes, and the great self-abnegation

[1] Monumenta Germaniæ Pædagogica, vol. ii, p. 72.

needed. Therefore, . . . another way has seemed good to adopt, that of admitting young men, who, by their good lives and their talents afford us ground to hope that they will grow up into virtuous and learned men, *in probos simul ac doctos viros;* of admitting also colleges, on those conditions which are expressed in the Apostolic briefs, whether these colleges be within universities, or independent: and, if within universities, whether these institutions themselves are committed to the care of the Society, or not. . . . Wherefore, we shall first speak of the colleges; then of the universities," etc.[1]

There were never wanting men of the former kind, already accomplished and of tried virtue, who offered themselves for this service of a lifetime. A noteworthy testimony to their numbers may be found in a dispute with Philip II of Spain, who objected to any moneys leaving the Jesuit Provinces of his realm, for the service and maintenance of the great central college in Rome; and this, notwithstanding the fact that Spanish members were being maintained and formed there. The general assembly, gathered in Rome, 1565, discussed the difficulty; and one of the circumstances mentioned was this: "The Provinces of Spain did not need the assistance of the Roman College as much as others; since many entered the Society, already mature in age and accomplished in learning, so that they could be employed at once in public positions; nor had they to be taught, but they were able to teach others. . . . It was finally recommended that, to lessen the burden of expense on the Roman

[1] Constitutiones S. J., pars iv, declarationes in procemium.

College, and in order that fewer scholastics need be called to Rome, each Province, as soon as convenient, should organize a general university; especially as there was already a sufficiency of students (members of the Order) and, besides, of Professors."[1] This was only twenty-six years after the foundation of the Society.

But, even with all the advantages accruing from these large contingents of learned men already formed, the idea of Ignatius, to train young men within the Order, was more practical for the formation of faculties; and it carried the general efficiency much further. Powerful and effective as the most pronounced personalties may be, when each striking character goes forward into the open field of battle and leads the way, they are not more powerful than when also qualified to move in the steady and regular march of the trained forces. Father Montmorency, referring to the strength which comes of uniformity, sociability, and harmony, said, *Homo unus, homo nullus,* "A man alone is as good as no man at all."

Ignatius then, having perpetuity and development in view, and therefore the steady and trained development of talented and virtuous young men, would not accept foundations, except on the basis of endowment, just described. He had not learned in vain the lessons of Barcelona, Alcalà, Salamanca, and Paris. How wisely he acted is shown by the troubles, which later legislation reveals, upon this very point of inadequately endowed colleges. The questions of ill-endowed colleges, small colleges, too many colleges

---

[1] Sacchini, pars iii, lib. i, nn. 36–42.

for the forces of a Province, are all excellently discussed and settled in the general assembly, which, in 1565, elected Francis Borgia to succeed Laynez. And "on the same day," says Sacchini, "the Fathers set the example of observing the decree which they had just made, with the same degree of severity with which they had made it; for, the letters of several Bishops and municipalities being read, in which foundations for five colleges were offered, they decided that no one of them should be admitted; and, besides, they gave the new General full authority to dissolve certain colleges already existing."[1] In a similar vein, this was the theme of an elegant apology delivered before King Stephen by Father Campano, Provincial of Poland, who requested the King to desist from urging on the Society the multiplication of its institutions.[2]

A tuition-fee paid by the scholar to the Professor, or to the institution, was nowhere contemplated. At Dijon, where Bossuet was afterwards a pupil, the magistrates when offering a college, in 1603, desired to supplement an inadequate endowment, by requiring a fee from the students. In the name of the Order, Father Coton, the King's confessor, remonstrated; and Henri IV himself wrote to the Parliament of Bourgogne, desiring another arrangement to be made; which was accordingly done.[3] The foundation was always to be received as a gratuitous donation, for which the

---

[1] Sacchini, pars iii, Borgia; lib. i, nn. 36 seq.

[2] Sacchini, pars v, Claudius Aquaviva, tom. prior; lib. iv, n. 81.

[3] Recherches sur la Compagnie de Jésus en France au temps du Père Coton, par le P. Prat, tom. ii, p. 296.

Order owed permanent gratitude. In turn, thenceforward, it gave gratuitously, and allowed of no recompense. "No obligations or conditions are to be admitted that would impair the integrity of our principle, which is: To give gratuitously, what we have received gratis."[1]

Thus then the faculty, a competent and a permanent one, is installed. It is not one conspicuous for leisured ease. Professors and Scholastics alike are working for a purpose. They are a "college," in the sense of the Society of Jesus. Yet, if there is not leisured ease, but a life of work and self-denial, the system has been found to result in all the consequences which may be looked for in literary "ease with dignity"; and perhaps in more, since no one does more, than he who, in his own line, has as much as he can well do, and do well. System and method, the great means for making time manifold, become so absolutely necessary; and the singleness of intention in a religious life intensifies results. Then, after the general formation has been bestowed, in the consecutive higher studies of seven or nine years within the Order, the plan of Ignatius leaves open to individual talents the whole field of specialties, in Science and Literature. Hence, to speak of our own day, Secchi or Perry devotes himself to astronomy, Garucci to archæology, Strassmeyer to Oriental inscriptions, the De Backers and Sommervogel to bibliography, others to philology, mathematics, and the natural sciences; while five hundred and more writers follow the lines of their own inclinations, either for some directly useful purpose, or because their pursuit is in itself liberal.

[1] Constitutiones S. J., pars iv, cap. vii, n. 3.

CHAPTER V.

COLLEGES FOUNDED AND ENDOWED.

What was the response of the Christian world, when it had become alive to the nature of this new power in its midst, and to the proposal which the new power made? What did the answer come to, in the way of providing temporalities, necessary and sufficient? Strange enough! Loyola's own short official lifetime of fifteen years does not appear to have been too short, for the purpose of awakening the world with his idea; which, like a two-edged sword of his own make, not only aroused the keenest opposition at every thrust, and at his every onward step, but opened numberless resources in the apostolic, the charitable, and educational reserves of human nature.

This man, who had inserted in the authentic formula and charter of his Institute that watchword of his movements, "Defence and Advance"; who had taken the whole world for the field of his operations, in defending and advancing; this cavalier of a new military type, who had only to show himself upon the field to gather around him the flower of youth as well as mature age, from college and university, from doctor's chair and prince's throne, left behind him, as the work of fifteen years from the foundation of the Order, about one hundred colleges and houses, distributed into twelve Provinces. The territorial divisions were named, after their chief centres, the Provinces of Portugal, Castile, Andalusia, Aragon, Italy, Naples, Sicily, Upper Germany, Lower Germany, France, Brazil, and the East Indies. Individuals under his orders had overrun Ireland, penetrated into Scotland, into Congo, Abyssinia, and Ethiopia. The East Indies, first traversed by Francis Xavier either on foot, or in unseaworthy vessels, signified the whole stretch of countries from Goa and Ceylon on the West, to Malacca, Japan, and the coast of China on the East. Some of this activity might be credited to apostolic zeal alone, were it not that, wherever the leaders advanced into the heart of a new country, it was always with the purpose, and generally with the result, that the country was to be occupied with educational institutions. De Backer notes this in another connection, when, in the preface to his great work of bibliography, "The Library of Writers of the Company of Jesus," he says: "Wherever a Jesuit set his foot, wherever there was founded a house, a college, a mission, there too arose apostles of another class, who labored, who taught, who wrote."[1]

What this means, with regard to its strategic value, there is no need of our being told. The Duke of Parma, writing, in 1580, from the seat of war in the Netherlands to Philip II of Spain, said: "Your Majesty desired that I should build a citadel in Maestricht; I thought that a college of the Jesuits would be a fortress more likely to protect the inhabitants

[1] Bibliothèque des Écrivains de la Compagnie de Jésus, Preface, 1869.

against the enemies of the Altar and the Throne. I have built it." [1]

Sixty years later, after the long generalship of Aquaviva, who during 34 years governed the Order with the ability of another Ignatius, the number of colleges was 372. Well might his immediate successor, Mutius Vitelleschi, writing to the whole Society about the Education of Youth, speak of the "beautiful and precious mass of gold, which we have in our hands to form and finish." [2]

One hundred and fifty years after the death of Ignatius, the collegiate and university houses of education numbered 769. Two hundred years after the same date, when the Order was on the verge of universal suppression, under the action of University men, Parliamentarians, Jansenists, Philosophers, and of that new movement which was preparing the Revolution, the Jesuit educational institutions stood at the figure, 728. The colleges covered almost the whole world, distributed into 39 Provinces, besides 172 Missions in the less organized regions of the globe.[3]

If we look at these 700 institutions of secondary and superior education, under the aspect of their constitution, that is to say, of their scope, their system, the supreme legislative and executive power which characterized them, we find that they were not so much a plurality of institutions, as a single one.

---

[1] Crétineau-Joly; Histoire Religieuse, Politique et Littéraire de la Compagnie de Jésus, tom. ii, ch. iv, p. 176; troisième édit. 1851.

[2] De Institutione Juventutis; Monumenta Germaniæ Pædagogica, vol. ix, p. 61.

[3] Monumenta Germaniæ Pædagogica, vol. ii; Pachtler, p. xx.

Take the 92 colleges of France alone.[1] In one sense, these may be considered as less united than the 50 colleges of the Paris University, for the Paris University was in one quarter of a city, which offers a material unity; these, on the contrary, were spread over the whole of France, presenting the characteristics of "national" education; just as the 700 were over the whole world, a cosmopolitan system. But, regarded in their formal and essential bond, they were vastly more of a unit, as an identical educational power, than any faculty existing. No faculty, whether at Paris or Salamanca, Rome or Oxford, ever possessed that control over its 50, 20, or even 8 colleges, which each Provincial Superior exercised over his 10, 20, or 30, and the General over more than 700, with 22,126 members in the Order. In the one General lay the power of an active headship; from him the facultative power of conferring degrees emanated; and he had one system of studies and discipline in his charge to administer, with a latitude of discretion according to times, places, and circumstances.

As to the numbers of students, and the general estimate to be formed of them, I will record such data as fall under the eye, while passing rapidly over the literature of the subject.

In Rome, the 20 colleges attending the classes of the Roman College numbered, in 1584, 2108 students. Father Argento, in his apology to the States at Klausenburg, in 1607, mentions that the schools in

[1] They are catalogued by Rochemonteix, Collège Henri IV, tom. ii, ch. i, p. 57, note.

Transylvania were frequented by the flower of the nobility; and, in his "History of the Affairs in Poland," dedicated to Sigismund III, he attests that from 8000 to 10,000 youths, chiefly of the nobility and gentry, frequented the gymnasia of the Order in Poland. At Rouen, in France, there were regularly 2000. At La Flèche there were 1700 during a century; 300 being boarders, the other 1400 finding accommodation in the village, but always remaining under the supervision of the faculty. Throughout the seventeenth century, the numbers at the College of Louis-le-Grand, in Paris, varied between 2000, 1827, and 3000; including, in the latter number, 550 boarders. In 1627, only a few years after the restoration of the Society by Henri IV, the one Province of Paris had, in its 14 colleges, 13,195 students; which would give an average of nearly 1000 to a college. Cologne almost began with 800 students, — its roll in 1558. Dilingen in 1607 had 760; in its *convictus*, 110 of the boarders were Religious, besides other Ecclesiastics; the next year, out of 250 *convictores* or boarders, 118 were Religious of various Orders, the secular Priesthood being represented among the students generally. At Utrecht, during the first century of the Order's existence, there were 1000 scholars; at Antwerp and Brussels each, 600; in most of the Belgian colleges, 300. As to Spain and Italy, which first saw the Society rise in their midst, and expand with immense vigor all over them, I consider it superfluous to dwell particularly upon them.

In many of the capitals and important centres throughout Europe, there were separate colleges for nobles. Elsewhere the nobility were mixed with the rest; thus 400 nobles and more were attending the Jesuit schools in Paris. It was studiously aimed at by the Order to eliminate, in matters of education, all distinguishing marks or privileges. Thus Father Buys endeavors, in 1610, to reduce the practice at Dilingen to the custom of the other colleges in the upper German Province.[1]

Most of the Papal Seminaries founded by Gregory XIII, at Vienna, Dilingen, Fulda, Prague, Gratz, Olmütz, Wilna, as well as in Japan and other countries, were put under the direction of the Society; as Pius IV did with his Roman Seminary; and St. Charles Borromeo with that of Milan.

Not knowing what the absolute average really was in these 700 institutions, we may still form some idea of what the sum total of students must have been at its lowest figure. For this purpose, we can take an average which seems about the lowest possible. I have not met with any distinct mention of a college having less than 300 scholars. There are indeed frequent complaints in the general assemblies, regarding what are denounced as "small" colleges. However, it seems clear from numerous indications, as, for instance, from the Encyclical letter of the General Paul Oliva,[2] that these colleges were called small, not primarily on account of an insufficient number of students, but because of insufficient foundations, which did not support the Professors actually employed. A document for the Rectors notes that

[1] Monumenta Germaniæ Pædagogica, vol. ix; Pachtler, p. 192, n. 3.
[2] Monumenta Germaniæ Pædagogica, vol. ix, pp. 110-2.

"thus far almost all the colleges, even such as have received endowments, suffer want regularly, and have frequently to borrow money."[1]

Hence we may be allowed to take, as a tentative average, 300 students to a college. At once, we rise to a sum total of more than 200,000 students in these collegiate and university grades, all being formed at a given date under one system of studies and of government, intellectual and moral.

If statistics, in that nicely tabulated form which delights modern bureaus, have failed us as we run over the whole world to decipher the indications, there is yet another view which we may catch of the same subject, and one that is equally valuable. It is the multitude of nations into which this educational growth ramified. At Goa, in Hindustan, the seminary, which was inferior to none in Europe, had for its students, Brahmins, Persians, Arabians, Ethiopians, Armenians, Chaldeans, Malabari, Cananorii, Guzarates, Dacanii, and others from the countries beyond the Ganges. Japan had its colleges at Funai, Arima, Anzuchzana, and Nangasaki. China had a college at Macao; and later on many more, reaching into the interior, where the Fathers became the highest mandarins in the service of the Emperor, and built his observatory. Towards the close of the eighteenth century a large number of colleges were flourishing in Central and South America. All of these disappeared, when the Order was suppressed. The youth,

---

[1] Arch. Rheni Sup., quoted by Pachtler; Monumenta Germaniæ Pædagogica, vol. ix, p. 110; see also the letter of the General John Paul Oliva, ibid. p. 106.

who could afford to obtain the education needed, went over to Europe, whence they returned, a generation quite different from what had been known of before. They returned with the principles of the Revolution. And the whole history of Central and South America has changed, from that date onwards, into a series of revolutions, which are the standing marvel of political scientists to our day.

To consult a graphic representation of how this educational Order looked on the map of the world, one may glance into the ninth volume of the *Monumenta Germaniæ Pædagogica*. There Father Pachtler, as in his other volumes of the series, sketches only the German "Assistency" of the Society of Jesus. The five Assistencies of the Order served the purposes of government, by grouping many Provinces together into larger divisions. In 1725, the German Assistency comprised nine out of thirty-two Provinces. The nine in question are those of Flandro-Belgium, French Belgium, the Lower Rhine, the Upper Rhine, Upper Germany, Bohemia, Austria, Poland, Lithuania. The map at the end of Father Pachtler's volume represents all this country, with the towns marked differently, according as they contained either universities of the Order, or colleges, or *convictus*, that is, boarding-colleges, or seminaries, or residences. The chronological order of their rise is presented in a table at the beginning of the same volume, with a note to indicate more in particular the grade or amplitude of each, as being a *Studium Generale*, otherwise called University or Academy, a College or a Gymnasium, as well as the annexes of each, in the shape of one or more *con-*

victus, one or more Episcopal or Papal Seminaries, a college of nobles, a *convictus* for poor scholars. By means of this map, a graphic presentation is afforded of one Assistency, from which, by a proper extension, the whole world may be portrayed to the imagination. In 1750, within the limits of this map, there were 217 colleges, 55 seminaries, 73 residences, 24 novitiates, 160 missions, 6 professed houses.[1]

The universities here spoken of, otherwise called *Studia Generalia*, or Academies, are quite typical, a special Jesuit development of the mediæval style. An exact and official form, drawn up for the University of Gratz, may be found in the same *Monumenta*.[2] As Father Pachtler remarks, it shows at a glance the inner working of a Jesuit university, and the general system prevailing over the whole Society. He entitles the document: "*Ordnung einer ausschliesclich von Jesuiten geleiteten Universität*," or "*Einer selbständige Universität*, 1658." The Latin title is: "*Forma et Ratio Gubernandi Academias et Studia Generalia S. J.*" It was the compilation of Father John Argento.

Upon this basis of the amount of work done, as well as its intrinsic character, shown by the results, I was going to draw some inferences with regard to the amount of the temporal endowments, which must have been required to support such a vast organization, and must have been vested in the Order by the Christian world. One might compare the work done with what Oxford accomplishes; and, seeing that the latter university supplies the facilities for higher edu-

---

[1] Monumenta Germaniæ Pædagogica, vol. ii; Pachtler, p. xx.
[2] Vol. ix, pp. 322-389.

cation, and that far from gratuitously, to only a couple of thousands among the nobility and gentry, then, since it spends upon this an annual revenue of $2,500,-000, how much would be required to conduct the education of a quarter of a million of students? Our arithmetic would feel oppressed by the calculation.

But the calculation is not necessary. It is quite evident that religious poverty gave the key to the situation, — poverty, self-abnegation, the resignation of all temporal considerations in life, by men who had no families to provide for, no station to acquire; who had themselves given up every station, from that of the clerical benefice, or the liberal and martial careers, to ducal coronets, princedoms, and even royalty; men therefore, who were bestowing with themselves, and in themselves, the essential endowment of education upon the world, and who needed only to have that supplemented with the few temporal necessities still remaining. And the conclusion to be drawn seems to be this. The Christian world, whether ruler or people, republic or municipality, was making a safe and lucrative investment, whether at home or abroad, in the midst of civilization or of barbarism, when it consigned the absolute use of sufficient temporalities to a world-wide faculty, inspired by the sentiment of religious devotion.

For what is the object of any religious society whatsoever? It is to complete in each of its members the duties of the man, the citizen and the Christian, with other duties called "religious," which, correlative with the former, are nevertheless distinct from them. They are duties which presuppose the moral virtues, the civil and Christian virtues, and tend to complete them with the highest qualities to which perfect Christianity aspires, those of self-devotion and religious self-consecration.

Hence the experiences, making a drama and a tragedy, when the Society abruptly disappeared. Supposing even that enough of competent men, with all personal requirements, could have been found to fill the void, what of their salaries and support? Take an instance. The revenues, which at Bourges had been enough for the support of thirty Jesuits, were found, after the Suppression of the Order, not to afford an adequate compensation for ten secular Professors.[1] Frederic II of Prussia, sending an agent to negotiate with Pius VI about retaining the Order in his States, expresses himself thus in a letter to Voltaire: "The surest means (to perpetuate a series of Professors) is to preserve a seminary of men destined to teach. In studying the sciences, they fit themselves for the office of instructing. It would be no easy task to fill instantaneously a vacancy left by a skilful professor. If the education of ordinary citizens be necessary, the training up of instructors must be no less so." And then, coming to the point before us, the King continues: "Besides, there are reasons of economy for preferring such a body of men to mere secular individuals. The professor taken from the latter class will cost more, because he has a greater number of wants. It is needless to remark that the

---

[1] Maynard; The Studies and Teaching of the Society of Jesus, at the Time of its Suppression, 1750-1773; Baltimore edit. 1885, ch. 2; The Jesuits in Germany, pp. 112-3.

property of the Jesuits would not be sufficient to remunerate their successors; and that revenues, which pass over to the administration of the government, always suffer diminution."¹ Speaking of Ganganelli, Pope Clement XIII, who was under pressure from various quarters to make him suppress the Order, Frederic writes to Voltaire in 1770: "For my own part, I have no reason to complain of him; he leaves me my dear Jesuits, whom they are persecuting everywhere. I will save the precious seed, to give some of it, one day, to those who should wish to cultivate a plant so rare."²

The testimony of documents is uniform upon the poverty of these men, whom Protestant historians like Grotius, Robertson, and others marvel at, for the authority they possessed in the world, for the purity of their lives, their success in teaching, and their art of commanding with wisdom as they themselves obeyed with fidelity. Their life was one of straitened circumstances and self-abnegation. We may see it illustrated in Dilingen.³ Or again, at the great royal college, founded by Henri IV at La Flèche, where three hundred boarders were supposed to be paying their own expenses, as *pensionnaires*, we find Louis XIII issuing a royal decree that his magistrates are to prosecute "les rétardataires et les récalcitrants par toutes les voyes raisonnables," persons who did not pay the expenses of their own children, but left that interest-

---

[1] 1777, 18 novembre; Œuvres de Voltaire, vol. xcv, p. 207; edit. 1832.

[2] Lettre à Voltaire, 7 juillet, 1770; Œuvres de Voltaire, tom. xii, p. 495; edit. 1817.

[3] Monumenta Germaniæ Pædagogica, vol. ii, pp. 358-9.

ing occupation to the college. With all that, says Rochemonteix, nothing came of it, neither of the royal injunctions, nor of judicial suits; things went on the same way, "the parents paying badly, and the treasurers lamenting."[1]

I will close this chapter with one case, because it serves to emphasize a particular sequel of the Suppression; that is, the revival of a tuition-fee. A recent author, writing in 1890, tells the history of the College of Saint-Yves at Vannes, in Brittany. He sums up its revenues at 6000 livres. Placed in the hands of the Order, this college, in 1636, that is, seven years after the Society had assumed charge, directed 400 students; later on, 900; and then 1200. In 1762, the faculty consisted of thirteen members, besides the four Fathers engaged in the adjoining house of retreats. All rendered various services, as is usual in a college of Jesuit instructors. To these we must add the requisite complement of the faculty, at least half as many more lay assistants, belonging to the Order, and to the same local community. Here then are twenty-two at the least, subsisting on 6000 livres a year; and meanwhile providing their house, their library, their physical cabinet, which was fully fitted up with all necessary instruments, and their observatory.[2] "The moment after the Suppression," he goes on to say, "it was quite another affair! Ten secular professors cost 11,000 livres for their salaries alone!"

[1] Le Collège Henri IV, tom. ii, ch. 1, p. 20.
[2] Fernand Butel, Docteur en Droit, etc.; L'Éducation des Jésuites autrefois et aujourd'hui, Un Collège Breton, ch. 1, p. 51; p. 19; p. 28; Paris, Firmin-Didot, 1890.

The author gives the list of their salaries. "To reëstablish equilibrium, one of the first acts of the parliament was to exact from each scholar a tuition-fee of twelve livres; and yet they complained, they could not make ends meet."

Observe, a tuition-fee! On the day after the Suppression, they begin to undo the very work, which, two hundred and thirty years before, the Order had begun to do at its birth, spreading education gratuitously, without drawing on pupils, or drawing on the public treasury.

Well might the General Vincent Caraffa say, in the time of the Thirty Years' War, "We abound rather in men than in revenues." And he says so, in the same breath and in the same sentence, in which he is asking Priests to offer themselves for life to the work of teaching the lower branches, a work which he calls laborious, in times which he specifies as disastrous, and in circumstances which he describes as having no provision made for the means of living.[1]

This brief sketch will go to show how the Christian world did, indeed, meet the proposal of the Order, and found seven hundred colleges. But it also shows how the Order endowed the world, and had even to make good, with its personal heroism, the defects in many of the foundations.

[1] Monumenta Germaniæ Pædagogica, vol. ix, p. 65.

CHAPTER VI.

THE INTELLECTUAL SCOPE AND METHOD PROPOSED.

As the second part of this book is intended to be a pedagogic analysis of the mental culture imparted, I need not sketch here, save in a general way, the intellectual scope proposed by Ignatius of Loyola, and the method which he originated. Both scope and method vary somewhat, according as the students contemplated are respectively external to the Order, or members of it. The latter are to be qualified for becoming future Professors, even though, in point of fact, only a certain proportion of them become so.

Studious youth in general, including Ecclesiastics and Religious of the various Orders, are considered by Ignatius as distributed amid two kinds of educational institutions. One of these he calls the Public School; the other, a University. The first is that which extends, in its courses, from the rudiments of literature up to the lower level of university education. He says: "Where it can conveniently be done, let Public Schools be opened, at least in the departments of Humane Letters."[1] In a note, he explains that Moral Theology may be treated in a gymnasium of this kind. Father Aquaviva, in 1588, puts this kind of school down as the lowest of three

[1] Constitutiones, pars iv, c. 7, n. 1.

ranks of colleges; and sums up the courses as being those of Grammar, Humanities, Rhetoric, Languages, and Moral Theology.[1] He also explains why the lowest Jesuit curriculum must fill these requirements, "in order that the Society be not defrauded of the end it has in view, which is, to carry the students on at least as far as mediocrity in learning, so that they may go forth into their respective vocations, Ecclesiastics to their ministry, lay students to their own work in life, qualified in some degree with a sufficiency of literary culture."[2] This curriculum served also the purpose of those, who, while members of the Order, were for some reason dispensed from the full course of studies.[3] If any grades are wanting in a college, it must be the lower ones which are omitted, the higher being retained.[4] Ignatius goes on to limit the courses in a gymnasium of this kind: "Let not higher sciences be treated here; but, to pursue them, the students who have made due progress in literature are to be sent from these colleges to the universities.[5]

Passing on to universities of the Order, he defines for their scope, first, in behalf of those who are to be Ecclesiastics, Scholastic Theology, Holy Scripture, and Positive Theology; secondly, for all students, Humane Letters, Latin, Greek, Hebrew, and other such languages as Chaldaic, Arabic, and Indian, subject to

[1] Formulæ acceptandorum Collegiorum, etc., summarium; Monumenta Germaniæ Pædagogica, vol. ii; Pachtler, p. 338.   [2] Ibid.
[3] Monumenta Germaniæ Pædagogica, vol. ii, Pachtler, p. 76, 5. Their curriculum was enlarged in 1829; ibid., p. 110, 6.
[4] Ratio Studiorum 1599; Reg. Prov. 21, § 4. Pachtler, Monumenta Germaniæ Pædagogica, vol. ii, p. 258.   [5] Constitutiones, ibid.

the demands of necessity or utility; moreover, Logic, Physics, Metaphysics, Moral Philosophy, and Mathematics. All these departments are to be provided for by Professors of the Order. If the departments of Civil Law and Medicine are added, they will be conducted by Professors not of the Society.[1]

As to the Scholastic members of the Society, their mental culture in the Order begins, of course, where their collegiate curriculum had closed, that is, at the end of their classical course. Their studies henceforth are defined by two objects; one, that of professing, as formed Jesuits in the future, what they are studying now; the other, that of being differentiated, according to talent and circumstance, into preachers, writers, directors of consciences, or managers of affairs.

In view of this two-fold object, all the examinations, arranged for members of the Order in the advanced courses, are regulated by one standard, that the Jesuit Scholastics must be found competent, at each stage, to teach the course in which they are being tested. Accordingly, they review their previous literary acquirements, in all the lines which the Society regularly professes; then, during three years, they apply exclusively to Philosophy and Natural Sciences; and, four years more, to Divinity and allied Sciences.[2]

This protracted course, therefore, as given more in detail by the subsequent *Ratio*, consists of Poetry, Rhetoric, and Literature; Mathematics, Physics, and

---

[1] Constitutiones, pars iv, c. 12.
[2] Constitutiones, pars iv, c. 5, n. 1.

Chemistry; Logic, Ontology, Cosmology, Psychology, and Natural Theology; Ethics, Natural, Social and Public Right, Moral Theology, Canon Law, Ecclesiastical History, Scholastic Theology, Hebrew, Sacred Scripture. The courses are to be pursued either in the same classes which external students attend, or, in their own university classes, when a general house of studies is formed as a "Scholasticate." In both cases, they have Seminary exercises of their own, beyond what is required in the most condensed university courses.

Those whom health and excellence have approved at every step are ordinarily to be withdrawn from studies, "when the course of Arts has been finished, and when four years have been spent on Theology."[1] Specialties are to be cultivated.[2] Subsequent legislation places these specialties in the interval between the Arts and Theology; and, again, after the latter.

This, in brief, is the practical idea of the Professorial Seminaries, philological, philosophical, scientific, and theological, through which the stream of future Professors is continually passing. Each one is subject, at every stage, to examination tests which include the most distinct reference to professorial capacity. The technical standard in the examinations is that of "surpassing mediocrity," which term is accurately defined, as we shall see later, when analyzing the *Ratio*.[3]

While the depleted ranks of the professorial body are thus regularly supplied, it is clear that more ser-

---

[1] Constitutiones, pars iv, c. 9, n. 3. [2] Ibid., c. 5, n. 1, C.
[3] Ch. xi. below.

vices remain available in the Order at large, than the single purpose of education would at any time require. But this only serves the wider scope which the Society has in view, much wider than education taken alone. And Ignatius makes mention of this expressly when he says, that the Scholastic students "may never come to profess the learning which they have acquired"; still "they are to consider that labor of studies as a work of great merit in the sight of God."[1]

So much for the widest and highest intellectual objects aimed at in these studies. Looking down now to its lowest limit, we perceive that education, as imparted by the Society to the external world, is to begin not below "the rudiments of grammar, in which boys must already be versed; they must know how to read and write; nor is any allowance to be made in favor of any one, whatever be his condition of life; but those who press these petitions upon us are to be answered, that we are not permitted" to teach the elements. This is the ordinance of Aquaviva, in 1592, and he simply refers to the Constitution.[2] He also notes, in the same document, that the new *Ratio Studiorum* elevates every grade, as it stood at that date, one year higher than it had been before. The document is from the German archives. Pachtler observes that most of the Latin schools, particularly in Protestant Germany, took children up from the alphabet.[3] The effect of the Jesuit system was that

---

[1] Constitutiones, pars iv, c. 6, n. 2.
[2] Monumenta Germaniæ Pædagogica, vol. ii, p. 311.
[3] Ibid., p. 310, note.

of a constant upward trend to what was higher, more systematic, and complete.

This brings us to the question of method. Here a number of elements occur, some of them essential, many of them subordinate. These latter, at least, were the products of ingenuity and industry on the part of the teaching body, and were productive of industry and life on the part of scholars. To illustrate the whole matter, I will refer to authors who were addressing the world, soon after the Society had taken its stand as an educational power, and when its institutions were conspicuous to the eyes of all.

First comes classification, which was an essential feature of the Jesuit system. Ribadeneira, the intimate friend of Ignatius, when writing the life of Loyola, in the year 1584, and describing the work of the Order, now forty-fours years old, observes: "Elsewhere one Professor has many grades of scholars before him; he addresses himself at one and the same time to scholars who are at the bottom, midway, and at the top; and he can scarcely meet the demands of each. But, in the Society, we distinguish one rank of scholars from another, dividing them into their own classes and orders; and separate Professors are placed over each."[1]

The division of classes, a thing so natural to us, was in those times a novelty. There were practically only two degrees of teaching; one superior, embracing Theology, Law, and Medicine; the other preparatory. The preparatory instruction had already been tending towards the later system of grading; the

[1] Ribadeneira, Bollandists, July, tom. vii, nn. 335 *seq.*

term "class" was an expression of the Renaissance. Father Rochemonteix, speaking of the Paris University, notes that the first authentic act, in which the term is used, dates from 1539.[1] From 1535, the division of studies, by means of classes, was already being accomplished. Still there was no definite number of grades. The study of literary models was defective. Grammar was beclouded with the subtleties of dialectics, to the great prejudice of written composition, as well as of the reading and imitation of models.[2]

Now it will be observed that Ignatius was studying in the University of Paris from 1528 to 1535; and his companions remained till 1536. By the time he published the Constitution as a rule of guidance, he had become surrounded by men, who were not merely graduates of universities, but had been Doctors, Professors, and Rectors in Portugal, Spain, France, Italy, Belgium, Germany. One consequence was that Ignatius, from the very beginning, formulated a complete system of graded classes. He relegated dialectics to its proper field, Philosophy and Theology. And, bringing into prominence the reading of authors, and the practice of style in imitation of the best models, he defined a method. This, after being elaborated during forty years, was then found to be not only new, but complete, and good for centuries to come. It arranged courses in a series, having reference to one another; it coördinated definite stages of the courses with definite matter to be seen; and, in the lower branches

---

[1] Le Collège Henri IV., tom. iii, pp. 5-7.
[2] Compare the ordinance of Father Oliver Manare, 1583, n. 114; Monumenta Germaniæ Pædagogica, vol. ii, p. 269.

it distributed the students, with their respective portions of the matter, into five grades, classifying precepts, authors, and exercises, as proportioned to each successive grade. Nothing more familiar to ourselves now; nothing newer to the world then! This was the *Ratio Studiorum.*

The grades of the gymnasium may include several divisions, according to the number of students; but the grading itself remains fixed, and leaves no element, either of actual culture, or of future developments, unprovided for, or without a location. Nor do these grades mean five years. They mean a work to be done in each grade, before the next is taken up. On this, the mind of Ignatius was most explicit. As an almost universal rule, they never mean less than five years. And, for one of them, the grade of Rhetoric, in which all literary perfection is to be acquired, the system contemplates two and even three years. In this point, too, we may note a characteristic view of Ignatius. It is that the longer term, whenever provided, whenever prescribed, urged, and insisted upon, is always for the talented student, the one who is to become eminent. To use his own words, when laying down the rules in this matter for the Rector of a University, his full idea will be carried out, when "those who are of the proper age, and have the aptitude of genius, endeavor to succeed in every branch and to be *conspicuous therein.*" [1]

To enumerate now some of the subordinate elements in the Jesuit method, I will quote from the same author, Ribadeneira. He says, speaking of young

[1] Constitutiones, pars iv, c. 13, n. 4.

scholars: "Many means are devised, and exercises employed, to stimulate the minds of the young — assiduous disputation, various trials of genius, prizes offered for excellence in talent and industry. These prerogatives and testimonies of virtue vehemently arouse the minds of students, awake them even when sleeping, and, when they are aroused and are running on with a good will, impel them and spur them on faster. For, as penalty and disgrace bridle the will and check it from pursuing evil, so honor and praise quicken the sense wonderfully, to attain the dignity and glory of virtue." He quotes Cicero and Quintilian to the same effect.[1]

This was not to develop a false self-love in young hearts; which would have been little to the purpose with religious teachers. "Let them root out from themselves, in every possible way, self-love and the craving for vain glory," says the oldest code of school rules in the Society, probably from the pen of Father Peter Canisius himself.[2] What is appealed to, is the spirit of emulation, and that by a world of industries; which, disguising the aridity of the work to be gone through, spurs young students on to excellence in whatever they undertake, and rewards the development of natural energies with the natural luxury of confessedly doing well. In the dry course of virtue and learning, satisfaction of this kind is not excited in the young, without a sign, a token, a badge, a prize. Then they feel happy in having done well, however little they enjoyed the labor before. Honor-

---

[1] Bollandists, ibid., 376–7.

[2] Monumenta Germaniæ Pædagogica, vol. ii, Pachtler, p. 169.

able distinctions well managed, sometimes a share in the unimportant direction of the class, brilliancy of success in single combat on the field of knowledge, of memory, or of intellectual self-reliance, the ordered discrimination of habitual merit, all these means and many others keep the little army in a condition of mental activity, and sometimes of suspense; "and if not all are victorious, all at least have traversed the strengthening probation of struggle."[1]

In all the courses of Belles-lettres, Rhetoric, Philosophy, and Theology, the institutions called "Academies" gather into select bodies the most talented and exemplary of the students. The young *literateurs*, or philosophers, having their own officials, special reunions, and archives, hold their public sessions in presence of the other students, the Masters, and illustrious personages invited for the occasion. In their poems, speeches, dialogues, they discuss, declaim, and rise to great thoughts, and to the conception of great deeds.

Civil discords are not the subject of their debates, but the glories of their native country, its success in arms, all that is congenial to the young mind and fosters the sentiment of love of country. Among the students of Rhetoric, forensic debates and judicial trials are organized; "and when the advocates of both sides have pleaded their cause in one or two sessions of the court, then," says a document I am quoting from, dated 1580, "the judge, who has been elected for the purpose, will pronounce his judgment in an

---

[1] L'Éducation des Jésuites autrefois, etc., par Dr. F. Butel, ch. 1 pp. 22–8. This author sketches agreeably the means touched upon in the text, and his references are useful.

oration of his own; this will be the brilliant performance; and, to hear it, friends will be invited, and the Doctors of the University and all the students will be in attendance."¹ In the programme for the distribution of rewards, there is described an interesting element, *puer lepidus*, "a bright young lad," and what he is to do and how he is to bring out the name of the victor, "whereupon the music will strike up a sweet symphony."² At another time, a set of published theses are defended against all comers by some philosopher or theologian. And, while games and manly exercises outside develop physical strength, gentility of demeanor and elegance of deportment have the stage at their service inside, for the exhibition of refined manners.

In all this, princes and nobles, future men of letters and of action, are mingling in daily life, in contest and emulation, with sons of the simplest burghers. Descartes³ notes these points sagaciously, when he recommends to a friend the College of La Flèche: "Young people are there," he says, "from all parts of France; there is a mingling of characters; their mutual intercourse effects almost the same good results as if they were actually travelling; and, in fine, the equality which the Jesuits establish among all, by treating just in the same way those who are most illustrious and those who are not so, is an extremely good invention."⁴

---

¹ Monumenta Germaniæ Pædagogica, vol. ii, Pachtler, p. 261. Addita quædam Exercitiis Litterariis Humanistarum, 1580; prior to the completed Ratio Studiorum.   ² Ibid., p. 262.

³ Lettre xc.

⁴ Compare Chateaubriand's Genius of Christianity, part iv, book vi, Recapitulation; translation by Dr. Chas. I. White; Baltimore, 1884, p. 637 *seq.*

As the new sciences came into vogue, they received at once the freedom of this city of intellect; and here they received it first. It has been said, indeed, that the Society of Jesus, "obstinately bound to its formalism, refused to admit anything modern, real, and actual, and that the national languages and literatures, as well as the new developing sciences, fared ill at its hands." This statement, as far as it concerns France, is examined by Father Charles Daniel, who to other valuable works of his own has added the neat little essay called, *Les Jésuites Instituteurs de la Jeunesse Française, au XVIIe et au XVIIIe siècle*.[1] As to Germany, we shall see indications enough on all these subjects in the *Monumenta Germaniæ Pædagogica*. For all countries there is a sufficiency of information, in the mere text of the *Ratio Studiorum*, in Jouvancy's classic commentary thereupon, *De Ratione Discendi et Docendi*, and other authentic documents, besides the actual practice visible in the colleges. But the whole question about the vernacular tongues, as if they were kept out of the colleges by Latin and Greek, is so far an anachronism for the dates and epochs, regarding which some moderns have agitated the question, that I shall tell a little anecdote, which will not be so much of a digression, but that it will place us back just where we are at present.

In 1605, Lord Bacon published his two books on the Advancement of Learning. The work is considered the first part of his "Novum Organum." He undertakes to "make a small Globe," as he says, "of the Intellectual World, as truly and faithfully as he

[1] Paris, Victor Palmé, 1880.

can discover.[1] His subject is identical, as far as it goes, with the much more extensive and exhaustive work of Father Anthony Possevino, a famous Jesuit, who had published, twelve years before, the results of twenty years' travel and observation, while fulfilling, in many countries, the important duties of Apostolic Legate, Preacher, Professor. I have two editions of his great tomes before me. The first is that of Rome, 1593; the other that of Venice, 1603; this latter is called "the most recent edition."[2] The only indication which I discern of Bacon's not having profited by Possevino is this, that he says: "No man hath propounded to himself the general state of learning to be described and represented from age to age."[3] Now, as this is saying too much, for it just indicates what Possevino's labors had been showing to the world during twelve years, I must conclude that there is no assurance whatever, but that Bacon profited by Possevino: he seems merely to have gone over the same ground in English, and done justice to the subject, in his own peculiar way. Accordingly, he did it. what justice he could, in English. Three years later he writes to Dr. Playfer, Margaret Professor of Divinity in the University of Cambridge, requesting that the Doctor would be pleased to translate the work into

---

[1] Works; Philadelphia edit. 1859, vol. i, p. 244.

[2] Bibliotheca Selecta in qua agitur de Ratione Studiorum, in Historia, in Disciplinis, in Salute Omnium procuranda. De Backer in his Bibliothèque des Écrivains de la Campagnie de Jésus gives the list of republications, either in whole or in part. Sommervogel's new work, royal quarto, Bibliothèque de la Compagnie de Jésus, 1890, has reached thus far only to the letter B; hence Possevino is not yet entered. [3] Ibid., p. 187.

Latin; and his lordship promises eternal gratitude. What reasons does the noble author urge for this request? Two reasons, of which the first is very noteworthy for our purpose: — "the privateness of the language, wherein it is written, excluding so many readers!" And the second is almost as worthy of note: — "the obscurity of the argument, in many parts of it, excluding many others!"[1] Here we have our domestic classic author, in the year 1608, endeavoring to get out of his narrow cell, the "privateness of the English language," into the broad world of the literary public, where the Jesuit with his tomes was enjoying to the full his literary franchise. This does not look as if the colleges, at that time, kept the languages down, but rather that they had in their gift the full freedom of the literary world, and sent students forth to walk abroad at their ease there, where Bacon humbly sued for admission!

I was going to quote from Possevino, describing in a graphic way the daily intellectual life of the great Roman College, with its two thousand and more students, besides the great body of Professors. But my limits forbid me to do more than refer to it.[2]

There are two views which may be taken of a coin and its stamp. One is taken direct, looking at it in itself; the other is indirect, observing the impression it leaves in the mould. It leaves a defined vacancy there. What kind of vacancy was left in the intellectual culture of Europe, when this intellectual system

---

[1] Ibid., p. 136.
[2] Ch. 10, of book 1, Ratio Collegiorum et Scholarum, etc., end of chapter; Roman edit.

was suddenly swept away? Before the Suppression of the Society, some of the institutions, which had thriven at all, had been inspired by a healthful rivalry. They found, when the Society was gone, that part of their life decayed. And, while they themselves began to languish, the place of the Jesuits they could not fill. Of some others, who lived a life barely discernible, we are given to understand, that their vitality consisted in the effort to keep the Jesuits out. I will take an instance from Bayonne.

A work has just been published on the municipal college of Bayonne, by the Censor of Studies, in the Lyceum of Agen.[1] In seventy pages, which concern transactions with the Jesuits,[2] the author, in no friendly tone, narrates the entire history from the documents of the Jansenist party. I will imitate this example of his so far as to narrate the following entirely in his own words.

Beginning his last chapter, entitled "Reform and Conclusion," he says in a tone somewhat subdued, but not more so than his subject:[3] "This then was the College of Bayonne, which, for a few years more, prolonged an existence ever more and more precarious; and it was finally closed in 1792, in spite of several generous efforts at restoring it.

"But already," he continues, "for thirty years, a great literary event had been accomplished in secondary education. A decree of the Parliament of Paris, dated

---

[1] Histoire d'un Collège Municipal aux XVIᵉ, XVIIᵉ, et XVIIIᵉ siècles . . . à Bayonne avant 1789. Thèse présentée à la Faculté des Lettres de Toulouse, par J. M. Drevon, censeur des Études au Lycée d'Agen, 1890. About 500 pages. [2] Pp. 160-234. [3] P. 429.

the 16th of August, 1762, had pronounced the expulsion of the 'ci-devant soi-disants Jésuites'; which decree was this time definitively executed. Now the Jesuits, in their five Provinces of France, possessed then nearly a hundred colleges. Judge of the immense void which was suddenly created in the secondary instruction of the Province, ill prepared for so abrupt a departure! There was a general confusion, and a concert, as it were, of complaints and recriminations. Where get the new masters? . . . The disciplinary and financial administration of the colleges, left vacant by the Jesuits, was confided to the bureaus, that is to say, assemblies composed of the Archbishop or Bishop, the Lieutenant General, the King's Proctor, and the senior Alderman. . . . Every one soon felt the inconveniences of this system. The municipal officers of the cities, the bureaus themselves hastened to petition the King, that their colleges might be confided to religious communities. Thus it was that the greater part of the old Jesuit colleges fell into the hands of the Benedictines and Bernardines, of the Carmelites and Minims, of Jacobins and Cordeliers, of Capuchins and Recollects, of Doctrinaires and Barnabites, and above all, of the Oratorians. But all these Religious, except the Oratorians, fell far short of the Jesuits. The greater part had not even any idea of teaching, etc." Then the author devotes a heavy page to the novel systems which were introduced. He closes the paragraph sadly: "All this agitation," he says, "was unfortunately sterile; and, as I have just said, secondary instruction, on the eve of the French Revolution, had not taken a step forward during fifty years."

CHAPTER VII.

THE MORAL SCOPE PROPOSED.

SWEET is the holiness of youth, says Chaucer. Nor less grateful to the eye are those gentle manners of youth, which another bard portrays as impersonated in his "celestial lights," who say: —

> We all
> Are ready at thy pleasure, well disposed
> To do thee gentle service.[1]

Christian morals and Christian manners make the perfect gentleman.

Plato had put it down that "he who hath a good soul is good"; and he insisted that no youth, who has had a personal acquaintance with evil, can have a good soul. He did not mean that a youth must be ignorant of what temptation is. There is no hot-house raising in this world which will keep off that blast. Every child, while keeping on the royal road of innocence, has enough in himself, and in the choicest of surroundings, to know the realities of life and its warfare. But Plato refers to a personal experience of the by-ways, which are not virtue, and which it is not necessary to travel by, in order to know enough about them. The educational means, the industry, the vigi-

[1] Dante, Parad. viii.

lance, which have for a result the preservation of youth in the freshness of innocence, signify a medium of respiration which is kept pure, and a moral nutriment which is good and is kept constantly supplied, until tender virtue has risen steadily into a well-knit rectitude, and is able thenceforth to brave manfully the incidental storms of life.

For this moral strengthening of character, no less than for the invigorating of mental energies, the system of Ignatius Loyola prescribes an education which is public, — public, as being that of many students together, public as opposed to private tutorism, public, in fine, as requiring a sufficiency of the open, fearless exercise both of practical morality and of religion. Since the time of Ignatius, Dupanloup has observed on this subject : —

"I have heard a man of great sense utter this remarkable word, 'If a usurping and able government wanted to get rid of great races in the country, and root them out, it need only come down to this, that it require of them, out of respect for themselves, to bring up their children at home, alone, far from their equals, shut up in the narrow horizon of a private education and a private tutor.'"[1]

The youthful material, on which the Jesuit system had to work, may be described from two points of view. There were home conditions; and there were conditions too of the educational system, which was commonly prevalent in those centuries.

As to the circumstances of polite society at the boys'

[1] De La Haute Éducation Intellectuelle, liv. iv, ch. 4. Compare Vasco, vol. i, n. 24.

homes, Charles Lenormant, speaking of those times, tells us that "it was the privilege of a gentleman to have from his infancy the responsibility of his own actions. The fathers of families were the first to launch their sons into the midst of the perils of the world, even before the age of discernment had begun."[1] Even when boys' homes effect no positive harm, still, only too often, they answer this description, that they undo the best of what the school training is endeavoring to effect, by the discipline of subordination and the practice of obedience.

It was this state of things which made the German Jesuits, in spite of themselves, petition for the requisite authorization to open boarding colleges in the north, as had already been done in Portugal and elsewhere. Reluctantly the authorization was given by the general assembly.[2] These *convictus*, or *pensionnats*, were known to make great inroads on the time of the Fathers, on their study, their religious retirement, and especially on that immunity of theirs from financial transactions, which they enjoyed as Religious. The Constitution of Ignatius offers no more than a bare foothold for the introduction of these colleges.[3] Yet they have proved to be the most prolific nurseries of the eminent men, whom the Society has sent forth into all the walks of life.

Not at home alone were effeminacy and dissolute-

---

[1] Essais sur l'Instruction Publique, par Charles Lenormant, membre de l'Institut; quoted by Rochemonteix, Le Collège Henri IV, tom. ii, ch. 1, p. 49, in his very instructive discussion on the Jesuit *internat*, or *pensionnat*.

[2] Monumenta Germaniæ Pædagogica, vol. ii, Pachtler, p. 78.

[3] Const., part iv, ch. 3, decl. B.

ness to be feared. There were conditions of life in the university system of the sixteenth century, which seemed considerably worse than those already described in the first chapter of this book. Possevino, who had spent ten years in the midst of the religious turmoils of France, and ten more in Papal legations to Germany, Poland, Hungary, Transylvania, Russia, Muscovy, Sweden, and Gothia, and, after that, four more years in visiting the universities throughout Europe, notices that there were five ways, whereby a general corruption of society had come about. First, he mentions the dissemination of bad books. Secondly, "the omission of lectures; or, when lectures were held, such disturbances during them, with noise and yells, that there scarce remained an appearance of human, let alone of Christian, society. Thirdly, factions. Fourthly, sensuality, to which cause must be referred that atrocious kind of iniquity, whereby the very walls of the schools were defiled with writing and the vilest pictures;[1] so that the tender age, which had come innocent, must go away more polluted with crime, than imbued with learning, becoming hateful to God himself. Fifthly, an aversion for Divine worship, inasmuch as disputations and graduating festivities and lectures have constantly been transferred to those days and those hours, when by Divine precept public worship is due."[2]

The means organized by Ignatius into a method of moral education I will sketch in the words of his

[1] Turpissimis signis.
[2] Bibliotheca Selecta, lib. i, ch. 44 ; Quasnam tetenderit insidias humani generis hostis, etc.

contemporaries. Ribadeneira, his biographer, says: "Those means are employed by our Masters, whereby virtue is conceived in the hearts of the pupils, is preserved and augmented. They are morning prayer, for obtaining grace from God not to fall into sin; night prayer and a diligent reflection on all the thoughts, words, and actions of the day, to do away by contrition of heart with all the faults committed; the attentive and devout hearing of Mass every day; frequent and humble confession of sins to a Priest; and if they are old enough, and great devotion recommends it, and their confessor approves of it, the reverent and pious reception of the Body of our Lord Jesus Christ; teaching and explaining the rudiments of the Christian faith, whereby the boys are animated to live well and happily. Besides, great pains are taken to know and root out the vices of boyhood, especially such as are somehow inborn and native to that age."[1]

Here, by the way, the reader may advert to the fact that the confessional, of which mention is made, never comes in as part of the external means of moral development; nor is a superior ever the confessor of those under his charge, except when desired to be so by the free choice of the subordinate himself. A general law of the Catholic Church ordains it thus.

Loyola's biographer goes on to the various means, whereby, in such a multitude of young persons, the bad element, which unfortunately will never die, is either suppressed and kept at its lowest stage of a struggling

---

[1] Ribadeneira, Bollandists, nn. 373 *seq.*

vitality, or else, if it happens to shoot up, is weeded out. The garden will be none the poorer for that.

Nil dabit inde minus!

There are, moreover, the division of students into categories and ranks, with their own officers from among the boys themselves; the degrees of honor and preëminence assigned to good conduct and virtue; especially the pious societies or Sodalities, into which none are admitted save the most studious and virtuous among the youths; and that with a discrimination in favor of superior merit, even among such as answer the general description. The Sodalities of the Society of Jesus, as the subject of a study upon the management of youth, and indeed upon the cultivation of all ranks in Christian society, from Peer and Field Marshal and Viceroy, down to the little boy beginning his career at school, would deserve a special discourse for themselves.

I will continue now from Possevino, describing the Roman College, which was an object of daily observation to the capital of the Christian world.[1] "Here," he says, "you have two thousand youths, among whom reigns a deep silence; there is no commotion. In the classes there is no reading of profane author or poet, who might inoculate the mind with defilement." I may remark that Ignatius had, from the very first, begun the method of expurgating authors, a task which was then carried on with diligence by the literary men of the Society. Our author resumes: "A hundred daily occasions of sin and idleness are pre-

[1] Bibliotheca Selecta, lib. i, ch. 40.

cluded; a continuous series is going on of lectures, repetitions, disputations, conferences." Then he portrays, as visible there in every-day life, many of the features which Ribadeneira has mentioned.

While idleness was under a ban, vacation was not debarred. Its principles, however, were defined on new lines. There was a sufficiency of rest to be provided; but then no new intermissions were to be granted. The "sufficiency" would appear spare luxury to our looser times.[1] "One week of doing nothing," say the Fathers of Upper Germany to the General Aquaviva, "is more hurtful to students, than four weeks in which some literary exercise is kept up"; and "parents take very much amiss this state of idleness, if the boys remain on our hands."[2]

In all this, there was no question of making religious men of the students. It was a question only of Religious making men of them. Father George Bader, Provincial of Upper Germany in 1585, left it in his instructions for the management of the *convictus*, at Dilingen, that "the Prefects were not to despair or despond, if they did not see at once, or in all, the improvement desired; nor were they to require the perfection of Religious from them, nor introduce among them such practices of life, as elsewhere the students could not keep up in their calling; but the directors

---

[1] Ratio Studiorum of 1599 and 1832, Reg. Prov. 37. The higher courses are allowed a midsummer vacation of between one and two months; in the lower or literary course, Rhetoric is allowed one month, the others classes less. Besides certain feast-days during the year, every week must have one day free, which, in the higher courses, is the whole day, but, in the lower, is only the latter part of it.

[2] 1602; Monumenta Germaniæ Pædagogica, vol. ii, Pachtler, p. 467.

should be content with having a manner of life followed, which was ordinary, virtuous, and pious."[1]

According to this idea, the religious teacher being a man, a citizen, and an ecclesiastic, his educational industry has produced its effect, when it has made accomplished men, worthy citizens, competent Ecclesiastics, or Religious; "when in the school," says Ribadeneira, "as in an arena, the students, foreshadowing the future, practise already, in their own way, those same virtues and duties, which in maturer years they will exhibit, in the management of the republic."[2] The rich material of the youthful mind and soul receives the manifold influence which the teacher's mind and heart possess; and receives it after the manner of the recipient, according to his future vocation.

What the Jesuit professors, in fact, were like, those who in after years showed themselves but little friendly to the Order did not omit to testify. "During the seven years," says Voltaire, "that I lived in the house of the Jesuits, what did I see among them? The most laborious, frugal, and regular life, all their hours divided between the care they spent on us and the exercises of their austere profession. I attest the same as thousands of others brought up by them, like myself; not one will be found to contradict me. Hence I never cease wondering how any one can accuse them of teaching corrupt morality. . . . Let any one place side by side the 'Provincial Letters' and the Sermons of Father Bourdaloue; he will learn in the former the art of raillery, the art of presenting things,

---

[1] Monumenta Germaniæ Pædagogica, vol. ii, Pachtler, p. 411.
[2] Bollandists, n. 374.

indifferent in themselves, under aspects which make them appear criminal, the art of insulting with eloquence; he will learn from Father Bourdaloue, that of being severe to oneself, and indulgent toward others."[1]

History is uniform in bearing witness that the general effects of their teaching corresponded to the example of these Professors, in spite of the fact, as Cretineau-Joly puts it, that even from the hands of religious men the impious can still come forth, as, in the school of the wise, dunces and dolts may still be found.[2] Man is still and always free. However, if it follows thence, that not only a positive, but a negative result may always be expected; such a double result may be set off by two consoling reflections, which I will mention, in order to complete the picture of this education in practice.

The first is, that since, from the school of virtue and religiousness, vice can still issue forth, and, as the General Vitelleschi says, a good education, though almost omnipotent, may, like the morning dew, evaporate and be lost in the first heat of manhood's passions,[3] what would be the results of the system, if it had less piety to enlighten, or less of an organized practice of virtue to confirm, the minds and hearts of the young?

Another reflection is this: that human nature, however erratic by defect of will, still remains beautiful,

---

[1] Lettre 7 février, 1746; Œuvres, tom. viii, p. 1128; edit. 1817.

[2] Crétineau-Joly, Histoire de la Compagnie de Jésus, tom. iv, ch. 3, p. 209; edit. 1851. This chapter and the following one, ch. 4, in Crétineau-Joly, pp. 158-297, contain the most varied information on our subject, regarding professors, writers, scholars, etc.

[3] Epistola de Institutione Juventutis, et Studiis Litterarum Promovendis, 1639; Mon. Germ. Pœd., vol. ix, Pachtler, p. 62.

thanks to the original gift of God. Whence it comes, that impiety is found beautifully inconsistent; and, in its lucid intervals, it makes the due acknowledgment, as he did, who once said : —

> O thou, that with surpassing glory crowned,
> Look'st from thy sole dominion . . .
> To thee I call. . . .
> To tell thee how I hate thy beams,
> That bring to my remembrance from what state
> I fell.[1]

The Society of Jesus has many a time been elegantly blessed and cursed by the same eloquent lips and pens.

The secret of this magisterial ascendency, as Ignatius of Loyola projected it, was to be found in the Masters' intellectual attainments, which naturally impressed youthful minds; and also in a paternal affection which, of course, won youthful hearts. Does anything more seem necessary for the full idea of authority? The committee appointed by the canton of Fribourg, for restoring the Fathers to their old college in 1818, mention as one reason for having done so, that "the will cannot be chained; it will not submit to restraint. You can win it, but not subjugate it." And they speak of that "most lively attachment" ever abiding in the hearts of students towards members of the Order, which they have known as the cradle of their youth.[2] The same Father Bader, whom I have quoted before, defines where authority lies, when he says: "Let not the Prefects consider their authority to consist in this, that the students are

---

[1] Paradise Lost, book iv.
[2] Notice sur le Pensionnat, etc. à Fribourg en Suisse, 1839, pp. 56 *seq.*

on hand in obedience to their nod, their every word, or their very look; but in this, that the boys love them, approach with confidence, and make their difficulties known." Speaking of penalties, he goes on: "The pupils should be led to understand that such reprehensions are necessary and are prompted by affection; and let it be the most grievous rebuke or penalty for them to know that they have offended their Prefect."[1]

Thus, in the education of the sixteenth century, there came into play a gradual reaction against the harshness and brusquer manners of earlier times. Speaking of conversation with the students, the General Vitelleschi, in 1639, gives characteristic directions: "It will be very useful if from time to time the Professors treat with their auditors, and converse with them, not about vain rumors and other affairs that are not to the purpose, but about those which appertain most to their well-being and education; going down to particulars that seem most to meet their wants; and showing them, in a familiar way, how they ought to conduct themselves in studies and piety. Let the Professors be persuaded that a single talk in private, animated with true zeal and prudence on their part, will penetrate the heart more and work more powerfully, than many lectures and sermons given in common."[2]

Here then I have touched on the secrets of success, those principles which commanded esteem, and shed about the Order an unmistakable halo of educational prestige.

---

[1] 1585; Monumenta Germaniæ Pædagogica, vol. ii, Pachtler, p. 411.
[2] Monumenta Germaniæ Pædagogica, vol. ix, Pachtler, p. 59.

CHAPTER VIII.

IGNATIUS ADMINISTERING THE COLLEGIATE SYSTEM. HIS DEATH.

The first two colleges were established in the same year, 1542,—one of them in the royal university at Coimbra in Portugal, the other at Goa in Hindustan. Though they were organized at an early date, only two years after the foundation of the Order, when as yet no system had been formally adopted, nevertheless these two first colleges, a good many thousands of miles apart, were found to have been established in precisely the same way. Francis Xavier, having been assigned to the apostolic ministry in the East, began a university there, in which all the sciences and branches were professed, just as in the European colleges. This became the base of operations for Japan, China, Persia, Ethiopia, and the other nations of the East. Forty years later, there were as many as one hundred and twenty Jesuits in the college.

In 1542, Ignatius had a select body of fifteen or sixteen young men studying in Paris; others he had placed in Padua or elsewhere. He availed himself of the actual universities until such time as he should have his own. War breaking out between the Emperor Charles V and the French King Francis, all Spaniards and Belgians were ordered out of France.

Such as were Italians remaining in Paris, the other young Jesuits crossed the frontier to Louvain, under the charge of Father Jerome Domenech. There the Latin oratory of the youth, Francis Strada, whom Lefèvre, on his way through Belgium, supplied with matter for his orations,[1] helped to build up the Order rapidly with two kinds of men, talented youths, who were captivated by the things they saw and heard, and men already eminent, who were equally attracted by the scope of the new Institute. In the young Strada preaching and the eminent Lefèvre going out of his way to subsidize him with matter, we catch a family glimpse of that intensified force which can be developed in a closely bound organization.

Conspicuously wanting in gifts of presence and of learning, Francis Villanova, sent by Ignatius to the university seat of Alcalà, won such an ascendency there by his other qualities as a Priest, that a commodious and flourishing college was soon founded. Father Jerome Domenech endowed one in his native city of Valentia, 1543. Lefèvre and Araoz, following awhile by royal request in the suite of the Princess Mary, daughter of the Portuguese King, and queen of the Spanish King, founded a college at Valladolid. In Gandia, his own duchy, Francis Borgia erected and richly equipped a university, which was the first placed in the hands of the Society.

Colleges at Barcelona, Bologna, Saragossa, arose within the next two or three years; also at Messina, Palermo, Venice, and Tivoli. It is evident that Ignatius had a world of administration already on his

Manare, Commentarius.

hands. As early as March 16, 1540, he had excused himself from granting an application, because of "much pains he was taking in sending some to the Indies, others to Ireland and to parts of Italy." Now, though his forces were increasing, yet he was husbanding them; and even so, while refusing many applications, he seemed to be everywhere. But this need not be so much a matter of wonder, if we consider that it is the right place, and the right move at the proper time, that commands other places, movements, and times.

At the death of Lefèvre, in 1546, the onward movement of these select men, coming in contact, either friendly or adverse, with every actual power in Europe, was so impressive for its strategic completeness, and so far-reaching in its results, that, as an historian remarks, "These ten men, so ably chosen, had accomplished to their entire satisfaction, in less than six years, what the most absolute monarch would not have ventured to exact of the most blind devotedness."[1]

Hardly had Lefèvre departed this life, when his place was taken by the last man whom he had dealt with, Francis Borgia, Duke of Gandia, the friend and cousin of the Emperor Charles V. Still wearing his ducal robes, until his temporal affairs could be settled, he came to Rome in 1550. He founds the Roman College, which is the centre and type of all Jesuit colleges.

It was begun on February 18th, 1551, at the foot of the Capitol, with fourteen members of the Order, and Father John Peltier, a Frenchman, at their head.

[1] Crétineau-Joly, tom. i, ch. 3, p. 150.

Doubling this number in the following September, the College moved to a larger building. The Professors taught Rhetoric, and three languages, Hebrew, Greek, and Latin. In 1553, the entire course of Philosophy and Theology was added. The number of Jesuit students among the auditory amounted, in this year, to sixty, and, in the following year, to one hundred. A few years later, Vittoria Toffia, niece of Paul IV, and wife of Camillo Orsini, provided the institution with a splendid property. Thenceforth, the number of Jesuit students alone was as high as 220, brought together from sixteen or more different nations, most of them familiar with many languages, all speaking by rule the tongue of the country in which they were residing, and all competent to speak and teach in the one universal and learned language of the time, the Latin tongue.

Of students not belonging to the Order, nearly twenty colleges are enumerated, at some periods, as following the courses of this central Roman College. They included the colleges of the English, the Greeks, the Scotch, the Maronites, the Irish, and the Neophytes; the Colleges named Capranica, Fuccioli, Mattei, Pamfili, Salviati, Ghislieri; the German College and the College Gymnasio; also the Roman Seminary. Of the 2107 students counted, as following the courses at a given time, 300 were in theology. The most eminent professors filled the chairs, in successive generations; theologians like Suarez and Vasquez, commentators like Cornelius a Lapide and Maldonado, founders or leaders in the schools of national history like Mariana and Pallavicini; Clavius, reformer of the Gregorian calendar; Kircher, universal in all exact sciences; and so of the rest; while the cycle of colleges over the world remained provided with their requisite forces, and maintained their own prestige.[1]

The emblem of this institution was Theology, enthroned, as it were, in a temple of imposing proportions. At her right and left two Maids of Honor stand; they are the Natural Sciences. One of them, representing Mathematics, is placing the celestial sphere under the feet of the august goddess seated; the other, representing Physics, is subjecting, in like manner, the orb of the earth. The legend attached reads: *Leges impone subactis.*

In forty or fifty years such an investment of talent, character, and virtue, had been made, by management within the Order, and by that power to which Ignatius always appealed, Divine Providence, that Rome had seen pass through this house the most distinguished men of the age, in every line of intellectual life, of moral eminence, and of all that could elevate the thoughts of noble and generous minds. For the young, in particular, three characters came, figures that were to fill the niches and terminate the aisles of contemplation, as the ideal choice of the bloom of youth — Stanislaus Kostka, a young Polish noble of seventeen, Aloysius Gonzaga, an Italian prince of twenty-three, and John Berchmans, a Flemish burgher of twenty-two. Being what they were, and leaving this life at such an age, they have appropriated in the Catholic Church the honors of the young.

[1] Compare Crétineau-Joly, tom. i, ch. 6; tom. iv, chs. 3, 4.

With regard to Germany, it is with a classic touch, as of Cæsar's style, that an historian introduces the subject thus: *Germania, quo gravius laboravit, hoc studiosius adjuta est; Ignatio nulla regio commendatior.*[1] Nor will the association be considered far-fetched, if, substituting for Cæsar's pen and Cæsar's sword, Loyola's legislation for letters and his strategic tactics, one catches a suggestive idea, on the present topic, from that statue of the same Roman General, which represents him as holding in one hand a sword, and in the other a pen, with the words inscribed underneath, *Ex utroque Cæsar.*

Of the services of those nine men, with whom he founded the Order, he spent a large part upon Germany. Lefèvre was there, Le Jay, Bobadilla, Salmeron, Laynez; not to mention the great Canisius (de Hondt), a young man already in the field, who was to stay there for half a century. It is of these men and their work that Ranke writes: "Of what country were these, the first of their Order amongst us? They were natives of Spain, Italy, the Netherlands. For a long time, even the name of their Society was unknown, and they were styled the Spanish Priests. They filled the chairs of the universities, and there met with disciples willing to embrace their faith. Germany has no part in them; their doctrine, their constitution, had been completed and reduced to form, before they appeared in our midst. We may then regard the progress of their Institute here, as a new

---

[1] The more heavily the strain of war bore upon Germany, the more assiduously were the succors sent in; no part of the field was more under Loyola's eye.

participation of Latin Europe in German Europe. They have defeated us upon our own soil, and wrested from us a share of our fatherland." [1]

In concert with the Duke of Bavaria and the Emperor Ferdinand, Ingolstadt and Vienna became the two first centres of operations. Ingolstadt was indeed destined to become soon one of the most representative universities of the Company, and the German centre of what has been called the "Counter-Reformation." [2] But Ignatius would not accept it, without the clearest enunciation of some fundamental principles in the educational work of his Institute. I will mention them.

First, the condition of all higher studies, and of lower studies as well, was such, that, as Ignatius said, it was useless to begin with the top, which without a good foundation will never stand. The disappointment of individual hopes and of general expectation would be the only result, with demoralization for the future. Let Literature, he said, and Philosophy be gone through satisfactorily; then Theology may be approached. Literature must come first of all. Hence Polanco, the secretary of Ignatius, writes to the Duke of Bavaria, in 1551, that the "Jesuits must begin by undertaking preparatory teaching, with Professors capable of inspiring their young students, little by little, with a taste for Theology." [3]

---

[1] History of the Papacy, vol. i, book v, § 3; The First Jesuit Schools in Germany; Foster's translation, p. 417.

[2] Compare Monumenta Germaniæ Pædagogica, vol. ix, Pachtler, Nr. 72; Nr. 91; Nr. 92, etc.

[3] This very instructive correspondence may be seen sketched in Genelli's Life of St. Ignatius of Loyola, part ii, ch. 8, pp. 342 *seq.* 1889.

Secondly, we may recall to mind what was mentioned before,[1] that Ignatius provides for Law and Medicine in his universities, but the professors of these departments are to be taken from without the Order. Now, quite as a counterpart to this, we find him declaring to the Duke of Bavaria, that it is at variance with his plan to lend any Professors or Lecturers of the Order for work outside of Jesuit institutions. Therefore a college must be founded for them, or the Duke cannot have them.

The reason for this reserve is not hard to discern. In an organization like his, there are no men at large to lend. And, were the most eminent men assigned for work outside of the Jesuit colleges and universities, the younger generation of the Order would practically be debarred from the influence of their type of eminence. And again, if there were eminent men laboring in a country, without the stable abode of a Jesuit college in the same place, there would be no propagating the distinctive work of the Order itself, by means of the men of that country. Yet, as he projected a native clergy for Germany, so he intended native Jesuits for the Germans. Besides, it does not seem possible to accept of a chair outside, except on the basis of some pecuniary consideration for the individual Professor. Now this is a situation which he does not accept. A Professed Father is not to sacrifice his religious life and independence, bound to a work outside of the Order's own houses, and that for a valuable consideration. Ignatius accepts of no obligations to fill chairs, save as accepting universities,

[1] Ch. 6, above, p. 84.

which contain those chairs.¹ And, as to pecuniary considerations, his principle is, *Gratis accepistis, gratis date;* "Give freely what you have freely received." To this cardinal principle the statutes of so many universities, if not of all, in which a Jesuit College conducted any of the faculties, distinctly refer, as the ground for exempting Religious of the Society from all pecuniary charges, incidental to university affairs.² No ingenious compromise was admitted which tended to relax this principle, regarding a pecuniary consideration.³ On the contrary, the most legitimate and ample revenues offered were not accepted as a recommendation for a university, if there were any conditions whatever not in keeping with the Institute.⁴

The German College in Rome was founded by Ignatius, to form German ecclesiastics for the Germans. At that time benefices and parochial cures, in the German Emperor's dominions, were generally vacant for want of Priests. It soon came to pass that Priests were found to be in waiting, for want of benefices. It was not merely for the ordinary cure of souls that this college received so much attention from Loyola. True to himself, ever contemplating something eminent,—*rarum et eximium facinus,* as he said once to

---

[1] Const., pars iv, c. 7, decl. E.
[2] Compare Mon. Germ. Pæd., vol. ii, Pachtler, Nr. 38, the theological faculty of the University of Würzburg, p. 303, n. 7 ; Mon. Germ. Pæd., vol. ix, Pachtler, Nr. 67, p. 162, and Nr. 68, p. 178, the theological and philosophical faculties of the University of Trier, etc.
[3] Compare Monumenta Germaniæ Pædagogica, vol. ii, Pachtler, p. 38, note about Perugia.
[4] Ibid., p. 51, note about Valencia.

the Scholastics of Coimbra, "that rare and excellent achievement, which is worth more than six hundred common ones,"—he was founding a seminary for preachers, professors, prelates. If the students sent from Germany, to be admitted and supported on this foundation, are not noblemen, "at all events," writes Ignatius in 1552, "let nobility of soul not be wanting to them."[1] This is the institution which caused so much vexation to non-Catholic Germany. It renovated the priesthood.

Thus, then, in a short official career of sixteen years, Ignatius had the gratification of seeing a new and vast educational policy crowned with success. In spite of the active opposition which powerful interests in Rome led against him — and a vigorous siege from the side of the schoolmasters was not to be despised, nor should it fail to be recorded,— in spite of the desperate hostility of the Sorbonne, which was but beginning its war upon the Society in France, with storms at Toledo and Saragossa flanking his movements in Spain; in spite of the open war with heresy in Protestant Germany, where acrimony, distilled to its last degree of concentration, was to embitter history, till the days of Ranke and Janssen should come, and begin to vindicate the truth of history; thanks to the labors of Ignatius, the monopoly of education was being broken down; the old universities were no longer either the sole depositories of superior instruction, or the arbiters of the intellectual life of Europe; and all the best learning, which the most accomplished

---

[1] Monumenta Germaniæ Pædagogica, vol. ii, p. 360, Letter to Father Kessel.

men could impart, was now being given gratuitously, and in as many centres of educational activity as the Society was allowed to create. And, whereas it is put down to the credit of Germany, that sixteen of the old universities had arisen on its soil, now, in the German Assistency of the Society, there arose more than sixteen Jesuit universities, besides two hundred colleges. And, in virtue of Papal charters, it was already an accomplished fact, that all the powers of universities, with regard to the degrees of Bachelor, Master, Licentiate, and Doctor, were vested in the head of the Order, who could delegate the same to subordinate Superiors.[1]

No wonder all the faculties of Christendom considered the Order an intruder and an aggressor. It might be considered so to-day. Free and universal education was at the doors of all. We, men of the nineteenth century, may flatter ourselves that it was the spirit of our age which breathed upon the Order of Jesus, three centuries before the time. Perhaps so. But we shall have to wait a few centuries more, even beyond the nineteenth century, before we come to such education given universally and given gratuitously. For it is one of the most palpable characteristics of all educational and other philanthropy which we know of, that it is an extremely expensive thing.

Let us now close our sketch of the great educator, Saint Ignatius of Loyola. All the particulars of his death have been preserved for us by those who were with him at the last. They were not his first compan-

[1] Compare Monumenta Germaniæ Pædagogica, vol. ii, Pachtler, Päpstliche Privilegien, pp. 1-8.

ions. Of these, the few who survived at the present date, sixteen years after the foundation of the Society, were scattered in various climes. The members with him were John Polanco, his polished secretary, André Frusis, a Frenchman, one of the most gifted of linguists and of *littérateurs*, Christopher Madrizi, a university Doctor of Alcalà, and Jerome Nadal, whom in Paris, long before, Ignatius had endeavored to enlist in the service of his Institute; but Nadal had rejected all overtures, pointing to the Bible under his arm, and saying he wanted no other institute save that. He was a man of the first quality in judgment and the governing cast of mind. Later on, when the exploits of Saint Francis Xavier in India and Japan had become the talk and admiration of Europe, Nadal entered the Order, so cautiously that one might say he did it reluctantly; yet he did it. His subsequent career showed that he had made a mistake, when he missed a place in the very first ranks.

Others were close by. Laynez lay in a sick-room; as was thought, on his death-bed; Mendoza too, and Martin Olave. The latter, some thirty years before, was a boy whom Ignatius met, when as a poor pilgrim he reached Alcalà from Barcelona, to take up his university studies. The boy gave him an alms, the first received by Ignatius in that city. Time had passed since then. The boy had become a Master of Arts, and, in 1543, a Doctor of the Paris University, remarkable in many ways for virtue and learning. Now, a man of mature age and great authority, he had embraced the Institute of Ignatius. He alone of the invalids died immediately after his master in religion.

The latter, on July the 30th, told them he was about to die. But, diseases having preyed upon him for years, the physicians did not confirm what he said; and Father Ignatius made no more statements on the subject. He spent the evening in his usual manner, transacted some business with perfect serenity of mind, and then was left alone till the morrow.

The morrow is just dawning, when they find him breathing his last. He declines to accept any potion. Joining his hands together, with his eyes fixed heavenward, and pronouncing the name of "Jesus," the founder of the Society of Jesus passes away from this life, in the Professed House at Rome.

It was the thirty-first day of July, 1556. He was sixty-five years of age. Thirty-five years had passed, since the Knight of the King of Navarre had, with such solemnity, changed his garb, hung up his sword and poniard in the sanctuary of Montserrat, and vowed himself to be a Knight in the Kingdom of Christ.

All the time since then he had spent in extreme poverty, in the practice of austerity, in the laborious travels of a pilgrim, in the more laborious pursuit of letters, under the stress of persecution, prisons, and chains, and under the relentless fatigue of a universal foresight, vigilance, and administration. He had proved himself a leader and commander of men, as nature had made him to be, and as history shows that he was.

In an especial manner, he is famous for his prudence. Approaching every enterprise with the most varied and exhaustive deliberation, spending forty days of meditation on determining a single point of the Constitution, throwing upon his premises every kind of light from consultation and advice, and having habitually in his room, for reference, only two books, the New Testament, and the Imitation of Christ, he thought out every plan to the last degree of definiteness and consistency. Having once reached such a definite conclusion, he was not easy to move thenceforth out of the direction taken. Quite otherwise. With the utmost vigilance, he applied himself and he applied all the means, whether they were persons available or measures necessary, to the execution of his purpose. Even when, as often seemed to be the case, he was starting from principles other than those of ordinary human foresight, apparently from a pure trust in Divine Providence, he did not exempt himself from applying, with the same circumspection and diligence as ever, the means adequate to execute what he had begun. Waiting fourteen hours, and fasting withal, in the ante-chamber of a prince, lest the propitious occasion should slip, writing out the same letter twice, thrice, and oftener, lest the right thing should not be said in the right way, and sending out thirty letters in one night, he exhibited, in the administration of great things and small, what had marked all his previous deliberation, the highest degree of consummate prudence and of practical perfection.

If, in all this, there are many eminent qualities to admire, there is a resultant fact more marvellous still. He did his work so that it went on without him. And hence, if, whenever he happened to be anywhere on the field of action, account had to be taken of such a man, it will not perhaps appear singular that his Order

THE COLLEGIATE SYSTEM. 123

too, even when ostracized and expatriated, is taken into account, if it is anywhere visible on the social horizon. While I am writing this, three hundred and fifty years after his time, the Bundesrath, on closing the Kulturkampf, and admitting all the exiled Orders of the Catholic Church back into the Empire of Germany, makes an exception of the Jesuits. It bans the Order of Jesus, and gives no reason, beyond the palpable fact that the Order is what it is. Evidently, Ignatius of Loyola did his work so as to make it go on without him; and go on just as he made it.

CHAPTER IX.

SUBSEQUENT ADMINISTRATIONS.

ACCORDING to a contemporary chronicle for the year 1556, the first announcement of the death of Ignatius caused such a profound sentiment of grief in all members of the Order, that a degree of stupor seemed for the moment to possess them. But this was only temporary. It was followed by a marked alacrity of spirit appearing everywhere. The Society was beginning its course.[1]

In the first general assembly, Father James Laynez was elected to succeed the founder, in the office of General Superior. The matters which concerned the assembly in its legislation, and the new General in his administration, were the proper temporal foundation of colleges, the admission of *convictus* or boarding-colleges, and other questions, which may be noted in the *Monumenta Germaniæ Pædagogica*.[2] Laynez governed the Order during nine years, till 1565.

Father Francis Borgia, who had resigned his dukedom, and by this example led Charles V to seek repose in the monastery of St. Yuste, was elected third General. His virtues and his presence, wherever he ap-

---

[1] Bollandists, J. P., n. 612.

[2] The pedagogic legislation, from this date onwards, is to be found in Monumenta Germaniæ Pædagogica, vol. ii, Pachtler, pp. 70-125.

peared, exercised such a magic influence that, when he had merely passed through Spain, colleges had sprung up as from the soil. Three Provinces had been formed in that country alone, within thirteen years from the foundation of the Society. But this multiplication of colleges, often not sufficiently endowed for their future development, was already seen to be one of the threatened weaknesses of the Company. The special legislation passed at the time of his election regarded the proper establishment, in every Province, of philological, philosophical, and theological seminaries, for the formation of Professors.[1] Instead of the proportionate number of Jesuit students being supported on each collegiate foundation, this legislation, and much more that followed later, ordained a system of concentration in seminaries of humane letters, philosophy, science, and divinity, which were conducted respectively by corps of eminent Professors selected for the purpose, and were maintained either on some munificent foundation specially made for this object, or by a due proportion of the other collegiate foundations. At this date it was that colleges for the formation of diocesan clergy, or " Bishops' Seminaries," as they are commonly called, were coming into existence, in accordance with the decrees of the Council of Trent. The manner of admitting them, as annexed to colleges of the Society, and thereby availing themselves of the Jesuit courses, was regulated by this assembly. In no case were they to be provided with a corps of Professors distinct from the faculty of the college.

[1] Pachtler, ibid., p. 75.

In 1573 Father Everard Mercurian, a Belgian, was elected to succeed Saint Francis Borgia. He was sixty-eight years old at the time of his election, and lived eight years after. He drew out of the Constitution various summaries of rules for the guidance of the chief officers in the Society. Those which concern studies are given in a few pages of the *Monumenta*.[1]

At his death, a young man thirty-seven years old, who had entered the Order only about twelve years before, was elected to succeed him. This was Claudius Aquaviva, son of Prince John Aquaviva, Duke of Atri. He was a man who, for his superior executive abilities and his services rendered to the Order in times most critical, has been regarded as a second founder. As to what his administration saw effected in the matter of education, the *Ratio Studiorum* bears witness. He governed the Society during thirty-four years.

Mutius Vitelleschi, one of the mildest and gentlest of men, but not on that account ineffective in his government, succeeded Aquaviva, filling a term of thirty-one years, from 1615 to 1646. Various pedagogic interests occupied the attention of the general assembly, by which he was elected; in particular, the promotion of Humane Letters, the means of supplying Professors, and the searching character of the examinations ordained, at every step in their studies, for the members of the Society.

The farther the Society advanced in history, the less there was of new legislation. The tension grew on the side of administration; and the urgency shown

[1] Pachtler, ibid., pp. 126-132.

by general assemblies evinces this. The philological seminary was developed for the junior scholastics; and a classic form drawn up for it by Jouvancy. As distinguished talents for preaching and governing were treated with the special favor of being allowed to compensate for some deficiencies, in the qualifications requisite for the degree of Profession in the Order, so special legislation provided for similar eminence in literature, in Oriental languages, in Greek and Hebrew.

Mathematics had, from the first, been a department of activity native to the energies of the Company. The schools of Geography and History developed in the seventeenth and at the beginning of the eighteenth centuries. The school of modern Physics then asserting itself, and running so close upon the field of Metaphysics, was subjected to regulations in the assemblies of 1730 and 1751.

After the restoration of the Order, social and educational circumstances being so immensely altered, the whole ground had to be surveyed again, with a view to adaptation; the curriculum had to be expanded, and, where necessary, prolonged to meet the growing demands of the exact sciences; and an indefinite number of specialties to be provided for, by the selection and fostering of special talents. These special lines are, in the terms of the latest general assembly, "Ancient Languages, Philology, Ethnology, Archæology, History, Higher Mathematics, and all the Natural Sciences." We are thus brought down, in the history of general legislation, to the very recent date, 1883, less than ten years ago.

Meanwhile the Generals, on whom rested the burden of supervising all this, discharged the functions of administration. Father Vincent Caraffa promoted and urged on the pursuit of Belles Lettres, and defined positions in Mathematics. Father Francis Piccolomini, in a general ordinance for all the higher studies, defined the stand to be taken by Professors, as representing the Society itself in their chairs; so, too, Father Goswin Nickel, with reference to certain new issues. Both he and his successor, Paul Oliva, had to face the new contingencies which arose from the charges of the Jansenists against what they called the loose moral teachings of the Jesuits. Father Oliva stimulated the pursuit of excellence in Humane Letters, in the Greek, Hebrew, Arabic, and Chaldaic languages. Positions of Descartes, Leibnitz, as well as of certain others in Philosophy and Theology, were animadverted upon by the Generals Tamburini and Retz. Father Ignatius Visconti urged again the pursuit of perfection in literary matters, and in the manner of conducting the schools of literature. And the General Aloysius Centurione, shortly before the Suppression, laid down the clearest principles with respect to the study of Moral Theology, and the examinations therein. Since the restoration of the Order, Fathers Roothaan, Beckx, and the actual General, Anthony M. Anderledy, have devoted their own attention and directed that of the Society to the ways of accepting, with undiminished energy, the altered and unfavorable situation, in which the present century has placed the Order, and hampers the revived Institute.

For this immense organization had been almost entirely destroyed by the stroke of a pen — the signature of Clement XIV given in pencil. They dispute whether he gave it at all; or, at least, whether he meant it. Howsoever that be, the Order, which had been erected on the principle of obedience, received the word and disappeared. The rock on which it had set its foot became the altar of a sacrifice; and that a sacrifice offered without a struggle or a remonstrance, to betray any change in the spirit, with which Ignatius, two hundred and thirty-three years before, had vowed obedience to the Vicar of Christ. An epigram had been written, on the occasion of the first centenary, under a picture of Archimedes and his lever; Archimedes is getting a foothold for his lever to move the world; and beneath is the epigram: —

Fac pedem figat, et terram movebit.

Its footing was now taken away, and it vanished from the world.

While the Catholic Bourbon courts were thus successful in accomplishing a manœuvre, which at fitful intervals they had essayed heretofore, the schismatical Empress, Catherine II of Russia, denounced it and endeavored to counteract it. She wrote to the Pope in 1783, "that she was resolved to maintain these Priests against any power, whatsoever it was"; and she was good to her word; the Society remained unsuppressed in White Russia. The Protestant King of Prussia, Frederick the Great, without exhibiting all the temper of the irascible lady, manipulated things as best he could to preserve the Society.

To sum up the Order's experiences, it may well be said that in public life there is no resurrection; and the State which dies is dead forever. From infancy on through maturity it goes its way decrepit to the grave. Yet Balmez observes, "the Society of Jesus did not follow the common course of others, either in its foundation, its development, or its fall; that Order, of which it is truly and correctly said, that it had neither infancy nor old age."[1] It rose again; and the flag of the Knight of Loyola, though worn and torn, was none the less fair for that:—

Jam se ipso formosius est.

For neither the violence of endurance, nor the vehemence of energy, although begetting intensest fatigue, is to be confounded with decay.

It was not decay, a century ago, when expropriation and exile were the confessed policy of the courts in Europe; when, as an American writer states it, in Portugal "Pombal cut the Gordian knot. . . . He commenced by the expulsion of the Jesuits and the expropriation of their property." Nor is it decay in the Order, when a liberal confederation in Switzerland, on obtaining the political ascendency in 1848, suppresses the Jesuit University at Fribourg, and provides in this wise, as an American writer records: "No religious society shall be allowed to teach; and persons hereafter educated by the Jesuits, or by any of the Orders affiliated to the Jesuits, shall be incapable of holding office in Church or State."[2] Policy

---

[1] European Civilization, ch. 46.
[2] National Education, part ii, vol. ii, p. 659; p. 74; New York, 1872.

like this, whether in the countries "expurgated," or in countries thereunto "affiliated," proves no decay in the Order.

But where decay may come in has been clearly pointed out by one of its Generals. Speaking of the Education of Youth and the Promotion of Humane Letters, Mutius Vitelleschi wrote, in 1639, "If ever the Society were to decline from that lofty position which it holds with so many provinces and peoples, such an event could come about in no other way than by failing to walk in the same steps, by which, with the Divine Grace, it has acquired that high esteem."[1]

Those steps had been taken in various paths, of which only two have concerned us here. For its men of action were largely identified with the general history of Europe; and its men of the word, who toiled in apostolic work, at home or abroad, have entwined their memories in the history of souls, often ungrateful, yet always worthy of the toil. But its men of the school did a work which we have sketched in a general way, and which we shall analyze in the second part of this essay; while its men of the pen deserve a passing word of notice here.

They concern us from a pedagogic point of view, in many ways. They wrote text-books, many of which are the basis of manuals in almost every line of education to-day, sometimes without the change of a word, and generally without acknowledgment. Besides that, their literary productions were, as a rule, the offspring of their labors in the schools. It might not be safe to estimate their standing as *littérateurs*,

[1] Monumenta Germaniæ Pædagogica, vol. ix, Pachtler, p. 57.

by the process which a Scotch Professor uses, who, in the course of forty-seven elegant lectures on Rhetoric and Belles Lettres, sees little occasion to recognize the existence of this Jesuit school of literature, except when he goes out of his way to salute Père Rapin in a somewhat questionable manner.[1] Many of those whom the Scottish Professor himself does honor to, in his pages, were Jesuit scholars,— Bossuet, Corneille, Molière, Tasso, Fontenelle, Didérot, Voltaire, Bourdaloue, himself a Jesuit. It would be safer then to determine the standing of these Professors, who were in control of a great literary age, by looking at the golden age itself, that of Louis XIV. The majority of the brilliant figures, whom Dr. Blair names as illustrating the epoch,[2] were all Jesuit scholars. Naturally, then, the fifty Professors of the Jesuit College at Paris were, as Cardinal Maury affirmed, a permanent tribunal of literature for all men of letters, a high court of judicature, a focus of public attention from which radiated the public opinion of the capital; in short, as Piron had emphatically said, "the Star-chamber of literary reputations."[3]

Devoted as they were to an austere profession, we may say of many among them, that they were not themselves romancers of a lively fancy or great poets; and so far agree with Voltaire, who made this very remark about his old Professor, Père Porée. Yet also,

---

[1] Blair's Lectures on Rhetoric and Belles Lettres, Lecture 26.
[2] Lecture 35.
[3] Eulogy pronounced by the Cardinal Maury on his predecessor in the Institute of France, the Jesuit De Radonvilliers, 1807.— Orateurs Sacrés, Migne, tom. lxvii, column 1161.

without inconsistency I believe, we may agree with the spirit of Père Porée's rejoiner, when the remark was reported to him, that "he was not one of the great poets." The Jesuit replied, "At least you may grant that I have been able to make some of them."

And, should results be gauged on a wider basis than mere poetry, not a few of the most prominent men in European history would seem to have been the outcome of this system, men, too, who represented every possible school and tendency, in their subsequent literary and public life. A few names show this. There are those of Descartes, Buffon, Justus Lipsius, Muratori, Calderon, Vico, the jurisconsult, founder of the philosophical school of history. There are Richelieu, Tilly, Malesherbes, Don John of Austria, Luxembourg, Esterhazy, Choiseul, with those of Saint Francis de Sales, founder of a religious Order, Lambertini, afterwards the most learned of Popes, under the name of Benedict XIV, and the present Pontiff, Leo XIII, also most erudite. These certainly represent many schools and tendencies, and they come, with many others, from the same schools.[1]

As authors of every kind, and in departments even far remote from the regular courses of the schools, Jesuit writers were, at the very least, so far related to Jesuit teachers, that, as we see in the bibliographical dictionary of the Society, all had been Professors, with scarcely an exception; and almost all had professed Humanities, Belles Lettres, Rhetoric.

When Father Nathaniel Southwell of Norfolk en-

[1] A classification of eminent students may be found in Crétineau-Joly, tom. iv, ch. 3, p. 207.

deavored, in 1676, to compile a dictionary of these authors, he recorded those whose works had the qualification of a respectable bulk to recommend them. He entered the names and works of 2240 authors who answered this description. This was 136 years after the foundation of the Order. The enterprise was repeatedly taken in hand afterwards. The possibility of ever accomplishing it was much jeopardized by the Suppression. But at length the two Fathers De Backer published a series of seven quarto volumes, in the years 1853–1861; and this first step they followed up, in the years 1869–1876, with a new edition, in three immense folios, containing the names of 11,100 authors. This number does not include the supplements, with the names of writers in the present century, and of the anonymous and pseudonymous authors. Of this last category, Father Sommervogel's researches, up to 1884, enabled him to publish a catalogue, which fills a full octavo volume of 600 pages, with double columns. The writers of this century, whom the De Backers catalogued in their supplement, fill 647 columns, folio, very small print. Altogether, the three folios contain 7086 columns, compressed with every art of typographical condensation.

Suarez of course is to be seen there, and Cornelius à Lapide, Petau, and the Bollandists. A single name, like that of Zaccaria, has 117 works recorded under it, whereof the 116th is in 13 volumes quarto, and the 117th in 22 volumes octavo. The Catechism of Canisius fills nearly 11 columns with the notices of its principal editions, translations, abridgments; the commentaries upon it, and critiques. Rossignol has 66 works to his name. The list of productions about Edmund Campian, for or against him, chiefly in English, fills, in De Backers' folio, two and a half columns of minutest print. Bellarmine, in Father Sommervogel's new edition, fills 50 pages, double column.[1]

Under each work are recorded the editions, translations, sometimes made into every language, including Arabic, Chinese, Indian; also the critiques, and the works published in refutation — a controversial enterprise which largely built up the Protestant theological literature of the times, and, in Bellarmine's case alone, meant the theological Protestant literature for 40 or 50 years afterwards. Oxford founded an anti-Bellarmine chair. The editions of one of this great man's works are catalogued by Sommervogel under the distinct heads of 54 languages.[2]

In the methodical or synoptic table, at the end of the De Backers' work, not only are the subjects well-nigh innumerable, which have their catalogues of authors' names attached to them, but such subjects too are here as might not be expected. Thus "Military Art" has 32 authors' names under it; "Agriculture" 11; "Navy" 12; "Music" 45; "Medicine" 28.

To conclude then our History of this Educational Order, we have one synoptical view of it in these twelve

---

[1] Bibliothèque de la Compagnie de Jésus, nouvelle édition, par Carlos Sommervogel S. J., Strasbourgeois, tom. i, from Abad to Boujart; large quarto edition, 1890.

[2] Doctrina Christiana, etc.; Traductions; Sommervogel, *sub voce*, *Bellarmine*, columns 1187-1204.

or thirteen thousand authors, all of one family. We have much more. This one work "attesting," as De Backer says in his preface, " at one and the same time a prodigious activity and often an indisputable merit," whereof three and a half centuries have been the course in time, and the whole world the place and theatre, is a general record of religion, letters, science, and education, in every country, civilized or barbarous, where the Society of Jesus labored and travelled. And where has it not done so? In many parts of the world it was the first to occupy the field with literary men, who then sent communications to their superiors, or to learned societies, about the manners of different countries, the state of religion there, of letters, science, and education, including reports of their own observations in geography, meteorology, botany, astronomy, mineralogy, etc. Original sources, from which later history in North, South, and Central America is drawing materials, are seen described here as they appeared; so too with regard to Japan, China, Thibet, the Philippine Islands, Hindustan, Syria, as also to-day with respect to the native tongues of the North American Indians. Here the record of published literature, described and catalogued according to date, marks the stages of mathematical and physical science, from the end of the sixteenth century onwards, and of magnetic and electrical researches all through last century; as well as the relationship between the books of Jesuit authors and similar or kindred ones, by persons outside the Society, in different countries and of divers religions.

In short, works composed in most of the tongues of the world exhibit the chief periods in universal culture, and the developments elaborated in the civilization of mankind.[1]

[1] In the matter of general philology alone compare the monograph, Die Sprachkunde und die Missionen, von Joseph Dahlmann S. J., 15 January, 1891, fiftieth supplement to the Stimmen aus Maria-Laach, 121 pages.

PART II.

ANALYSIS OF THE SYSTEM OF STUDIES

CHAPTER X.

AQUAVIVA. THE RATIO STUDIORUM.

So centralized an Order as the Society of Jesus, which formed its Professors for every country, and sent them from one place to another, undertook, in doing so, to exhibit a definite system of education, of courses, of method. Besides such a unity of method, it professed also a consistent uniformity of doctrine.

Before its time there was no one method which could be considered universal; because there was no teaching body itself universal. The Order, as it branched out into the world, found a variety of systems in vogue; and the Jesuit Professors conformed, as best they could, to the local traditions of populations very diverse, in universities which were distinct and mutually independent. But, while they endeavored to better such systems, in accordance with the plan of their own Constitution, it was clear that they fell short of realizing the idea of their founder. Hence variations and dispensations were part of the usual order of the day.

Yet there is a best way of doing everything; and, not least, in education. In such a best way, some elements are essential at all times, while others are accidental, and vary with time, place, and circumstance. The ideal system will preserve in its integrity all that is essential, and then will adapt the general principles with the closest adjustment to the particular environment.

Besides the unity of method desired, which I may define to be *the best way best adjusted to circumstance*, there was need, as I have just said, of a consistent uniformity of doctrine; lest, in the same chair of philosophy, of divinity, or of science, or in chairs placed side by side, one Professor should say Yea to a question, and another Nay to the same question, with no more material a reason evident for the difference, save that one taught here and the other there, one spoke yesterday, the other speaks to-day. The educational effects, however, are far from being immaterial; for, contradictory statements eliding one another, it is quite possible that the students understand less the next day than the day before. And, as to the Professors themselves, nothing can imperil more the harmony and efficiency of an educational organization, than disagreement of opinion in the function and act of teaching. In philosophy, the occasions for dispute spring off at every turn. Theology, as every one knows, is made to bristle with them. And, among men who are themselves educated to the highest degree of mental culture, interests and questions like these are far more absorbing than money, place, or power elsewhere. If anywhere ideas rule, it is among men of profound thought; as the intense intellectuality of the mediæval universities had shown, with all the consequences of unlimited vagaries in an unbridled scholasticism; or, again, as the whole history of the intellectual Greek world had evidenced, whether in the early ages of the

Christian Church, or in the heathen generations before.

Whatever, then, a man may think privately, and be free to think, in matters of mere opinion, the genius of education imposes limits on the manner and matter of his actual teaching; and the speculations of a thinker, a writer, or an investigator, are not to be confounded with the best results of an educator, who, doing his work in the best way, is to effect a definite and immediate object. That object is nothing less than the equipping of fresh young spirits with principles of thought and habits of life, to enter fully appointed on their respective paths of duty. In this view, therefore, definiteness of matter, no less than unity of method, were required from the first for an effective system of education.

During forty years, the individual enterprise of experienced and responsible men had been interpreting the values and measuring the results of existing methods. The Society itself had mounted into such a position, as practically to command the whole field of secular education. Its own system must have been excellent already. Nor could that system have been uniformly excellent, but for some uniformity which characterized it. Still the unity was defective. The Provinces were petitioning for an improvement. Evils obstructed the way to something better. For these reasons, the matter was taken in hand by one General after another. And the final outcome of their work was a "Form," or "Method of Studies," *Formula*, or *Ratio Studiorum*.

On the nineteenth day of February, 1581, Father

Claudius Aquaviva was elected fifth General Superior of the Society. Taking up this educational project where his predecessors had left it, and, like them, availing himself of his almost boundless resources for obtaining information, he began by putting the work through every possible stage of consultation, to which the traditions of his office, and his own executive ability prompted him; and, when all prudent means had been exhausted in deliberating, he then used the executive power which was vested in him; and he required that what had been so laboriously designed, by the united efforts of many, should henceforth be reduced to practice, with the good will of all.

It will be interesting to review briefly the process of elaboration. In the general assembly which elected Aquaviva, a committee of twelve Fathers from different countries was appointed to draw up a method of studies. How far their work proceeded does not appear. Three years later, in 1584, the General named a Commission of six, John Azor from Spain, Gaspar Gonzalez from Portugal, Peter Buys from Austria, Anthony Guisani from Upper Germany, Stephen Tucci of Rome, and James Tyre to represent France. This last-named Jesuit, a Scotchman, was not unknown in the lists of controversy to his countryman, John Knox. They were all experienced in the administration of colleges, and versed in the subjects of all the faculties. Entering on their labors, they worked during six winter months in the Pœnitentiaria of St. Peter's in Rome; and, during the next three summer months, they resided in the Quirinal. The eyes of the chief authorities in the Catholic world were turned in expectancy towards them. Indeed, some of the chief interests of Catholic Christendom seemed to depend upon them.

They spent three hours a day in consultation. The rest of their time they devoted to consulting authors and conning over methods, in the three fields of letters, philosophy, and divinity. The documents which they studied are enumerated by themselves as being the minutes of previous deliberations held at Rome, or in the more prominent colleges of the Order; the letters, consultations and laws of the universities, and other such documents, sent at different times up to that date from Italy, Spain, France, Germany, Poland; the fourth part of the Constitution, as the standard of guidance; the canons of the general assemblies; the rules and statutes of the schools; moreover, the customs and regulations of the Roman College.[1]

After nine months of consecutive labor, they presented the results to the General, in August, 1585. Father Aquaviva submitted the document for examination to the Professors of the Roman College. Then he took the whole matter under his own personal consideration, with his four General Assistants, who represented each a certain number of Provinces. At this stage, the report was printed, not as a rule determined on, but as the preliminary outline of a rule. The copies struck off were few, just enough for the use of the Provinces. The General's letter, which accompanied the report, defined the precise stage at which the process was now understood to be.[2]

---

[1] Monumenta Germaniæ Pædagogica, vol. v, Pachtler, p. 29.
[2] Ibid., vol. v, p. 9 *seq*.

He says that, in a matter of such grave and universal consequence, it was not his intention to prescribe anything, without first learning the opinions of the chief Doctors of the Society. Accordingly, he had been content with reading the results of the Commission's labors, decreeing nothing, changing nothing, except so far as was necessary to put it in shape for distribution. He now required the Provincial Superiors, immediately upon receipt of the present letter, to select at least five men, who were the best qualified in point of learning and judgment, along with other members, who were eminent in literature, and whom the Provincial might think fit to convoke. To these the report was to be submitted, for each to examine privately, and with great care. On certain days, several times in the week, they were to meet and hold consultations; to put their conclusions in writing, as well with regard to the practical method of studies, as with regard to the speculative opinions which they favored; they were to note whatever they thought should be added, or be made clearer, or otherwise regulated, for the greater perfection of the work. If any of the Fathers, designated for this Provincial committee, could not possibly attend the meetings, still they were to send their opinions in writing to the Fathers actually in session; so that full account might be taken of the public opinion in that Province. The criterion they were to follow, in making up their minds, was not so much their own private sentiment or their own leaning this way or that, as the general good of the whole Society, the practice of the universities and schools, and, in fine, the judgment of Doctors most approved for their authority and solidity of doctrine.

Aquaviva refers to the idea and intention of Ignatius with respect to the present undertaking; and he adds: "I would have all steadfastly keep this object in view, that they endeavor to find out reasons, not how a final decree may be prevented, as if the enterprise were hard, and could not possibly be carried out (for we have made up our mind to carry it out, since it is necessary, and is recommended by the Constitution); but how the difficulties, if any such there be, may disappear, and the whole Order may combine in one and the same arrangement; for otherwise the final result would only be the greater detriment of the Society."

He calls their attention to an important point, in what is now styled Pedagogics, or the Science of Education. It is, that, in the form now sent out, the Fathers had taken pains to explain their reasons for arriving at conclusions. That would not be done in the System to be drawn up later, which would contain only the statement of directions for all to follow. In these words, we have a most important distinction laid down between the science which underlies the system of education, and the practical method itself which rests upon the science. The *Ratio Studiorum*, as subsequently promulgated, is a practical method. The science is sketched, as need arises, in the preliminary *Ratio* of 1586.

At the same time, Father Aquaviva despatched another letter, about which he says, in a postscript to the foregoing, that the six points provisionally laid down in it are to be subjected to the same examination as the preliminary *Ratio* itself.

In this supplementary epistle, he premises that it will require much time and consideration to issue the final code of rules; and therefore, as a direction for the time being, he issues the following:—

First, Professors shall adhere to St. Thomas Aquinas as their standard in theology.

Secondly, they shall take care, in their manner of teaching, always to consolidate faith and piety.

Thirdly, he lays down a principle of still wider application, and one which seems vital in the whole theory and practice of teaching: "Let no one defend any opinion which is judged by the generality of learned men to go against the received tenets of philosophers and theologians, or the common consent of theological schools." This touches a vital element in education. If we suppose that the teacher's art lies, not in giving forth the lucubrations of his own private thoughts and theories, but in imparting solid results, approved and ascertained, to those who come for such results, and wish to receive them in the most approved way, then the Professor in his chair ought not to mistake himself for the author in his study, nor should he practise on living men, whose life is all before them, what he might, with more propriety, first practise on the leisured world, and test elsewhere, either in the printed page, or in conference with his equals. The Professor, as such, is not the original investigator. In mathematics, he is notoriously not so. In that branch, the best teacher is the man who walks along a definite line, turns neither to the right nor left, and finishes in a definite time; or else his scholars will never finish. To a certain degree, the same holds in all courses. If a man is theorizing, when he ought to be instructing, he goes off the line of perfect system, however much pains he takes with his matter; just as much as if, taking no pains whatever, he neglected his matter altogether, went behind it, or around it, gave histories of his branch, methods of teaching it, and descanted on pedagogics, to young people who were never sent to him for that purpose. They are sent to learn definite matter, and to be formed therein on a good plan, by the man who understands it. Then, as Loyola said in another connection, "when they have experienced in themselves the effects thereof," they will be qualified for all the rest, for understanding the plan itself on which they have been formed, and enjoying all the practical results of it; and, if their line of life invites, for understanding other plans too. This is practical wisdom in education; neither dilettantism nor speculation.

Fourthly, Aquaviva lays down a principle regarding the public advocacy of opinions. He is not referring to authorities denouncing, or Professors repudiating, them; but merely to certain conditions for putting them forward: "If opinions, no matter whose they be, are found in a certain province or city to give offence to many Catholics, whether members of the Society or not, that is, persons not unqualified to judge, let no one teach them or defend them there, albeit the same doctrines may be taught elsewhere without offence." The word "defence," in a context like this, means publishing and sustaining theses against all comers in public disputations; wherein the Professor represents the school, and the school is put to the account of the Order. The principle seems discreet. If a corporate body does not want to be compromised, it is not for the member to compromise it. If he wants to use the perfect freedom of his opinions, and deliver himself of his own pronouncements, he ought first to assure himself that his circumstances are such as to set him free from representing others. This is an elementary principle of social and urbane existence.

The fifth point concerns the march of improvement in the advancement of opinions. It describes the method of discreet development: "In questions which have already been treated by others, let no one follow new opinions, or, in matters which in any way pertain to religion, or are of some consequence, let no one introduce new questions, without consulting the Prefect of Studies, or the Superior. If, then, it still remains dubious, whether the new opinion, or the new question, is permissible, it will be proper for the said authority, in order that things may proceed more smoothly, to learn the judgment of others in the Society upon the subject; and then he will determine what appears best for the greater glory of God." In the sixth and last point, Aquaviva calls attention to a former decree, upon the manner of treating the Aristotelian philosophy.[1]

So much for this letter of Aquaviva. On the sense and purport thereof he invited the communication of views from the Order at large, as well as on the docu-

[1] Monumenta Germaniæ Pædagogica, vol. v, p. 12 *seq*.

ment which he encloses, the preliminary *Ratio Studiorum*. To this we may now turn our attention.

The six Fathers, who drew it up, state, in their introduction, that there are two mainstays and supports of the Society of Jesus, "an ardent pursuit of piety and an eminent degree of learning," *ardens pietatis studium et præstans rerum scientia*. If piety is not illumined with the light of learning, it can be, no doubt, of great use to the person who possesses it, but of scarcely any use in the service of the Church and of one's neighbor, in the administration of the Word and of the Sacraments, in the education of youth, in controversies with those who are hostile to the faith, in giving counsel, answering doubts, and in all other offices and functions, which are proper to men of the Order. All these call for an endowment of learning not common, but excelling in its degree.

To acquire such learning, it is of supreme consequence that we set before ourselves what path we enter on, what arts we employ, and what means we use; because, unless a ready and tried method be adopted, *ratio facilis ac solers*, much labor is spent in gathering but little fruit; whereas, if the labor of studies be guided by some sage rule, great results are compendiously obtained, at the cost of little research.

Then the Commission goes on to say: "We have undertaken to teach, not only members of the Order, but youth from the world outside. The number of this latter class is vast; it includes brilliant talent, and represents the nobility. We cannot imagine that we do justice to our functions, or come up to the expectations formed of us, if we do not feed this multitude of youths, in the same way as nurses do, with food dressed in the best way, for fear they grow up in our schools, without growing much in learning. An additional spur is felt in the circumstance, that whatever concerns us is public and, day after day, is before the eyes of all, even of those who are not well disposed towards us." The Fathers consider it unnecessary to enlarge upon that harmony of views, so much commended in the Constitution, as to matters of public policy or teaching; they say, " sufficient regard could not, up to this, be paid to such harmony; for, when no common order or form was as yet prescribed, every one thought that he could hold what sentiments he liked, and teach them to others in the manner he himself preferred; so that sometimes the members of the Order disagreed as much among themselves, as with others outside." [1]

After describing, in vivid terms, the manner in which they had conducted their deliberations, and arrived at conclusions, and how, when any keen dispute had arisen among them,[2] they had divided and distinguished the disputed matter, and had examined it during two and even three days, till they came to settle at last on what all of them accepted, the critics come to the Practice and Order of Studies;[3] and upon this they enlarge, in successive chapters, under the following heads:—

The Sacred Scriptures. The Length of the Course in Divinity. The Means of finishing that Course in Four Years. The Method of Lecturing. The Ques-

---

[1] Monumenta Germaniæ Pædagogica, vol. v, p. 26 *seq.*
[2] Disputatio acris oriebatur. [3] Ibid., Nr. 8, p. 65.

tions which are either not to be treated by the Theological Professors, or are to be treated only at a Certain Part of the Course. Repetitions. Disputations. The Choice, Censorship, and Correcting of Opinions. The Private Studies of Students. Vacations. The Degrees of Bachelor, Master, Doctor. Controversial Theology. Moral Theology. Hebrew. The Study of Philosophy, which includes Physics. Mathematics. Literature, that is, Grammar, History, Poetry, Rhetoric. Seminaries for Literature and the Higher Faculties. The Professors of Literature. The Grammar to be used. Greek. Different Exercises in the Classics. Incitements to Study. The Method of Promotion. Books. Vacations in the Lower Classes. Order and Piety. The Respective Objects and Exercises of the Classes of Grammar and Humanity. The Class of Humanity. The Class of Rhetoric. General Distribution of Time during the Year.

These are the matters handled in the publication of 1586. In the course of treatment, this document contains, by way of a running commentary, the complete theory of Education, or Science of Pedagogics, as understood by these critics. It will not be possible, within the brief limits of this work, to give more than a bare sketch of the pedagogical elements contained in the one hundred and fifty pages of the *Monumenta Germaniæ Pædagogica*.[1]

A second, partial edition of this preliminary *Ratio* was sent out by Father Aquaviva, in 1591, to which an entertaining bibliographical history is attached.[2] In

[1] Vol. v, pp. 67-217.
[2] Monumenta Germaniæ Pædagogica, vol. v, p. 15 *seq.*

1593, the fifth general assembly of the Order met, Claudius Aquaviva presiding. By this time, during the interval of seven years which had elapsed since the first edition, the book had been subjected to examination in all the Provinces; observations and criticisms had been returned; it had been re-committed to the Fathers at Rome, and revised by the General with his Assistants; and had again been sent out for trial. The Provincials and Deputies, meeting in 1593, brought with them the reports of how the system worked. Its slightest defects were noted.[1] Most asked for an abridged form.

Amid the very grave questions then pending, the assembly took some action on the *Ratio*. It was re-committed once more to the competent authorities for revision. And it assumed its last and definite form, in what was probably its ninth edition. This last issue, in the year 1599, after fifteen years spent on the elaboration of it, is the RATIO STUDIORUM.

One hundred and twenty-seven years later, the great old University of Paris seems to have become a disciple of its educational rival, the Society of Jesus. Querard observes that the Rector, Rollin, "without saying anything about it, translated the *Ratio* for his *Traité des Études*."[2] Indeed, as M. Bréal, historian of that University, observes, referring to the

---

[1] As an instance of the minute criticism brought to bear upon it in Germany, consult Monumenta Germaniæ Pædagogica. vol. v, p. 218 *seq*. Similar animadversions are to be understood as coming from other quarters.

[2] Supercheries littéraires dévoilées iii, 446, f; Sommervogel, Dictionnaire des Ouvrages Anonymes et Pseudonymes, etc., S. J., *sub voce, Ratio*.

suppression of the Order: "Once delivered from the Jesuits, the University installed itself in their houses, and continued their manner of teaching."[1]

In all general works on education, there is question of this System. Its form is that of a practical method, without reasons being assigned, or arguments urged. It is a legislative document, which superseded all previous forms. The General's letter, which accompanied it, ordered the suppression of them all, promulgating this one to the exclusion of the rest.

The sentiment, to which the last words of this letter gives expression as a fond hope, was fully responded to by the course of events, in the one hundred and seventy-four years which were to elapse before the general suppression of the Order: "It is believed," he said, "that it will bring forth abundant fruit, for the benefit of our scholars," *Quae nostris auditoribus uberes fructus allatura creditur*. Aquaviva's letter is dated the eighth day of January, 1599.[2]

[1] Quoted by Ch. Daniel, S. J., Les Jésuites Instituteurs de la Jeunesse, etc., last ch. p. 297.

[2] Monumenta Germaniæ Pædagogica, vol. v, Nr. 11, p. 227.

CHAPTER XI.

FORMATION OF THE MASTER. HIS COURSES OF LITERATURE AND PHILOSOPHY.

It seems an apt distribution of our subject, to consider, first, the formation of the Master, and secondly, the formation of the Scholar. The Master's development will conduct us chiefly through the higher studies; the Scholar's, rather through the lower. Thus the two persons, about whom the science of education revolves, will be directly under inspection; while the elements which go to form them will, at the same time, pass under review.

Without theorizing on pedagogy, the Jesuit system itself, merely as observed and realized, results in the formation of Professors. There are several reasons, apparent on the surface, why it should do so. The studies, which the members of the Order pursue, are the same courses as the Order professes for the world at large. But, for the Jesuit members of the divers courses, a most elaborate system of examinations at every stage, with a specially searching manner of testing the students, is made to regard one objective point, which is the capacity of the Jesuit to teach what he has learnt, and this, as evinced, while under examination. The manner, in which this point is judicially determined, consists in referring the examiners to a standard, called "mediocrity." After a personal and oral disputation with the young Jesuit, lasting either half an hour, or one hour, or two consecutive hours, according to the stage at which he happens to be, a preponderating vote of the four or five examining Professors must aver that he has "surpassed mediocrity." The learning, prudence, and sincerity of the examiners are appealed to without further sanction, except at the very last stage in the young man's progress, when success under the ordeal will entitle him to Profession in the Society. Then each examiner's prudence is stimulated, and his sincerity bound down, by an oath. Only at one initial stage, that of the first examination in the course of his three years' Philosophy, is a certain margin allowed the beginner, in favor of bare mediocrity.

"Mediocrity" is defined to be that degree of intelligence, and comprehension of the matters studied, which can give an account of them to one asking an explanation. "To surpass mediocrity" designates the student's ability to defend his entire ground with such erudition and facility as show him qualified, in point of actual attainments, to profess the philosophy or theology studied. The final degree in the Order, which is that of Profession, requires this competency for all Philosophy and Theology together. Here then we see, that the capacity to teach is made the criterion of having learned sufficiently well. Passing through all the grades with this mark of excellence, the man who, after a general formation of seventeen years, and the requisite development of other qualifications, is then appointed to profess in a chair of the higher faculties, has been very much to the manner born of "surpassing mediocrity," and of doing so with the characteristics of a Professor.[1] How the same principles, if not in the same form, affect the conduct of the literary curriculum, we shall now see in the rest of this chapter.

The literary curriculum has been already finished by the Jesuit, before entering the Order. But, after his admission, special means are taken to have him revise those studies, extend them, and grasp them from the standpoint of the teacher. It happens in Jesuit history, and the nature of secondary education will always have it so, that the largest amount of teaching has been done in the arena of these literary courses. And it was no small part of the general revival of studies, effected by Ignatius of Loyola, that justice was done to literature, as well by students who were to enter on philosophical or scientific courses,[2] as by those who contemplated embarking on life in the world. We noticed, on a former occasion, the reasoning of Aquaviva with respect to this policy.[3] The literary courses in question are those of Grammar, Humanities, and Rhetoric, which fill from five to seven years. The Fathers of 1586 urge the importance of these studies for the English and German students in Rome, as if special difficulties were experienced with them.[4]

---

[1] Monumenta Germaniæ Pædagogica, vol. v, p. 252, Ratio Studiorum of 1599, Reg. Prov. 19, § 11.

[2] Compare Lord Bacon, The Advancement of Learning, book ii, p. 186, 1st column; Philadelphia edit. 1846.

[3] Chapter vi, above, p. 83.

[4] Monumenta Germaniæ Pædagogica, vol. v, p. 129, Ratio Studiorum of 1586, c. Stud. Philos.

If we inquire what were the results of the stringent regulations adopted to enforce this policy, and what degree of proficiency was attained in the Jesuit courses of Belles-Lettres and eloquence, we have only to consult the concordant testimony of history upon the "handsome style" and literary finish of the scholars. An interesting answer, from a domestic point of view, is casually afforded us by a remark, which the Fathers of Upper Germany make, when in 1602 they send to Aquaviva some animadversions of theirs upon the *Ratio*. They say that students in the class of Rhetoric might deliver their own orations, "since there are generally found in that class, particularly among those of the second year, young men who often surpass even their own Professors in genius, and in the variety and fluency of their language."[1]

The bearing of all this is obvious, in determining the grade of those students who ask for admission into the Order. It is after a full gymnasium course of this kind, that the life of the Jesuit is to begin. And these are the studies which he will have to possess after the manner of a teacher. He will review them as soon as his two years of novitiate are over.

Those years of novitiate are blank, under the aspect of secular pursuits. But, in other respects, being a time for reflection and for internal application to the affairs of his mind and heart, they are worth a long season in the process of developing character, by habits of assiduous labor, of acquiring a taste for retirement and virtue, and practising the spirit of docility to counsel. Indeed, on issuing from this period of

[1] Monumenta Germaniæ Pædagogica, vol. v, p. 491, n. 32.

intense application to the knowledge of self, the young religious student is already started on his career of knowing men, and dealing successfully with human characters. Henceforth, ecclesiastical knowledge and other acquirements will be proper to his state, as a Religious; but, for the special vocation of the Society of Jesus, he returns to secular studies.

In view of his approaching " regency," or Professorship in the curriculum of letters, the critics of 1586 give this advice: "It would be most profitable for the schools, if those who are about to be Preceptors were privately taken in hand by some one of great experience; and, for two months or more, were practised by him in the method of reading, teaching, correcting, writing, and managing a class. If teachers have not learnt these things beforehand, they are forced to learn them afterwards at the expense of their scholars; and then they will acquire proficiency only when they have already lost in reputation; and perchance they will never unlearn a bad habit. Sometimes, such a habit is neither very serious nor incorrigible, if taken at the beginning; but, if the habit is not corrected then, it comes to pass that a man, who otherwise would have been most useful, becomes well-nigh useless. There is no describing how much amiss Preceptors take it, if they are corrected, when they have already adopted a fixed method of teaching; and what continual disagreement ensues on that score with the Prefects of Studies. To obviate this evil, in the case of our Professors, let the Prefect in the chief College, whence our Professors of Humanities and Grammar are usually taken, remind the Rector and Provincial, about three months before the next scholastic year begins, that, if the Province needs new Professors for the following term, they should select some one eminently versed in the art of managing classes, whether he be, at the time, actually a Professor, or a student of Theology or Philosophy; and to him the future Masters are to go daily for an hour, to be prepared by him for their new ministry, giving prelections in turn, writing, dictating, correcting, and discharging the other duties of a good teacher."[1]

This advice was in keeping with an ordinance of the second general assembly, held in 1565, nine years after the death of Ignatius. It had been resolved, that at least one perfect Seminary of the Society should be established in each Province for the formation of Professors and others, who would be competent workmen in the vineyard of Christ, in the department of Humane Letters, Philosophy, and Theology, so as to suffice for the needs of the whole Province. This was to be done as soon as convenient in each Province.

Henceforward, it became a matter of general observance that all should have spent "at least two years in the school of eloquence," besides repeating grammar, if that were necessary.[2] "And if any are so gifted as to promise great success in these pursuits, it will be worth while seeing whether they should not spend three years in them, to lay a more solid founda-

---

[1] Monumenta Germaniæ Pædagogica, vol. v, p. 154, n. 6; Humanitatis Doctores quos et quales, etc.

[2] Vitelleschi, 1639, Monumenta Germaniæ Pædagogica, vol. ix, p. 60, n. 4.

tion."[1] To such a solid foundation in Humane Letters corresponds a special privilege in the crowning of a member's formation, inasmuch as the Society admits to Profession one who is altogether eminent in literature, even though in Theology he may not have surpassed mediocrity; a privilege which was extended to great proficiency in the Indian and Oriental languages, as also to a marked excellence in Greek and Hebrew.[2]

Examining more in detail this literary formation, we may take up the programme for the seminary of the junior members, as drafted by Jouvancy. He drew it up in pursuance of a decree to that effect, passed a hundred years later, by the general assembly of 1696. This decree required that, "besides the rules, whereby the Masters of Literature are directed in the manner of teaching, they should be provided with an Instruction and Method of learning properly, and so be guided in their private studies even while they are actually teaching."[3] The method in question is outlined in the first part of Jouvancy's little book, entitled *Ratio Discendi et Docendi*, "The art of Learning and of Teaching." A cursory glance at this part shows that, while addressing Masters on the subject of their own private studies, his directions bear chiefly upon their efficiency as teachers.

Jouvancy divides his subject into three chapters: first, the knowledge and use of languages; secondly, the possession of sciences; thirdly, some aids to study.

---

[1] Ratio Stud., Reg. Prov. 19; Monumenta Germaniæ Pædagogica, vol. v, p. 242.

[2] Monumenta Germaniæ Pædagogica, vol. ii, pp. 84, 93.

[3] Ibid., vol. ii, p. 101.

As to languages, they are three in number: Greek, Latin, and the native tongue. Laying down some principles on style in general, he says: "If a correct understanding, according to Horace, be the first principle and source of writing well, it follows that style, which is nothing else than a certain manner of writing, has two parts; first, the intelligent thought or sentiment, properly conceived; secondly, the expression of the same; so that, as man himself is made up of soul and body, all style likewise consists of the underlying thought and the manner of its expression." Thought must be true, perspicuous, and adapted to the subject. To think truly or justly of things, there is required mental power and insight, which distinguishes what is really the gist of a subject-matter from what is only a deceptive appearance, or is superficial. Assistance is to be had for all this from the reading of good books, from accurate reflection and protracted thought, which does not merely skim over the subject, or touch it in a desultory way; again, from the analysis of parts, causes, adjuncts; finally, from the prudent judgment of others, or what is called criticism. As to the ways of acquiring proper diction, Jouvancy says: "I would have you avail yourself of books which treat of this matter, not so as to imagine all is done by thumbing them; you will gain much more by the plentiful reading of the best writers"; and again, "'abundance of diction,' *copia verborum*, will be easily acquired by reading much." It is by reading, writing, and imitating the best authors that a good style is formed; and only the best authors are to be read, "lest the odor of a foreign and vicious style cling to the mind, as to new vases."

Coming to treat of one's native tongue, Jouvancy lays down these points: " The study of the vernacular consists chiefly in three things. First, since the Latin authors are explained to the boys, and are rendered into the mother-tongue, the version so made should be as elegant as possible. Wherefore, let the master elaborate his version for himself, or, if he draws on any writer in the vernacular, let him compare first the Latin text with the version before him; thus he will find it easy to perceive what is peculiar to either tongue, and what is the respective force and beauty of each. The same method is to be observed in explaining and translating histories in the lower classes. Secondly, all the drafts of compositions, which are dictated in the vernacular, must be in accord with the most exact rules of the mother-tongue, free from every defect of style. [Thirdly,] it will be of use to bring up and discuss, from time to time, whatever has been noticed in the course of one's reading, and whatever others have observed regarding the vicious and excellent qualities of speech. The younger Master should be on his guard against indulging too much in the reading of vernacular authors, especially the poets, to the loss of time, and perhaps to the prejudice of virtue."

The interest here manifested in the vicious and excellent qualities of the mother-tongue was a contribution of the schools to the development of modern languages. Nor was the severity, which is here prescribed, with reference to the use of poetry, a barrier to the formation of some good poets among the Jesuits themselves. Friedrich von Spee is considered a distinguished lyric poet of the seventeenth century. Denis, as the translator of Ossian into German, helped to inaugurate the later period of German literature. In Italian prose, Bartoli, Segneri, Pallavicini, have ranked as classics; Tiraboschi, as the historian of literature; Bresciani, in our days, as the popular novelist. As writers of French prose, Bourdaloue and Bouhours appertain to the choicest circle of Louis XIV's golden age; Du Cygne, Brumoy, Tournemine, besides others already mentioned in these pages, took their place as literary critics. And, in their several national literatures, Cahours, Martin, Garucci, have attained their literary eminence as art-critics.

Reverting to solidity of thought as the basis of style, Jouvancy eliminates the false ornaments of a subtle and abrupt style, by reducing the conceptions to a dialectical analysis: "What does the thing mean?" And he gives examples.

In the second chapter of the same part, the *Ars Discendi*, he comes to the acquisition of those sciences, which are proper to a Master of Literature. He says: " The erudition of a religious master is not confined to mere command of languages, whereof we have spoken heretofore; it must rise higher to the understanding of some sciences, which it is usual to impart to youth. Such are Rhetoric, Poetry, History, Chronology, Geography, and Philology or Polymathy, which last is not so much a single science as a series of erudite attainments, whereof an accomplished person should at least have tasted." History he divides into Sacred,

Universal, and Particular. "As to the histories of particular nations, writers of the respective nationalities record them;" "and if you do not add Chronology to History, you take out one of History's eyes." For Geography, he designates the books and maps which were then to be had. And, for all the branches, he indicates standard authors.

Now, in this little rhetorical sketch of Jouvancy's, we may take note of two features, one pedagogical, the other historical. The distinctively pedagogical cast is put upon these private studies, in as much as they are magisterial, being pursued with express reference to the Master's chair. The historical feature, to be noted here, is common to the Jesuit educational literature in general; which, in its many departments, marked several epochs and, as a whole, made an era in education.

Thus, at the time of the *Ratio Studiorum*, there were indeed several guides of the very first rank, in the path of a literary formation. They were three in number, Cicero, Quintilian, and Aristotle. From these the Professor of Rhetoric had to derive his matter and make clear his method. The *Ratio* names them as his text-books for the Precepts.[1] From these sources the literary activity and experience of many generations of Professors, in several hundred colleges of the Order, tended to mark out the best line to follow, for the attainment of literary perfection. The literary course, in which they themselves were proximately formed for the duties of teaching, served but to organ-

---

[1] Rt. St. 1599, Reg. Prof. Rhet. 6; Monumenta Germaniæ Pædagogica, vol. v, p. 404.

ize the matter, and to digest it. The numberless pedagogical text-books, issued before Jouvancy, and after him, exhibit the progress of the movement during the several centuries. And, at present, the system may be seen in its most developed form, if one consults the newest guides, like Father Kleutgen's *Ars Dicendi*, or Father Broeckaert's *Le Guide du Jeune Littérateur*. But, long before our day, the most ordinary systems of literary instruction have embodied the method; and the commonest text-books have it.

A similar epoch was made, as early as 1572, by the Grammar of Father Emmanuel Alvarez, *De Institutione Grammatica Libri Tres*, a work adopted by the *Ratio*, then republished in editions so numerous as to baffle all calculation, translated either entire, or in part, into thirteen languages; while one portion, well-known in our times as a "Latin Prosody," is credited to divers authors or publishers.[1] The latest editions of this Grammar, issued in different languages, are of the last twenty-five years. This era of development in grammar superseded the subtleties and metaphysical abstractions of mediæval methods.[2]

In history, not to mention the voluminous James Sirmond, whose researches among original sources were made before the sixteenth century had closed, Father Denis Petau (Petavius), early in the following century, composed his great work on Chronology, lay-

[1] Sommervogel fills twenty-four columns with a partial enumeration of the editions of Alvarez; Bibliothèque de la Compagnie de Jésus, 1890, *sub voce, Alvarez*.

[2] Compare Monumenta Germaniæ Pædagogica, vol. ii, p. 269, n. 114; Manare's Ordinance for Germany.

ing down the exact basis in this respect for Universal History, both sacred and profane.[1] Geneva and Holland alike reproduced the work. Labbe's publications on ancient and modern History and Chronology, the greater part of his eighty works being upon these subjects, with several abridgments and geographical adjuncts; Father Buffier's "Practical History," which was published for the schools in 1701, and then rapidly went through divers editions, to be supplemented in 1715 by his "Universal Geography," his treatise on the Globe and his Maps, all of which went through some scores of French, Italian and Dutch editions; these and other works of the kind indicate the line of pedagogical development going on at the same time in the various colleges. Hence, the "New Elements of History and Geography for the use of the Scholars of the Collège Louis-le-Grand," which was an abridgment of Buffier's book, could say, with some propriety, on its first page: "How great has been the carelessness of an age, otherwise so judicious and cultivated as ours, in not having as yet made the science of History and Geography an essential part of the education of youth? The public and posterity will perhaps be grateful to the College of Louis-le-Grand, for having shown in this regard an example, which ought to do honor to our time."[2] Thus the same resources were at the service of Jesuit education as, in the general literary world, helped to form the Jesuit historians: Mariana, historian of Spain; Damian Strada, of the War in the Netherlands; Balbin, of Bohemia; Narus-

---

[1] Rationarium Temporum, Paris, 1632.
[2] Daniel, Les Jésuites Instituteurs, etc., ch. 10, p. 216.

zewicz, of Poland; Katona, of the Kings of Hungary; Damberger, of the Middle Ages; Francis Wagner, of Leopold I; G. Daniel, historiographer royal of France.

Geography is not to be separated from History. Up to the end of the sixteenth century, Ptolemy's Geography, corrected, modified, altered, according to the reports of navigators, had been the scientific standard, but uncertain, vacillating, and self-contradictory. From the earlier part of the seventeenth century, the astronomical observations, sent from the far East by the Jesuit missionaries, emphasized the need of a general reform, already sufficiently evident. Father Riccioli, assisted by Father Grimaldi, who is known in science as one of the precursors of Newton, undertook, in his *Geographia Reformata*, the reform of Geography by means of Astronomy.[1] For this purpose, he created first his own metrology, identifying, and reducing to a common denomination, all the measures received in reports from different parts of the earth. The first eclipse of the moon which he makes mention of, among his astronomical reports, had been observed on the night of November 8, 1612, by Father Scheiner at Ingolstadt and by Father Charles Spinola at Nangasaki in Japan. At the time that Riccioli was writing, the Jesuit missionaries had multiplied in China. Adam Schall died in 1666, holding the post of President of the Mathematical Tribunal at Pekin; he was followed by Ferdinand Verbiest; and then a long line of imperial

[1] Geographiæ et Hydrographiæ Reformatæ Libri xii, Bologna, 1661, in folio.

astronomers of the Celestial Empire, Koegler, Hallerstein, Seixas, Francesco, De Rocha, Espinha, continued to send their reports, either to the colleges of their respective Provinces, or to other mathematical centres, or to the learned societies in Europe, whereof not a few Jesuits were members. Meanwhile, scientific returns from Hindustan, Siam, Thibet, on one side of the globe, and from San Domingo on the other side, poured into the Collège Louis-le-Grand, and made of this educational centre an indispensable auxiliary to the Bureau of Longitudes. All this, reacting on education, was received with satisfaction by the general world, and drew the pedagogic bodies steadily, though with some difficulty, on the line of progress. The University of Paris was quite tardy in following up the steps of the Jesuits.[1]

As to Mathematics in education, it is evident that a similar process of development must have been the history of this branch, with the limitation however, that mathematical science has not been so nearly created anew within these last centuries, as some other departments. Father Christopher Clavius, "the Euclid of his time," was engaged by Gregory XIII in reforming the Calendar, the same which we use to-day; he died in 1612. His death intervening, while his complete works were being republished, Father Ziegler superintended the new edition, till it was finished in five tomes. Francis Coster, at Cologne, Hurtado Perez, at Ingolstadt, Henry Garnet, an Englishman,

---

[1] See the pleasant sketch in Daniel's Les Jésuites Instituteurs, etc., chs. 2-5; also Maynard's The Jesuits, their Studies and Teaching, ch. 4, Scientific Condition of the Jesuits, etc.

and Grienberger, successor of Clavius, both at Rome, belonged, with other mathematicans of the Order, to the sixteenth century. The writers of the preliminary *Ratio*, 1586, require that, in a brief course of Mathematics, "Euclid's Elements" "be seasoned always with some application to Geography or the Sphere"; then, in the following year, the rest of Father Clavius' "Epitome of Practical Arithmetic"[1] is to be finished;[2] and special courses are provided for members of the Order, who give promise of eminence.[3]

Indeed, whether as Professors of officers for the army and navy, or as constructing and directing observatories, the members pursued every branch of Mathematics, pure and applied. Father L'Hoste's "Treatise on Naval Evolutions" was used in the French navy, as "the Book of the Jesuit."[4] Of this book the Count de Maistre writes quaintly in 1820: "An English Admiral assured me less than ten years ago, that he had received his first instructions in the 'Book of the Jesuit.' If events are taken for results, there is not a better book in the world!"[5] Eximeno, at the school of Segovia, instructed young nobles in Mathematics and the science of Artillery. And so, in general, courses were provided, according as the needs of respective localities required. The Republic of Venice struck a gold medal in honor of Vincent Riccolati, the Jesuit engineer, just as the King of Denmark honors De Vico, the astronomer, with a gold medal struck in

---

[1] Rome, 1583, 8vo, pp. 219.
[2] Monumenta Germaniæ Pædagogica, vol. v, p. 141, De Mathematicis.   [3] Reg. Prov. n. 20.   [4] First edition in 1697.
[5] De l'Église Gallicane, liv. i, ch. 8, p. 46; edit. 1821.

his honor, and having the words inscribed, "Comet Seen, Jan. 24, 1846."[1]

Kircher, Boscovich, Pianciani, Secchi, Perry, honored with the fellowship of so many learned and scientific Academies, and exercising a distinct influence to-day, either by the far-reaching effects of their researches, or by their actual contact with science, may be looked upon as belonging to our most recent times.[2]

It is remarked that to the Order was due the multiplication of observatories, in the middle of last century. Father Huberti superintended the building of an observatory at Würzburg; Father Maximilian Hell, the court astronomer, built one at Vienna. At Manheim, a third was erected by Mayer and Metzger; at Tyrnau, one by Keri; at Prague, another by Steppling; one at the Jesuit College of Gratz; similarly at Wilna, Milan, Florence, Parma, Venice, Brescia, Rome, Lisbon, Marseilles, Bonfa. In short, Montucla remarks: "In Germany and the neighboring countries, there were few Jesuit colleges without an observatory. They were to be found at Ingolstadt, Gratz, Breslau, Olmütz, Prague, Posen, etc. Most of them seem to have shared the fate of the Society; though there are a few which survive the general destruction."[3]

[1] The medal is in the Coleman Museum of the Georgetown University, where De Vico, with Sestini, was astronomer for some time.

[2] For an historical sketch of Bavarian Jesuits, under the aspect of scientific eminence, see Monumenta Germaniæ Pædagogica, vol. ix, pp. 445-6, where Father Pachtler gives the Prospectus of a new scientific and literary review, to be issued in Bavaria, 1772. The Suppression forestalled it.

[3] Histoire des Mathematiques, t. iv, p. 347; quoted by Crétineau-Joly, t. iv, c. 4, p. 283, who contains a large amount of literature

These few indications go to illustrate the pedagogical epochs made by the system of the Order. And the young member, who is being formed to contribute his own share towards carrying on the education of the world, passes all these branches under review. One of them, Mathematics, is conducted outside of the philological seminary, which we have so far been considering; it is left for his course of Philosophy, which he will pursue during three years, before actually embarking on the life of the class-room, or his "regency." We may now suppose that the time has arrived for his entering the class-room, as a Master of Grammar and Elementary Literature.

When he does so, he has possessed himself, in that philosophical triennium, of positive intellectual attainments, neither meagre nor common. He has surveyed the whole field of natural thought and investigation, in the various branches, mental, physical, and ethical. To enumerate them, there is Logic, including dialectics, and the criteria, objective and subjective, of truth; Ontology, or general metaphysics; Special Metaphysics, in its three divisions : — Cosmology, which immediately underlies physics, chemistry, and biology; Psychology, which underlies all the anthropological sciences about the human compound, its principles, and the formation of its ideas; Natural Theology.

upon this subject. According to late researches, made by MM. C. André and G. Rayet, astronomers of the observatory of Paris, the number of observatories established in the whole world, towards the close of the last century, was 130. Of this number, 32 were founded by Jesuits, or were under their direction. — Victor Van Tricht, La Bibliothèque des Écrivains de la Compagnie de Jésus, etc., appendice 1er, p. 221; 1876.

All this is theoretic or speculative philosophy. There is besides the science of moral life, which comprises Ethics, Natural Right, and Social Right. Concurrent with Philosophy, there has been a double course of Physics and Chemistry, during one year, with a course of higher Mathematics, varying from one year to three; as well as a half-year's course of Geology, Astronomy, and some other subsidiary matters. This is the general formation. The principle which guides individual cases was laid down by Ignatius in these terms: "In the superior faculties, on account of the great inequality of talents and age and other considerations, the Rector of the University will consider how much in each line individuals shall learn, and how long they shall stay in the courses; although it is better for those who are of the proper age, and who have the requisite facility in point of talent, that they should endeavor to advance and become conspicuous in all."[1] During all this course of higher natural sciences, some attention has still been paid to accessories; literature has not been entirely neglected; oratory has been practised, and poems presented on stated occasions. And then the new Master is introduced into his course of "regency."

[1] Constitutiones, pars iv, c. 13, n. 4.

CHAPTER XII.

YOUTHFUL MASTERS.

WHEN Ignatius of Loyola was governing the Society, the multiplicity of affairs which he had to administer, and the absorption of mind which they demanded, did not prevent him from devoting to every minute element the attention which it specially invited. Hence he required the young Scholastics, who were reviewing their literary studies at Valencia, to send him their orations and a poem. So, too, with the Masters of the lower classes at Messina, in Sicily. This college had opened with the higher courses of letters; but the very next year such numerous throngs of younger boys came asking for admission, that the system, begun with Rhetoric and Humanities, was carried down to meet their needs; and the entire course was distributed into five grades. Ignatius required the teachers of these lower grades, no less than those of the higher, to write each week, and send him an account of the affairs of his class.[1]

It is indeed an eventful moment, when a man becomes a teacher of others. They may be boys. But, whether they are boys merely blossoming into life, or youths on the verge of manhood, the teacher of them has to be a teacher of men; and perhaps more so

[1] Bollandists, J. P., n. 871.

with the boy than with the man, inasmuch as his control of the younger student has to be so much the more complete. It is not merely such a control as will address the intellects of men mature, whose characters are already far advanced in the way of formation, or are perhaps fixed for life; but it must be such as will form a whole human nature, which is still pliable and docile.

As an almost universal rule, the Jesuit Scholastic, after his course of Philosophy, takes his place in a college to teach Grammar or Literature. If it be asked, why should this be an almost universal rule, several reasons are at hand. In the first place, the candidate for admission into the Order has been accepted with special reference to this work. If this reference was expressly overlooked, the candidate so admitted is in an exceptional category. In the second place, the whole tenor of what has to be said in the present chapter will show the pedagogical policy in the arrangement. But, in the third place, not to pass over too summarily one special fitness, I will say a few words upon it at once.

The manner of teaching the young is oral and tutorial. All through the Jesuit System the manner followed is oral: in the examinations of the lower classes, where writing is admitted, it is only as a specimen of style and composition that writing enters the examination exercises. With the younger students, the manner of teaching is oral in its most specific sense. It is not that generic quality which will suit as well the lecturer or the public speaker. But it is the tutorial manner, which includes a fund of sympathy, of that tact which supposes sympathy, of such a superiority, both moral and intellectual, as knows how to stoop, and elevate the boy by stooping, and does it all naturally, instinctively, gracefully. In the ordinary course of human affairs, this magnetic power of the teacher is more intense, according as in years he is nearer to the subject on whom his ascendancy plays, and by whom it is spontaneously admitted. I mean that inestimable and precious subject, the mind and heart of the impressionable boy, who is about to develop into manhood, first young, and then mature.

The youthful subject is rich, though not in positive acquisitions already made its own; for, in this respect, it may rather be considered *parum fructuosa*, as Sacchini says; that is, bearing little fruit as yet, either of judgment or positive acquirements. But it is rich in its promise, as it struggles upward into the sunshine of varied and beautiful truth. This is the fact which imposes upon liberal education the duty of omitting nothing that is either beautiful or polished, in imagination, thought, or style. It justifies Belles Lettres and the most finished course of Literature, as being the chosen garden of flowers and fruit, to entertain withal, richly and exquisitely, the youthful promise of mind, sentiment, and heart.

Or, inverting the figure, if we liken the mind itself in youth to the choice and prolific soil of a garden, we may note that, to till such soil, there is need of a gardener who has a delicate hand and a light touch. He must not be a lecturer who stands off, nor a speaker who declaims, nor a text-book monger who reads, and hears recitations of what a book says; nor is he to dole out methods and analyses to an inquisitive sense and emotional fancy, which, in the youthful soul, are the temporary vesture of an unfolding intellect; even, as in nature around, things tangible and palpable are bursting, to the boy's inquisitive eyes, with the great intellectual truths which they contain. Analyses, text-books, lectures are not the powers with the young mind. But, often enough, we see where the real power lies; when young men, scarcely as yet approaching the prime of life, exercise over impressionable and brilliant youths, not much beneath themselves in age, such a personal influence as bids fair to rank them among the greater forces of human nature — forces which are great in leading, because they know so well how to follow. That other form of ascendancy, more purely intellectual, and originating in wide learning and maturity of scholarship, belongs to the University Professor of a later stage of life. Hence it appears that youthfulness in the Master is an advantage for the tutorial teaching of the young.

The critics who drew up the preliminary *Ratio* in 1586 were of opinion that the Masters in the literary courses should be assigned to their work, not after their course of Philosophy, but before.[1] They would except from this arrangement only the Professor of Rhetoric; perhaps, also, in the chief colleges, the Professor of Humanity or Poetry; besides, of course, those "whose age or deportment shows that they are too young to become Masters as yet, or too far advanced in years to be kept back from their Philosophy." In support of this view, they urge several

---

[1] Monumenta Germaniæ Pædagogica, vol. v, p. 151 *seq.*

reasons, which do not much concern us here; as, for instance, that, if young men have once tasted of the subtleties of the philosophers, they can hardly bring themselves to take pleasure any more in the insipid subject-matter of Grammar; they will pore over philosophical lore; they will branch off, during class, into philosophical digressions, which may serve for show, but not for utility. The critics also express a fear that these philosophers will bring into the school-room a style of language infected with philosophical terms; and they quote the eminent Jesuit, Annibal Codret, to the effect that, if Philosophy has been tasted beforehand, nothing brilliant in literary style can subsequently be guaranteed. But, these arguments notwithstanding, the Society, when it came to sanction a final arrangement, in the legislative document of 1599, seems to have entertained a higher idea of the younger members, and of their ability and resolution to shake off any deleterious effects of scholastic Latin, when they advanced to the chair of purest Latinity. Hence the legislation ordains that Philosophy is to be studied before undertaking to teach Letters.[1]

There are several reasons, however, which, as urged by these critics, are quite relevant to our present topic. They urge that Grammar studies require a certain fervor, or alacrity, which is rather to be found in persons who are younger, and so far are nearer to the thoughts and sentiments of boyhood. The fuller results of education, in this respect, are not to be had

[1] Ratio St., Reg. Prov. 28; Monumenta Germaniæ Pædagogica, vol. v, p. 260.

from them when older. If authority or experience is felt to be wanting, it can readily be supplemented by the Prefect of Studies, who is constantly in attendance on the classes of Grammar; and his direction finds a sufficient response in the teacher's aptitude and docility. Indeed, docility to counsel is so indispensable a requisite, on the part of young teachers, that the General Mutius Vitelleschi observes: "If they were to show themselves impatient of correction, and were to refuse the necessary aids for becoming efficient, they should on all accounts be removed from teaching, even if they had filled only half a year; since it is more just and expedient that one suffer shame, than that many be injured."[1]

Unless singular talents, or the bare force of circumstance, recommend another course of action, it is not desirable that new teachers should at once become Masters of the higher class of Grammar or of Humanity, though otherwise not unfit for these grades. On all accounts, say the critics, the rule should be that they start with the lowest classes, and then, year after year, advance to the next higher grade, with the best part of their scholars. A certain crudeness and inexperience which, at the beginning, are unavoidable in their management, will cause, as long as it lasts, not so much evil with the younger as with the older students. Inexperience wears away with practice. Then again, if the Masters go up each year, and the scholars go with them, the same students are very much with the same teachers. The young people have not to pass so often from one

[1] Ibid., vol. ix, p. 59.

kind of management to another. Frequent change entails a waste of time, until each party comes to know the other, and understand his own as well as the other's part.[1] In 1583, Father Oliver Manare, visiting the German Provinces by the General's authority, had noticed this point, in his ordinance for the management of *convictus*, or boarding colleges; that "frequent changes were burdensome to the students themselves, because they were forced to accommodate themselves often to new teachers or prefects."[2]

In the same sense, these critics, whom we are following, consider it undesirable that a Master should resign his post in less than three years. Frequent and manifold changes provoke complaints on the part of the outside world. Besides, the Master's own efforts at acquiring perfection in the magisterial art will be cut short. When there is no prospective permanency in a position, the mind is not so seriously applied to the work in hand.[3]

In all this, a most important question regarding boys is being faced by these critics; and a definite practical solution is adopted. The question is, which of the two alternatives to adopt, whether to submit boys to one person's dominant influence, or to pass them on through the hands of divers experienced and permanent Professors, stationed respectively in the different grades. This latter alternative, if it is understood to mean that one Professor remains perpetually in one grade, and another in another, scarcely

[1] Ibid., vol. v, Rt. St. 1586; Humanitatis Magistri, n. 5, p. 153.
[2] Monumenta Germaniæ Pædagogica, vol. ii, p. 415.
[3] Ibid., vol. v, n. 3, p. 152.

seems to merit consideration with them, except as regards the two highest literary classes, — of Poetry and Rhetoric, — where the requirements of erudition are so considerable as to need a lengthened term of years for filling the chairs worthily. But, if the alternative regarding permanent Professors means that the same teachers remain constantly within the limits of the same curriculum, then the question seems to be the one which the critics of the preliminary *Ratio* argue about in both senses, for and against; and they finally arrive at a solution, or rather a compromise.[1]

The severest thing they say against the plan is in this wise, when speaking directly of the two highest grades: "Perpetuity of that kind may give occasion to mere idleness and indifference; for after acquiring, in the first years, some esteem and name for their learning (in Poetry or Rhetoric), Masters prefer to enjoy the fruit and name of the labor already undergone, however moderate that was, rather than wear themselves out with new labors. Hence they make no new acquisitions in the learning and accomplishments proper to their branch; they get rooted in very much the same spot, and teach what they have taught before over and over again, though with some variations. What is worse, as if they were quite worn out with their prolonged exertions, they say that they cannot any longer stand all the labor of exercising their students; whence everything freezes, and they ask for an assistant, who, if he is unlearned, does more harm than good; if learned, then why are two doing the work of one?"

[1] Ibid., vol. v, n. 4, p. 152.

The solution which they arrive at is a compromise, which recognizes peculiar advantages in both arrangements. It is embodied in several rules of the *Ratio Studiorum*.[1] As many perpetual Professors as possible, for Grammar and Rhetoric, are to be provided; and some candidates for admission to the Order, who seem qualified for this field of work, though apparently not likely to succeed in the higher studies of the Society, may be admitted on this condition, that they devote themselves in perpetuity to this work of zeal. Thus such exigencies are provided for as postulate a perpetuity of professorship within the same limited curriculum.

On the other hand, the normal process is that which arranges a constant succession of teachers in the college, but not a constant change with the same boys. The same boys go hand in hand with the one Master, with whom they have most to do. And no one is to take charge of them, however transiently, says the General Vitelleschi, "whether on account of fewness of numbers, or merely to supply for another in his absence, of whom it is not certain that he is qualified for the post."[2] The very frequent mention, in all these discussions, of something like domestic tragedies resulting from the change of masters, seems to show two things; first, it justifies the practice of keeping the same Professor over the same boys for a certain term of years, if not until the class itself dissolves into higher courses; secondly, it shows what a usual condition it was for masters to have won the

---

[1] Ibid., vol. v, p. 260; Reg. Prov. 24, 25.
[2] Ibid., vol. ix, p. 60; letter of the year 1639.

most absolute attachment to themselves, in the exercise of their magisterial duties, both on the side of parents and on the part of the scholars. Thus, speaking of the Professors mounting with their classes, the critics say: "They will have observed what their disciples need; they will take them up to the next class. And hence, that changing of Masters, which has caused so many tragic scenes, will not be felt so much."[1]

Add to these elements of permanency and identity, another which is most fundamental of all, the identity of their formation as Masters; so that the young Jesuits, as the General Visconti sums up the matter in 1752, "must have the most accomplished Professors of Rhetoric, immediately after their novitiate, men who not only are altogether eminent in this faculty, but who know how to teach, and make everything smooth for them; men of eminent talent and the widest experience in the art; who are not merely to form good scholars, but to train good Masters"; and that "two years entire must be given to Rhetoric, according to the custom of the Society, which term is not to be abridged, unless necessity is urgent."[2] Add, moreover, the uniformity of plan, "so that the form of our schools may be everywhere as much as possible the same, and, when Masters are changed, itself need undergo no change."[3] It follows that, though the flow of new blood is constantly entering the pedagogic body, and a constant renewal is taking place, neither the permanency nor the identity of the teaching body and its system is found to depend upon the same individuals remaining at the same posts. Naturally,

[1] Ibid., vol. v, p. 154. [2] Ibid., vol. ix, p. 130, n. 2. [3] Ibid., n. 6.

such conditions are not to be looked for, except in the special circumstances of a religious community, with perfect organization in the body, with the conscientiousness of a self-denying formation actuating the members, with the landmarks of traditions, and a statutory method to show the way; and, finally, with executive officials adequate to control.

As to this last-named condition of executive superintendence over persons and things in the system, several rules for the Prefect of Studies of these literary courses will explain themselves. The *Ratio* of 1599 says: "Let him have the rules of the Masters and scholars, and see that they are observed, as if they were his own. Let him help the Masters themselves and direct them, and be especially cautious that the esteem and authority due to them be not in the least impaired. Let him be very solicitous that the new Preceptors follow with accuracy the manner of teaching, and other customs of their predecessors, provided that these were not foreign to our method; so that persons outside may not have reason to find fault with the frequent change of Masters. Once a fortnight, at least, let him listen to each one teaching."[1]

This moral identity being secured, in the ways, means, and views of the teaching body, the individual and personal elements, which each Master brings to bear upon the work before him, are no more interfered with, or hampered by community of method, than are all the varieties of race, nation, politics, and environment, slighted or interfered with by a single

[1] Ibid., vol. v, p. 352.

system of collegiate institution being placed in their midst. It was in view of being everywhere, that the system was cast in its precise and adjustable form, so that, in spite of being everywhere, it should be found equally manageable and effective. And similarly, in spite of the system itself being one, the play of individual talents can be various, as are the movable factors in any great organization.

We may close this chapter by observing several far-reaching consequences of the foregoing principles. In the first place, those who, after personal experience in the classes, come to take charge of colleges in the capacity of Rectors, are found, say the critics of 1586, to take full and accurate account of studies and Professors alike; for they themselves "have borne the burden of the schools, and know how to sympathize with others from their own experience"; a fact which is the more conducive to the end in view, as "colleges have been instituted for the study of letters. Besides, not unfrequently there arise in the classes, especially of the smaller colleges, difficulties which can scarcely be overcome, except by a Rector who has personal experience to guide him; otherwise, whether he chances to solve the difficulty aright, or solves it awry, he will not do much good either way, since they do not give him the credit of knowing how."[1] The "smaller colleges" spoken of here, as more liable to encounter internal difficulties, are contrasted elsewhere by these critics with "the greater and principal ones, in which there are many counsellors or referees at hand, to whom the Masters can have recourse for

[1] Ibid., vol. v, p. 149.

assistance; and the schools themselves have sufficient authority." But, in what they call the minor colleges, "the authority of the schools depends for the most part on the reputation and authority of the individual Masters," who happen at a given time to be filling the posts.[1]

In the spirit of this personal and experienced concurrence with all the affairs of the college, the Rector is required so to moderate the other concerns of his office, as to be prompt in fostering and advancing all literary exercises. He is to go often to the classes, those of the lower faculties as well as of the higher.[2] Every month, or at least every other month, he is to hold general consultations with all the Masters below the course of Logic, the several Prefects being present; and, after the reading of some selection from the *Ratio*, concerning the Masters or the piety and good conduct of the students, he is to inquire what difficulties occur, or what omissions are noticed in the observance of rules.[3] Books are never to be wanting, in the sufficiency desired by the members generally, whether they are engaged in teaching, or are pursuing their studies.[4] To this regulation, which concerns the chief authority in a Province, the revised *Ratio* of 1832 adds: "The same is to be said of literary periodicals for the use of the Professors; of museums, physical apparatus, and other equipments, which are needed by a college according to its degree." The General Visconti observes somewhat emphatically,

[1] Ibid., p. 153.
[2] Rt. St., Reg. Rect. 3; Monumenta Germaniæ Pædagogica, vol. v, p. 268.
[3] Ibid., n. 18, p. 272.
[4] Reg. Prov. 33; Monumenta Germanniæ Pædagogica, p. 262.

that "in buying books the Rectors will never consider the money of their colleges ill spent."[1]

Jouvancy applies the same principle to publishing the literary productions of the Masters. He first sketches the series of literary productions expected from them, — the annual addresses of inauguration to be given by each Professor in his own class, the public and solemn one to be delivered, on the same inaugural occasion, by the Professor of Rhetoric, the poem to be composed and read by the Master of Poetry; then, during the year, a certain number of addresses to be delivered; and, at the end, a tragedy composed by the Professor of Rhetoric, a minor drama by the Professor of Poetry, both to be acted on the stage. Jouvancy goes on to recommend that no public occasion be allowed to go by, without receiving the tribute of some such literary work. Then he adds: "Nor is that expense to be considered useless which is incurred for printing and publishing good poems. In all these matter, splendors should be added to literary exercises, and to the exhibition thereof, in such wise that everything meanwhile tends to solidity of erudition."[2]

A second consequence of the literary cast, marking the whole Order, is the vantage-ground on which it placed the Jesuits, with regard to all the learning and the learned men of Europe. The fluent and elegant command of the Latin language gave at once a mastery over the vehicle of intercourse, in which all learning was conveyed. Our critics of 1586 sum up the bearings of this particular advantage under several

---

[1] Ibid., vol. ix, p. 131.
[2] Jouvancy, Ratio Discendi; c. Ordo Studendi.

heads: The members of the Order deal with so many nations; scholastic disputations, whether in Philosophy or Theology, are always conducted in Latin; the members write so many books; they can do justice to the ancient Fathers of the Church; they have to deal constantly with learned men.[1]

A last consequence, which I shall present, is suggested by an observation of the same writers, in the same place. It throws no little light upon the history of the Society, and it shows the practical adjustment of the educational system to the times. They say then, it is by the studies of Belles-Lettres, more than by the higher faculties, that the Society has, in a short time, been propagated through all the principal parts of Christendom. Nor can it be preserved better or more solidly, than by the same means through which it was first introduced. Unless they endeavor to maintain this honorable distinction, with which God has been pleased to grace the Society, there is reason to fear that they themselves may yet lapse into the barbarism, which they are far from admiring in others. "As to the other faculties, which are brilliant enough of themselves, there is no trouble in cultivating them. But, natural inclinations feeling a repugnance for less conspicuous pursuits, people have, as it were, to drag themselves to these lower faculties. They should take lesson, therefore, by good husbandmen, who bestow more care on transplanted and exotic growths than on native shoots."[2] And they proceed to quote the rule, formulated in the words of Ignatius, by the General Everard Mercurian,

[1] Monumenta Germaniæ Pædagogica, vol. v, p. 144.   [2] Ibid.

who required the institution and preservation of the literary seminary.[1] So that we end here this discussion on the lower faculties, at the point where we began.

In all well-assorted plans each element has a reference to every other. Men must match the work, and the work be suited to the men. Were the men not formed, the best system would settle into an inert state; and, the more consistency and vitality of its own it offered to contribute, the more inept and inert would it look, a memorial of what it might do, dead to what it can. In itself, and in its effects, it might appear to be out of date, as not being understood. Only the practical working of a thing, by the man who understands it, shows it off for what it is worth. This is a rule quite universal, wherever practical insight is needed for the working of a mechanism. It must be worked intelligently to be understood. Once it is understood, the practical intelligence grows.

[1] Ibid., vol. ii, p. 126; Reg. Prov. n. 50.

CHAPTER XIII.

THE COURSES OF DIVINITY AND ALLIED SCIENCES. PRIVATE STUDY. REPETITION.

1. Having finished his course of teaching literature, the Jesuit returns to his higher studies. Divinity and its allied sciences stand out in prominence for their intrinsic dignity; but they have, besides, a studied preëminence assigned them in the system before us. The almost universal rule, of intermitting the higher studies with a course of literary teaching, undergoes a special exception in the case of those "theologians, whose number is few, and use so manifold";[1] of whom Aquaviva says that, "according as the higher courses are developed, the fewer proportionately, out of many students, become qualified to profess those exalted sciences."[2] The same policy holds with respect to those who have an eminent talent for oratory. Laynez, himself a great preacher, and a competent judge in the matter, relieved Father Francis Strada of the office of Provincial, to set him free for the ministry of the pulpit; and he wrote, as he did so: "If only he had a sufficiency of those whom he could put in the office of Provincial, he would relieve all preachers of that

[1] Rt. St. 1586; Monumenta Germaniæ Pædagogica, vol. v, p. 150.
[2] Formula Acceptandorum Collegiorum, b; Monumenta Germaniæ Pædagogica, vol. ii, p. 339.

office, that they might devote themselves entirely to spreading the seed of the Divine Word."[1] Of these and others, "who give eminent promise of being equal to the graver occupations, or for whom an immediate need exists in that direction,"[2] an immediate application is to be made to the study of Theology.[3]

All who graduate in these higher courses do so, as "qualified to profess"; just as they had graduated in Philosophy and its cognate branches.[4] But, though a master in the matter of his philosophical triennium, no student is called upon to profess any of those branches, until he has graduated also in Theology. Here we may advert to several lines of strict parallelism in the system, both with regard to admitting any students, whether Jesuits or not, to the respective courses of study, and with regard to admitting Jesuits themselves to profess in the chairs.

As a condition for admitting any students at all into the higher courses, the Society introduced a much-needed reform, in requiring that literary qualifications of a sufficiently high grade should precede matriculation. Thus the University of Ingolstadt ordains that no one shall be admitted to Academic, that is, University lectures, except after one year of Rhetoric; and it adds very strict regulations about the election of courses, repetitions, disputations, etc., in the three years' curriculum of Philosophy.[5]

---

[1] Hist. S. J., Sacchini, pars ii, Lainius, lib. viii, n. 219, ad annum 1564. [2] Rt. St. 1586, ibid.
[3] Rt. St. 1599, Reg. Prov. 27; Monumenta Germaniæ Pædagogica, vol. v, p. 260. [4] Chapter xi, above, p. 155.
[5] Statuten der philos. Fak. Ingolstadt, 1649; De Auditoribus; Monumenta Germaniæ Pædagogica, vol. ix, p. 284.

In like manner, to be admitted as a student of Divinity and its correlative sciences, it is necessary to have graduated in the course of Arts, that is to say, Philosophy and its branches. Thus the University of Würzburg ordains that no one shall be admitted as an auditor of Scholastic Theology, unless he be *Magisterio insignis*, "a Master of Arts"; it excepts only the members of religious Orders in attendance, and also *Principis Alumnos*, "the Prince's scholars." Others, who have not so graduated, it will admit to Moral Theology and its supplementary branches. It will not even examine, for the Mastership in Arts, any one, whether a Religious or not, who has studied Philosophy in a private institution or a monastery.[1] To apply for Academic Degrees, "they must prove that they have followed all the courses in some approved public University."[2]

The curriculum, now before the student, is a quadriennium, or four-year course. It is prolonged into a fifth and sixth year, for reviewing the whole ground of one's studies; for preparing a public defence against all comers; and, in the case of Jesuit students, for an immediate preparation to fill the Professor's chair, the pulpit, or to discharge other functions. Hence the University of Cologne specifies, in general, a sexennium, or six-year course for Theology.[3]

---

[1] Qui non in Academia, sed privatim in aliquo Auditorio aut Monasterio audierunt philosophiam.

[2] Nisi probent se omnes materias publice audivisse in aliqua Academia probata: Würzburger Promotionsgebrauche, 1662; Monumenta Germaniæ Pædagogica, vol. ix, p. 387.

[3] Rhetius S. J. für Reform der theol. Fak. zu Köln, November, 1570; Monumenta Germaniæ Pædagogica, vol. ii, p. 217.

Not unlike to this is the parallelism which we may notice, in appointing the members of the Society to Professors' chairs. Though qualified to teach literature after his own complete course of letters in the seminary, yet, as we have seen, no one is to be put over the classes of Grammar or Humanity who has not first studied his Philosophy. And so again, at this stage, though apparently competent to teach Philosophy, and approved as being qualified to profess it, yet no one is to be put in a chair of that course who has not also studied his Theology.[1]

The reasons for this are assigned by the critics of 1586. The philosopher, they say, who has not yet become a theologian, will not be so safe in his conclusions, in his proofs, in his manner of expression. He will be of an age less mature. His learning will be less superabundant. He will scarcely be able to answer the arguments of unbelievers. Nor will he treat Philosophy in a way to render it useful to Theology. In fine, the proprieties of things cannot be well observed, if he who has just filled a chair of Philosophy has to sit down as a mere student in Theology.[2]

The branches of this theological course are Scholastic Theology, Moral Theology, Sacred Scripture, Hebrew and Oriental Languages, Ecclesiastical History, and Canon Law. The general category of students is naturally more limited than in the philosophical curriculum. There the auditors were young men,

---

[1] Rt. St., Reg. Prov. 28; Monumenta Germaniæ Pædagogica, vol. v, p. 260.

[2] Ibid., vol. v, p. 133, n. 10, Studium Philos.

COURSES OF DIVINITY. 195

who would betake themselves, at its close, to Medicine, or other walks of life. They may have taken to Law; though Possevino, himself eminent in jurisprudence, would seem to imply that Canon Law must have been pursued first.[1] The students now are chiefly Ecclesiastics, with various careers before them; or they are Religious of different Orders; or, finally, the members of the Society itself. The principal object of our consideration is the formation of these latter, as qualified to profess. The pedagogical elements before us may be ranged under three heads: Private Study; Repetition, which includes Disputation; Lecturing, which is supplemented by Dictation.

2. As to the method of private study, all the auditors of the course are directed to look over, prior to the lecture,[2] the text in Aristotle, St. Thomas, etc., which the Professor is about to explain.[3] Then, while the lecture is being delivered, they take down notes; the copying of mere dictation is not favored. After the lecture, they are to read over the notes which they have taken down. Let them endeavor to understand their annotations. Understanding what they have written, they are to make objections to themselves against the thesis established, and endeavor to solve their own objections. If they cannot find a solution, let them note the difficulties, and take occasion to ask the Professor, or reserve them for disputation. Such is the method of private study prescribed for the members of the Order,[4] and laid down in more general

---

[1] Biblioth. Selecta; de Cultura Ingeniorum, cap. 27.
[2] Prævidere. [3] Prælegere.
[4] Monumenta Germaniæ Pædagogica, vol. v, p. 450, n. 4.

terms for the other students.¹ To develop habits of such study, and to afford the requisite leisure, a certain custom, then prevailing in Portugal, of keeping the Professors of Philosophy and their students during two hours and a half consecutively in the lecture room is discountenanced by the critics of 1586: "That the philosophers should remain two whole hours and a half in class, as is now done, is burdensome to the Professor and troublesome to the students; for these latter should get accustomed to private study, lest, like parrots, they seem to be always talking by rote."²

This curtailing of class hours was characteristic of the Society's system. In 1567 the General Father Francis Borgia wrote, through his secretary Polanco, correcting, in this respect, a school-regulation which had been followed in the lower classes of the German Province. The secretary writes: "It is found by experience, in the schools of the Company, that to teach three consecutive hours in the forenoon, and three more in the afternoon, is injurious to the health of our Masters, and does no good to the health of the scholars; for which reason it is now ordained that in our schools the morning classes shall not last longer than two and a half hours, and the same in the afternoon."³

Nothing intensifies more the results of studies than concentration, nor dissipates them more than division of attention, while a given pursuit is in progress.

---

[1] Ibid., p. 460, n. 9.

[2] Rt. St. 1586, Studium Philos. n. 12; Monumenta Germaniæ Pædagogica, vol. v, p. 134. Compare also the German Province, where, in 1586, four hours are reduced to three, ibid., vol. ii, p. 283.

[3] Monumenta Germaniæ Pædagogica, vol. ii, p. 154.

This principle applies to the number of courses taken up at one time, the conduct of private studies in any single course, and the degree to which the appointed teachers and the standard authors have full justice done them. On this head, the critics of 1586 give recommendations, derived from the Constitution, for the direction of all the students in general, and for the members of the Order in particular. The recommendations are embodied briefly in the *Ratio Studiorum*.[1] With Aristotle in Philosophy, or with St. Thomas in Theology, one commentary is to be designated, and that a specially chosen author, suited to the individual's capacity. In the second year of Theology, one of the Fathers of the Church can be added, "to be read at odds and ends of time, or after the fatigue of a long stretch of study. Another can be substituted, if after a while they ask for another. But care should be taken that they do not spend too much time on this reading, as if they were getting up a sermon."[2]

All this, no doubt, tends to make the student "a man of one book," who, as the adage says, is much to be feared. However, when he goes through every course, and is everywhere a man of concentrated attention, while, for the purpose of public disputation and the attempted refutation of his own and the Professor's conclusions, the side avenues of various authors and systems are studiously and necessarily kept open, it is probable that, after being "a man of

---

[1] Ibid., vol. v, p. 108, De Privato Studio Scholasticorum; ibid. p. 133, n. 11, Studium Philos.

[2] Ut concionabundi.

one book," in many courses successively, he will also be well-rounded by the time his formation is complete. With students in general, this can be accomplished by the age of twenty-five; with the Jesuits themselves, about the age of thirty-three.

3. I come now to the subject of Repetition, of which two chief forms offer themselves. One is just what the word of itself indicates; it belongs to all the faculties, but chiefly to the lower courses. I shall call it by the generic name of Repetition. The other has place principally in the higher; it is Disputation; of which a preparatory exercise, called *Concertatio*, prevails also from the lowest class of Grammar upwards.

Repetition then rehearses in full class, under various forms or modifications of that exercise, what the Professor has explained in class. Just before the close of the hour spent on his lecture, the Professor of Philosophy or Theology signifies that he is ready for questions on the matter treated; he asks sometimes an account of the lecture, and he sees that it is repeated. The revised *Ratio* of 1832 puts it, in more general terms, thus: "He is often to require an account of the lectures, and to see that they are repeated"; and then it desires that, after the lecture, either in the class-room, or somewhere near, he remain accessible to the students for at least a quarter of an hour, to answer their questions.[1] This is all from the Constitution of Ignatius.

The Repetition, which he is to see to personally,

---

[1] Rt. St., Reg. comm. Prof. sup. fac. n. 11; Monumenta Germaniæ Pædagogica, vol. v, p. 290.

is that which takes place in small circles of about ten students each. "At the close of the lectures let them, in parties of about ten apiece, repeat for half an hour what they have just heard; one of the students, and, if possible, a member of the Society, presiding over each party, *decuria*."[1] Neither the preliminary, nor the final, *Ratio* demands that the Professor himself preside over any of these parties. But "those who do preside will become more learned, and will be practising to become Masters themselves."[2]

It must be admitted that the tenor of many remarks in the earlier document of 1586, shows the presence of Jesuits among the auditors to have acted on the course as a leaven and a relief; although the concurrent testimony of historians, about the Jesuit schools, indicates little or nothing there of that license of manners, such as Possevino described for us in a former chapter.[3] In a special manner, those Jesuit students, already young priests, who, having gone through their four-year course, were now reviewing in a biennium, of a fifth and sixth year, all their long studies of the higher sciences, stood ready at hand for many functions in the arena of direction and presidency, either over the repetitions or the disputations, or in the chair; to which as many of them as were needed would be officially assigned, when their private studies left them at last free.[4]

[1] Rt. St. 1599, Reg. Prof. Phil. n. 16; 1832, n. 9; Monumenta Germaniæ Pædagogica, vol. v, pp 340, 332.

[2] Rt. St. 1586, Repetitiones, n. 3; Monumenta Germaniæ Pædagogica, vol. v, p. 99.

[3] Chapter vii, above, The Moral Scope, p. 101.

[4] Monumenta Germaniæ Pædagogica, vol. v, p. 268; Reg. Rect. n. 6.

To say a word upon this class of Jesuit students, they show us the Professor's formation at its last stage. They are reviewing all Theology, Philosophy, Sacred Scripture, Canon Law, Polemical or Controversial Theology, and ecclesiastical erudition generally. The last of their rules for self-guidance says: "In particular, they are to devote themselves most of all to that pursuit, to which they feel chiefly drawn, without, however, omitting any of the rest."[1] Meanwhile, they present, in various ways, specimens of their talent and erudition; they throw into the form of a digest, "from their own genius," all Theology, under certain heads and principles; they can choose some "splendid subject,"[2] and deliver ten public lectures thereupon to the auditors who choose to attend, which, we may observe, was precisely the status of all Professors in the mediæval universities. In their acts of public defence, five of which are prescribed during the two years, they are free to follow or to leave the opinions of their late Professors.[3]

These students then are assistant and extraordinary Professors. They have begun the work, which some of them will continue when called upon to become Professors in ordinary. They are already in training for that independent work, which the revised *Ratio* of 1832 shows some anxiety about preserving; for it says to all who occupy any chair in these faculties, that, in case they adopt a standard author to follow in their lectures, which is a custom rather

---

[1] Monumenta Germaniæ Pædagogica, p. 456; Institutio pro biennio, n. 14.   [2] Præclara aliqua materia.

[3] Ibid., p. 454.

prevalent in more recent times, they must nevertheless deliver each year some special question elaborated independently by themselves.[1] This independence of style, perfect command of the matter, with express leave for the incipient Professor, in the course of his final biennium, to relinquish the opinions of his late Professors, are made the subject of many a remark by the critics of 1586. Withal, it is clear enough that for a younger man to leave an approved opinion safely, it is very necessary for him to know well what he is about; and doubly necessary when he comes forward in a public defence; for his own late Professors are among the Doctors present, and are there to assail him in all his tenets.

These, then, or others presiding over the circles, "one person repeats, the others listening; they propose difficulties mutually, and, if they cannot solve their own objections, they consult the Professor."[2] The one who repeats is to do so, not from his notes, but from memory. Thus "the memory is exercised; practice is afforded those who are to be Masters, so that they accustom themselves to develop their thoughts before others; it makes them all keep alive and attentive during the lecture, to take down the necessary notes, as they might not do, if they were free from such repetition."[3] There are several other possible forms of conducting this exercise.

---

[1] Reg. comm. Prof. sup. fac., n. 9; Monumenta Germaniæ Pædagogica, p. 288.

[2] Constitutiones, pars iv, c. 6, H.

[3] Rt. St. 1586, Repetitiones; Monumenta Germaniæ Pædagogica, vol. v, p. 99.

When once the first crude repetition is over, the series of disputations begins, daily, weekly, monthly, yearly. Without counting in the "Grand Acts" of public defence against all objectors, at stated times and by specially designated persons, we may enumerate as many as seven ordinary rehearsals of the same matter.

First, before going to the lecture hall, the student looks over the text. This is done easily enough in St. Thomas or Aristotle, if one of these is the standard. As Ignatius expected would be done, many standard works have been published by writers of the Society.[1] Their recommendation is, as he intimated, that they are "more adapted to our times"; and they have incorporated recent researches in progressive branches. In the sense of this adaptation to times and circumstances, the theologians in Cologne, making their announcement for the year 1578, say that they follow St. Thomas as a general rule, but not so "as to treat all that he treats, nor only what he treats. . . . Every age," they say, "has its own debated ground in matters of doctrine, and this brings it to pass that Theology is not only constantly enlarged with a variety of new disputations, but assumes, as it were, a new cast."[2] And the critics of the preliminary *Ratio*, treating of the Scripture course, lecture at some length all whom it may concern, — theologians, professors, preachers, — precisely on this ground, the need of amplifying and adapting the course of Scripture to the conditions of the times.[3] Accordingly, works

---

[1] Constitutiones, pars iv, c. 14, B.
[2] Monumenta Germaniæ Pædagogica, vol. ii, p. 245.
[3] Ibid., vol. v, p. 68.

always new and adapted to latest needs, have poured forth from the writers of the Order. And such as furnish the conditions of a text, which may readily be followed, also supply the conditions for conning over, before going to the lecture hall, what the Professor means to treat. If no such standard is being followed, still, as I find noted in a documentary report of 1886, "the Professors should always, as far as possible, throw out directions enough for the students to look up the subject before coming to the lecture."

In this connection many familiar names of authors occur. For Scholastic Theology and Philosophy, there is, in the first place, the prince of modern theologians, Francis Suarez, with his library of tomes; there are the three Cardinals Toletus, Bellarmine, De Lugo; Valentia, Vasquez, Lessius, Franzelin; and, in the modern school of Scholastic Philosophy, the elegant Liberatore, Kleutgen, Tongiorgi, Pesch, along with the writers of Louvain, Stonyhurst, Innsbruck, and elsewhere; in Positive Theology and Controversy, Canisius, Becanus, Petau, Sardagna; in Exegesis, Maldonado, Salmeron, À Lapide, Menochius, Patrizi, Cornely, with the school of Maria Laach; in Moral Theology, an endless number, Sanchez, Laymann, Busembaum, with his two hundred editions, Gury, Ballerini.[1]

Secondly, the student hears the Professor's lecture. Thirdly, one of the forms of regular repetition is gone through. Fourthly, the daily disputation takes

[1] Consult the five volumes of Nomenclator Litterarius Recentioris Theologiæ Catholicæ, by H. Hurter, S. J., 1871-1886.

place, at least among the Jesuit Scholastics: "At home, every day except on Saturdays, free and feast days, one hour is to be appointed," during which, after a preliminary summarizing of the matter for defence, the disputation follows; and, if time remains over, difficulties may be proposed. "In order to have some time remain over, the president must have the syllogistic form of discussion rigidly observed; and, if nothing new is being urged, he will cut off the debate."[1]

Fifthly, there is the weekly disputation: "On Saturday, or some other day, as the custom of the University has it, let them hold disputations in the schools during two hours, or longer still, whenever there is a large concourse of persons who come to hear."[2] Sixthly, the more solemn disputation follows, every month, or nearly so: "Each month, or, if the students are few, every other month, let disputations be held on a certain day, both morning and afternoon. The number of defendants will correspond to the number of Professors whose theses they defend."[3] Seventhly, towards the close of the scholastic year, though no time is to be set aside for the purpose, so as to prejudice the continuous course of the Professor's lectures, yet "all the matter of the year is to have been gone through, by way of repetition, when the time of vacation arrives."[4] The whole of this

---

[1] Rt. St., Reg. comm. Prof. sup. fac., n. 12; Monumenta Germaniæ Pædagogica, vol. v, p. 290; compare also Monumenta Germaniæ Pædagogica, vol. ix, Ordnung Einer Selbst. Univ. der Ges. J. 1658, pars ii, c. 4, p. 355; De Repetitonibus et Disputationibus Scholasticorum S. J.

[2] Ibid., n. 14.   [3] Ibid., n. 20.   [4] Ibid., n. 13.

matter forms the subject of the year's examination for the Jesuit members of the course.[1] To all these argumentative repetitions may be added the discursive form, in the shape of lectures given by the students themselves, or dissertations read on stated occasions.[2]

It is evident that the members of the Society are the chief subjects of this completeness of formation; and that for two reasons. In the first place, no other students, even if *convictores*, that is, boarders in the Jesuit colleges, can be brought under such a thoroughness of system. Secondly, other students are not in the same way subject to the regular gradation of examinations from year to year. When they are competent, they may apply for admission to the requisite public tests, or Acts of Defence; and, in the philosophical courses, they become Bachelors, Licentiates, and Masters of Arts; in Theology, Bachelors in the first and then in the second grade, Licentiates, Doctors. "No degree is to be conferred on any one who has not stood all the tests, which, according to the custom of Universities, must precede the conferring of these degrees." The character of each degree, its conditions, tests, formalities, are treated of fully in the "Form and Method of conducting Academies and *Studia Generalia S. J.*," 1658.

Here, then, the spirit of the Constitution is fully observed, with regard to repetition and also disputation. The Fathers remark that Ignatius "recom-

---

[1] Monumenta Germaniæ Pædagogica, vol. ii, p. 95; Congr. gen. 11.
[2] Reg. Prof. S. Script., n. 19, 20; also Statuten der philos. Fak. Ingolstadt, 1649, Monumenta Germaniæ Pædagogica, vol. ix, p. 291.
[3] Monumenta Germaniæ Pædagogica, vol. ix, pp. 359-381.

mends nothing with more urgency than disputation, and constancy in its exercise; so much stress does he lay upon it, as not to let the students of Letters and Grammar go without it."[1] In the lower classes it takes the form of *concertatio* and mutual challenges, in the matter of Grammar and literary doctrine. Here it is in its full form; and we may pass on to consider it in the next chapter, not as a manner of repetition, but on its own merits.

I will make the transition, by quoting an important passage or two from the preliminary *Ratio*. They bear not only on disputation, but on that very essential point, where it is that the vital power for actuating the whole system lies; and what is the intrinsic value of any system, as a mere code of legislation.

The critics say that, to counteract the apparent decline of disputation, and to restore this exercise to its ancient form and splendor, everything depends on the vigilance and diligence of those in authority. "Without this, nothing will be effected, even though, for the proper administration of this department of studies, many laws and precepts are put down in writing."[2] Elsewhere, acknowledging in another connection that there is indeed a multitude of points defined for observance, the same writers go on to make these pertinent reflections: "The perfection of doctrine, like the perfection of moral life, stands in need of many aids; whence it is that there is no people under the direction of more laws than the Christian people, nor any Religious Order more under the obli-

---

[1] Rt. St. 1586, Disputationes; Monumenta Germaniæ Pædagogica, vol. v, p. 103. [2] Ibid.

gation of Constitution and Decrees than our own." They undertake to prove the advantage of this, both from the side of those in authority, and of those under authority. "Aristotle and St. Thomas," they say, "are both of opinion that as few points as possible should be left to the private opinions of a judge, and as many as possible should be determined by the clear definition of law. They prove it; for it is easier to find the few wise men, whose wisdom is equal to the task of determining fixed rules of guidance, than to find the multitude, which otherwise is required to pass judgment in all contingencies of time and place; there is the sanction of greater maturity in laws which' have stood the test of time and experience, than in the off-hand decision of the present hour; there is less of a corrupting influence on law-givers, when they are defining things in general and for the future. Wherefore, whatever can be despatched by general law is so to be despatched; what cannot be provided for by such law is to be left to the judge, as the living rule. Under this head come the particular decisions to be passed in given junctures, whereof the general law cannot take cognizance." So far Aristotle and St. Thomas; and the Fathers of 1586 agree with them.[1]

[1] Ibid., vol. v, Commentariolus, p. 45 *seq*.

CHAPTER XIV.

DISPUTATION. DICTATION.

1. Many wise things had been said by the experienced masters of old on the subject of disputation. Thus Robert of Sorbon, the founder of the College of the Sorbonne, had put it down in one of his six essential rules for the scholar, that "nothing is perfectly known unless masticated by the tooth of disputation."[1]

Our Jesuit critics mention incidentally, in one place, that "their age is eminently versed in disputation."[2] They are cautioning the Professor of Scripture against using disputation at all, lest he come thereby to relinquish his own eloquent style of commentary. For every chair has its own character; and that which the *Ratio Studiorum* of 1599 attributes to the chair of Scripture includes, among a number of qualifications, this one, which is mentioned in the last place, that, "as far as possible, the Professors be well versed in eloquence."[3]

---

[1] Nihil perfecte scitur, nisi dente disputationis feriatur; see the Life and Labors of St. Thomas of Aquin, by Bede Vaughan, 1871, vol. i, ch. 16, p. 388. The two chapters on Paris, in this learned work, are replete with information pertinent to our subject.

[2] Monumenta Germaniæ Pædagogica, vol. v, p. 71, n. 5; De Scripturis.

[3] Reg. Prov., n. 5; Monumenta Germaniæ Pædagogica, vol. v, p. 234.

On the other hand, in the proper arena of disputation, they caution Professors against its abuse. Taking note, in one place, of the discord which can arise among learned men, they illustrate their point with some instances, taken precisely from a disputatious tendency, from that exaggerated scholasticism which had run into dialectic excesses. They say: "For the disturbance of harmony, it makes very little difference whether discord arises in great things or in little. It is not only the importance of a question, it is also the spirit of emulation, that fosters contention; so that sometimes a war of words and the bitterest altercation is kept up on a single term and phrase. Forsooth, what is more trivial than to ask whether God is in imaginary space? Yet what tragic scenes does not this very question give rise to!" [1]

Excesses of this kind being guarded against, the Fathers lay down the thesis that, when employed in its proper place, no exercise is more useful than disputation. You will see not a few wholly taken up with reading, writing, arranging, and paging what they have written; but they eschew most carefully all disputation, neglecting it, looking upon it as an idle occupation, having all their Theology locked up, not so much in their memory and intelligence, as in their paper books. Men of authority, they go on to say, have always been persuaded that Philosophy and Theology are learnt, not so much by hearing, as by discussing. For, in this exercise, you have a most certain test how much a man understands of what he

[1] Commentariolus, Monumenta Germaniæ Pædagogica, vol. v, p. 53.

is writing about or teaching; also how much solidity there is in one's own private cogitations, since it happens not unfrequently that what appears brilliant in one's private room is seen to drag in the mud, when it comes to disputation.[1] Then, too, while we are hard pressed by our adversary, we are forced to strain every nerve of our wits, and, when others are bearing down heavily upon us, we knock out of our brains many things which would never have come into our heads, while we stayed in the quiet of leisure and rested in the shade. We hear things which others have found out, and which either throw light on doubtful points, or indicate the path to some other point. Or, if what is said does not commend itself to our judgment, we see through the opponent's artifice; we meet him with more facility, and establish our own thesis with more stability. The auditors, meanwhile, can take note of the good points one Professor makes, the strong points of another, and, after the example of their Doctors, they quicken their wits for the fray, observing where the arguments limp, which are the distinctions that tell, how the whole doctrine of a Professor hangs together. In short, it is well established by the authority of the gravest men, and by the test of experience, that one disputation does more good than many lectures; not to mention the other consideration, that there is nothing more calculated to render our schools illustrious, than making our students competent to win great approba-

---

[1] Cum non raro, quæ splendescere videntur in cubiculo, sordeant in Scholasticis concertationibus.

tion and applause, in public sessions and disputations.[1]

These critics express their mind upon the need which exists, of reviving considerably the fervor and dignity of this exercise, and so restoring it to its former educational influence. But we can observe for ourselves, how congenial an element the whole exercise must be in a system like this, which is preëminently oral — oral examinations, oral and self-reliant defence and attack, free and open lecturing, with the influence of eye, voice, and person, to bring everything home, even though all the while there is no question of oratory, but of mere teaching. In the earlier stages, too, of the scholar's life, however much has been made of the acquirement of style, "forging the word with Grammar," as Robert of Sorbon had said, "and polishing it with Rhetoric," to make it glow on the written page, yet from the very first, also, no less account has been taken of the ability to express one's thought, with perfect presence of mind, without depending upon note or book. In the higher faculties, this holds good more than ever. Now the time has come for matter of the most approved kind. And the independent, self-possessed delivery of one's thoughts, with the power to force them home unto conviction, or to maintain them against all odds, appears not only as the scope proposed in the system, but also as the historical result, effected in the public career of the Order.

[1] Monumenta Germaniæ Pædagogica, vol. v, Disputationes, n. 8, p. 102.

Father Laynez, at the Conference of Poissy, contended thus with Peter Martyr and others; Possevino at Lyons with Viret, using, not so much the severe syllogistic form, as copious and learned discussion. Maldonado was double-handed, either syllogistic or discursive. In the Conference at Sedan, in 1572, he argued first in dialectic form; then, on the demand of his opponents for a different kind of weapon, he took with the same facility to discursive exposition. Edmund Campian, in England, on being removed from the rack more dead than alive, was immediately brought face to face with Newell and Day, able champions as well of the Queen's spiritual supremacy, as of the doctrine of Justification by Faith alone. He proceeded to argue: "If faith alone justifies, it justifies without charity; but without charity it does not justify; therefore faith alone does not justify." Now for the answer, clear and incisive as the propositions. Deny or distinguish major or minor proposition, if you want to deny the conclusion; for, those premises standing, the inference remains intact, since the syllogism is perfect in form. And so argumentations proceed.

To revive disputation in its best style, the critics devote several pages to a most valuable analysis of the conditions and method of the exercise.[1] Their suggestions are embodied in the final *Ratio*. The Rectors are to show their lively and active interest in the disputations, by attending on public and private occasions alike, and by the various arts which such interest will inspire. As argument "freezes except in

[1] Ibid.

a crowd," the critics require that the attendance of all be insisted on, when the days and hours of disputation arrive. This susceptibility of human nature, which the Fathers touch upon, when they speak of disputation freezing except in a concourse, is not without an exact counterpart, when, in another connection, they are speaking of the humanists, or Professors of the literary classes. There they adopt the view that the literary seminary of the Province should be in the same great college, along with the faculties of Philosophy and Theology; for, say they, among other reasons, "the humanists would languish in obscurity, if they had not the philosophers and theologians to be witnesses, spectators, and applauding auditors of their literary achievements." And again they plead sympathetically, "the philosophers and theologians, when composing the prefatory essays for their disputations, call for the taste of the humanists, by whose verses and orations, moreover, they are refreshed from time to time."[1]

Continuing their remarks, the Fathers define the limits of the weekly disputations to be two hours, not more, assigning four regular objectors for that time. The Professors, belonging to different faculties, should invite one another reciprocally to the private disputations in their classes, at least for an hour or so, that the intellectual contest may wax warm by the meeting of these Doctors. Other Doctors, too, not of the faculty, can be invited for the same purpose. But, continues the *Ratio* of 1599, in undertaking to push the arguments which are being urged, "they should

[1] Ibid., p. 147, Separandae sint Seminaria, etc.

not take the thread out of the hands of an objector, who is still ably and strenuously following it up."[1] Meanwhile, the students who receive the commission to act as objectors, on occasions of some publicity, must be the more qualified members of the course; the others have the practice of their private arena, until they can take part with dignity in a public tournament.

If argument freezes except in a crowd, so, too, it palls, if it never comes to a conclusion; and no useful point of doctrine is carried away by the listeners. Truth is lost in clouds, and there is no gain to good humor. Acrimony or melancholy may well be the only outcome of an unfinished or revolving argumentation. It will not revolve, if the disputants keep to strict syllogistic form. But when both or all parties become heated, and wit becomes lively, the syllogism may suffer, and then, when will they finish? To obviate this inconvenience, two persons are charged with the responsibility of the performance, one the Professor himself, who is presiding over his own disputation, the other, the General Prefect of Studies, who controls the whole series of disputations, as they follow one another in turn.

Of the Professor it is said, that he is to consider the day of disputation as no less laborious and useful than that of his own lecture; and that all the fruit and life of the exercise depends upon him. The earlier *Ratio* lays even more stress upon the private disputations, "which are wont to grow more frigid

---

[1] Reg. comm. Prof. sup. fac., n. 16; Monumenta Germaniæ Pædagogica, vol. v, p. 292.

than the public ones." He is to assist the two disputants, "so as to be himself apparently the person contesting in each; let him signify his approval, if anything specially good is urged, excite the attention of all when any first-class difficulty is proposed, throw out a hint now and then to support the respondent or direct the opponent; call them back to strict syllogistic form, if they wander from it; not always be silent, nor yet be always talking, so as to let the students bring out what they know. What is brought forward, he can amend or improve; let him bid the objector proceed, so long as his argument carries weight with it; carry on the objector's difficulty for him farther; nor connive at it, if he slips off to another track. He is not to allow an argument which has been well answered to be kept up, nor an answer that is not solid to be long sustained; but, when the dispute has been sufficiently exhaustive, let him briefly define the matter, and explain it."[1]

The General Prefect of Studies is required to keep the series of disputations in due form; arguing himself but sparingly, and thereby discharging the duty of general direction with more dignity. He is not to suffer any difficulty which comes under debate, to be agitated this way and that, "so that it remains as much of a difficulty after as before"; but when such an agitated question has been sufficiently mooted, he will see that an accurate explanation of it is given by the Professor who is presiding.[2]

---

[1] Monumenta Germaniæ Pædagogica, vol. v, p. 292; Rt. St. 1599, Reg. comm. Prof. sup. fac., n. 18; Rt. St. 1586, Disputationes, ibid., p. 106.   [2] Ibid., p. 102, n. 7; p. 276, n. 6.

With the last public act, or general defence of Philosophy and Theology, the formation of the future Professor closes. This public defence occupies four or five hours, in two sessions. If the defendant is not a member of the Order, special care is taken to honor it with all solemnity, and with the attendance of all the faculties, of guests invited, Doctors from without, and princes or the nobility.[1] This act will be followed by the solemnity of conferring the final degree upon the Licentiate. When the student is a Jesuit, much more is made of thoroughness in a searching examination then, as at all times previously. He has now passed through a long series of yearly examinations, which were almost always disputations, and that, not with equals, but with four or five Professors.[2] So that, on viewing him at the close of his formation, we are enabled to conceive, with more distinctness, the meaning of that standard, "surpassing mediocrity," which, in a former chapter, I endeavored to define.[3]

2. On turning our attention now to the Professor's chair, and examining his manner of lecturing, of explaining, of teaching, whether in the field of Letters, Science, Philosophy, or Theology, we have, on the one side, to suppose him complete in his formation, and, on the other, to regard the scholar as undergoing formation. Here, then, we begin the second part of this analysis. The style of teaching and of manage-

---

[1] Rt. St., Reg. Prof. Stud., nn. 12, 21; Monumenta Germaniæ Pædagogica, vol. v, pp. 278, 282.

[2] Ibid., Reg. Prov., n. 19, p. 244.

[3] Chapter xi, above, p. 157.

ment, which is distinctively the Jesuit type, is presented in the *Ratio Studiorum* under its practical and ideal aspect. There is also a manner of instruction which is not considered an ideal method, however much it may sometimes recommend itself as practically expedient. I will touch upon this latter, the negative side of the question, first, to be free, in the next chapter, for approaching the matter on its positive and constructive side.

In putting dictation down as not being the ideal form of teaching in the Society, I do not speak of the proper use of dictation. The *Ratio* itself leaves room for it. It is the abuse of dictation that merits and receives a protracted examination of its value, at the hands of the critics. The discussion is of the highest importance. In analyzing a style of instruction, with which they are not in harmony, they bring out the essential elements of all true teaching. And, if we approve at all of their principles, the implied disapproval for the rejected form becomes only aggravated, on contemplating an exaggerated development of the same; that is to say, when, instead of dictating what has the merit of being one's own laborious production, the teacher is seen to become the servile dependant on a text-book printed by somebody else; and neither does the teacher show any of the qualifications necessary to have composed the book, nor does the scholar expend the industry which would have been necessary to copy it. But it is left to speak as best it may, is read by the teacher, instead of his teaching, is read by the scholar as the talk of some third person, and is found, in the last issue, to have spoken just articulately enough for the pupil to have learnt a memory lesson, and perhaps to have gathered information which may or may not adhere to his mental structure. But, as to anything like mental training, or what is properly education, the final result of a long series of years seems to show that, if there has been any of it, possibly the man who wrote the book had it; and with him it has remained. So must it always be under such conditions. For when the living Master has contributed so little in the way of live education, the scholar must, of necessity, go away with somewhat less.

These critics say trenchantly: "Let no dictation be given, unless the explanation of very much all that is dictated has gone before, or accompanies, or follows the dictation; where the custom does not exist, let no dictation be introduced; where it does, an effort should be made to do away with it, as far as possible." Then they support their position by many quotations from the Constitution of Ignatius.[1]

They go on to state that this habit of dictating was a thing unheard of till within the last forty years; "yet the auditors were not less learned then than now." In fact, but a slight acquaintance with the old university system of Europe will show how jealously the empire of the spoken word was maintained — the spoken word, as distinct, not only from reading what the Doctor had himself composed, but also from consulting even notes, while actually lecturing. He might have the text of Aristotle, or Peter the Lom-

[1] De Ratione et Modo Prælegendi; Monumenta Germaniæ Pædagogica, vol. v, p. 82.

bard, before him; he might himself have written and published works; the student might, with permission, take down notes in shorthand, from which in part, but chiefly from memory, he would commit the whole lecture to writing,[1] on his return from school. It was not mere want of facilities that determined the system so. But the objective point was, not to have learning in one's papers and bound up; still less to have it in books, bought for the learning that is in them, and left afterwards with the learning still remaining there. The object was to make learning one's personal possession, and to profess the live mastery of it, with voice, eye, and person showing how live it was.

These Doctors continue: "The common impression in men's minds is, that dictating is not lecturing; also that it is one thing to write after the manner of polishing off a treatise, a different thing to have at hand merely some brief heads and references. And, should the matter which is dictated be from some author, the labor of taking it down is superfluous."

The living voice actuates the mind more; it expresses, it impresses; it arouses, suspends the attention; it explains. All these effects are nowhere in a dead-and-alive dictation. Nor do they give satisfaction, who append the explanation afterwards; for then both times seem to be lost, that taken up with dictation and that with the explanation. First, while the dictation was going on, the auditors were intent upon writing rather than understanding; particularly as, before the end of a sentence is come to, the

[1] Ad literam legibilem.

beginning of it has already slipped from the mind; and the writing has to go on, without allowing any of that time to breathe, which is frequent enough if the Professor lectures and explains. Secondly, when the time for explanation comes after the dictation, the students are tired; they think they have all their learning now, down in their papers; so they go off, or they yawn, or they read over their copy, to see if anything is wanting.

After dictating, the Professor thinks that he has now done his part. What follows, that is, the work of explaining, he gulps down, as best he can, — a laborious work, requiring memory, promptitude, facility of development, fluency of speech; whence he will gradually vanish away into a nonentity, as we see actually taking place in some universities.

More time is lost. For, while he goes over his dictation to explain it, he has to take up again things which were clear enough, in order to follow out the whole thread of his matter. If he had lectured, he would have said those things once for all. Then, since it must be something polished and finished in style that a man dictates, the poor scribes have to take down much that is not necessary.

As if they had wearied themselves with this general assault on dictation, the Fathers go on to relieve their feelings by exclaiming: "What an amount of tedium meanwhile to those who are not writing, especially to Prelates and other illustrious persons present! Must they be told not to come while the dictation is going on, and to appear only afterwards when the matter is being explained? If so, they will be in attendance barely half an hour, and what they will hear will be meagre enough; and the person they listen to will be one accustomed to languid dictation, one who relies on his papers, and is but little practised in the oral development of his thoughts. Besides, the students themselves ought to get accustomed to make things their own when they hear them, and to exercise their own judgment in selecting what to write. Thus they will understand things better, and be kept more on the alert."

Not to disguise inconveniences, from whatever side they come, these critics take note of the difficulties which are thought to exist; that, unless the matter is dictated, the students cannot do justice to it, that the lecturer is too quick, or, out of the many things he says, they do not know how to select the necessary elements for annotation; and, while phrase is piled upon phrase, they are at a loss, their notes are disordered, inept, and sometimes simply wrong.

To this the critics promptly make answer: Those who are to lecture in future are either such as are now beginning their career of Professorship, or such as are long accustomed to dictation. For those who are now beginning, previous exercise is to be recommended in the most approved form of lecture, or *prælectio*. And they sketch the form. As to the others who are long habituated to dictating, the critics ask such Professors to give this form of lecturing the benefit of a trial. If they despair of being able to adopt it, let them go their own way, until another generation of Professors is ready to take their places. Dictation can also be permitted, where our

Professors have often tried to give it up, but with the consequence that the students took fright, and abandoned the classes. "Yet," continue the Fathers, "they would not be apt to abandon the courses, nor complain so much, if all the Professors would devote themselves to brilliant lecturing,[1] and would put away dictation. For, if one dictates and nurses the lazy folks, and another does not, who doubts but that sloth will still be dearer to the slothful than the labors and thorns of study? Yea, by dictation they are made daily more and more lazy, so as to be always asking for more and more time; whereas, without dictation, they become daily more prompt, and need less time for everything."[2]

The final *Ratio* of 1599 embodies these suggestions, without being absolute in excluding all dictation, for which it suggests the form most useful and in accord with the spirit of true lecturing. It deprecates the dictation of what may be found in authors within reach of the students. "Let the Professor refer his hearers to those authors who have been copious and accurate in their treatment of any matter." As to what the critics of 1586 recommend, that, if dictation be given, the lecture should extend to five quarters of an hour, the *Ratio* says nothing about it.[3]

Possevino, in his *Bibliotheca Selecta,* has a chapter on this question, "Whether mental culture suffers by

---

[1] Ad prælegendum egregie.
[2] Rt. St. 1586, De Ratione ac Modo Prælegendi; Monumenta Germaniæ Pædagogica, vol. v, pp. 81-5.
[3] Monumenta Germaniæ Pædagogica, vol. v, Reg. comm. Prof. sup. fac., nn. 9, 10, p. 288.

the dictation of lectures?" He answers in the affirmative, and he speaks on the subject with his usual erudition. He refers to the Pythagorean "acoustic" disciples, who were never copyists, and not even talkers, until, by a prolonged silence for years, they had thought enough to be able to talk well, to put questions, and make comments. He quotes the cynicism of Diogenes, about writing at the expense of true exercise. He notes the plan of Xeniades the Corinthian, who gave a written compendium to the young people, but one so short that they had to have the best part of their learning in their heads. The Socratic method was eminently one of living speech. And, as to Aristotle's "peripatetic" school, which was conducted while *walking about* the Lyceum, that was certainly neither in practice nor in principle favorable to writing. Coming to speak expressly of dictation and citing a pleasant old rhyme:—

Quod si charta cadat, secum sapientia vadat,[1]

Possevino goes on to plead for the chests of the students, and says that the ink is the price of their blood, and the end of their studies becomes the end of their lives. Hence one singular result of it all is, that scholars even employ amanuenses to go to school instead of themselves, and bring back in writing what was said. But all that money, says Possevino, could have been reserved for the buying of books, to supplement real study.

Then he enforces what he has said with a piece of university history, wherein perhaps no one of his time

[1] Why, if the paper drops, the wisdom too must be off!

was better versed. The University of Paris, two and a half centuries before, had legislated against dictating, and against the Doctors who used it, and who were dubbed *Nominatores ad pennam.* One century before, the Cardinal Legate had again formulated a law on the subject. And finally the Jesuits, "of whom a great number are chiefly engaged in this profession, taught by experience the evils of that system, have long understood the necessity, not merely of moderating it, but simply doing away with it. Wherefore the Fathers in the universities of Portugal have already published a part of Natural Philosophy, whereby writing is dispensed with, room is left for quickening genius, and much material stored up to bring into the arena of discussion."[1]

[1] Possevinus, Biblioth. Selecta, lib. i, de cultura ingeniorum, cc. 25–6; edit. Venet. 1603, pp. 21-2. He refers to the publication of the Conimbricenses, a consolidated work of the faculty of Coimbra, just as the "Wirceburgenses," later on, and at present, under Father Cornely, the writers of the Cursus Scripturæ Sacræ are publishing their works as a corporate whole.

CHAPTER XV.

FORMATION OF THE SCHOLAR. SYMMETRY OF THE COURSES. THE PRELECTION. BOOKS.

WHAT is developed to perfection can make other things like unto itself; it is prolific. So the Aristotelian principle has it: *Perfectum est, quod generat simile sibi*. This is the outcome and test of perfection. Having followed the Master, therefore, till he was complete in his own formation, we have now turned to look in another direction, and see him reacting upon those whom he is to form. Though much has been said already, implicitly or otherwise, on the method and principles of this reactive process, yet something remains, especially with regard to the lower faculties, the literary courses. In this chapter, we may consider the attitude which the Professors take, singly and as a body, towards the students and towards their own courses; and then their chief manner of imparting knowledge, or what is called in the *Ratio* the *prælectio*. In the next chapter we can survey the principal class exercises, and the method of school management, throughout the lower grades. And, in the chapter after that, I shall sketch the system of grades from the lowest to the highest.

1. One of the first most general rules lays it down that the authority, in whose hands is the appointment

of Professors, "should foresee far ahead what Professors he can have for every faculty, noting especially those who seem to be more adapted for the work, who are learned, diligent, and assiduous, and who are zealous for the advancement of their students, as well in their lectures (or lessons) as in other literary exercises."[1] "They are to procure the advancement of each of their scholars in particular," says Ignatius.[2] The Professor "is not to show himself more familiar with one student than with another; he is to disregard no one, to foster the studies of the poor equally with the rich."[3]

These are the regular and "ordinary Professors, who take account of their students in particular."[4] There can also be in a university one or more of another kind, "who, with more solemnity than the ordinary lecturers, treat Philosophy, Mathematical Sciences, or any other branch, after the manner of public Professors."[5]

In the lower, or literary courses the Masters must "be good and skilled," who "seriously, and with all the attention of their mind, work for the advancement of their scholars, as well in what concerns learning, as in the matter of morals. They will have to take care that besides the Christian doctrine, which is so integral a part of our Institute, they also give frequent exhortations, suited to the capacity of the boys, and not

[1] Rt. St. 1599, Reg. Prov., n. 4; Monumenta Germaniæ Pædagogica, vol. v, p. 234.
[2] Constitutiones, pars iv, c. 13, n. 3; Monumenta Germaniæ Pædagogica, vol. ii, p. 55.
[3] Reg. comm. Prof. sup. fac., n. 20; Monumenta Germaniæ Pædagogica, vol. v, p. 292.   [4] Constitutiones, ibid., C.   [5] Ibid.

devised for empty ostentation; let them endeavor to instil solid affections of piety and love for the things of God, and a hatred for sin."[1]

What is meant by "good and skilled Masters" in these courses, we have already seen from Jouvancy's sketch of the accomplishments proper to a teacher of Literature.[2] If anything remained to be said on this topic, it would only be to note and reject false standards, by which the position or efficiency of Professors might possibly, but incorrectly, be measured. Thus, some five years ago, that is to say, three hundred years later than the drawing up of the *Ratio*, I find two such false standards distinctly repudiated; one is the idea of gathering in just enough of doctrine beforehand to be able, when occasion calls for it, to develop the attainments of a Professor; another is that which would look only to the environment around, and would measure the intellectual formation of men, and the supply of learning, by the estimate commonly formed of the article, and the actual demand for it.

2. If we regard not individual Professors, but the whole moral body or faculty of them, there are two characteristics which it may be difficult to find, or at least to ensure, outside of an organization such as the Society of Jesus. One is the very strict unity of educational matter presented to the studious world. The other is the degree of coördination and subordination of courses professed. A word upon each.

The unity of matter in question, as designed for

---

[1] Vitelleschi, 1639; Monumenta Germaniæ Pædagogica, vol. ix, p. 59.   [2] Chapter xi, above, p. 162.

the purposes of education, is prescribed on the strength of a double maxim; first, that the sifting of many opinions, by the varied and multiplied activity of many minds, leaves a residue of matter, quite solid enough to support a compact and reliable system of teaching; secondly, that, in point of fact, such matter, which I have called "a residue," is nothing else than the basis of truth, divine and eternal; since, in clearing away the ground, all the criteria of each order, the natural and supernatural, have been faithfully and assiduously regarded.

Hereupon, intellectual concord is felt to be the result in the entire teaching body. Of this concord the critics say, that it is the condition and cause of a wider and profounder learning in the faculties at large. Each Professor is engaged, "not in tilling some patch of his own, but in contributing his industry to the general field of all." Where is the gain, they ask, "if what one establishes, another upsets, not as if he had always excogitated something better, but for fear he should be thought to profit by the fruits of another's genius? Sometimes it really makes no difference whether one or other tenet is held; but, if we are bent on receiving no support from another, then, for all our labor, we get no other fruit but dissension."[1] I presume there is not a university anywhere but will bear witness, by its internal history, to the justice of this remark.

Nor do these Fathers apprehend that reputation for real science will suffer by such concord, since

---

[1] Monumenta Germaniæ Pædagogica, vol. v, Commentariolus, p. 43.

"reputation for science does not come from opinions contradicting one another, but from their having agreed." They express no lofty esteem for the notoriety which may be had, by fighting no less with friends than with foes, and reserving admiration for only what is at a respectable distance, and "turning up one's nose at what is near."[1] This pungent remark seems to be a new and pedagogical application of the old proverb, *Nihil vicinia molestius,* "Nothing more annoying than one's neighbors!" They hold that, upon a basis of concord, there is always room and liberty for the exercise of talent; first, in those questions which are manifestly indifferent; secondly, in thinking out new distinctions and reasons, whereby truths already certain may be made more secure still; thirdly, in attacking the same, either when publicly disputing, or also when actually teaching, if what they acutely urge against a position, they more acutely refute; fourthly, in proposing new opinions and questions, but after they have sought the approval of the responsible authorities, lest the labor be spent amiss. The most learned men have always been persuaded that there is more subtlety shown, more applause merited and comfort enjoyed, in pursuing the lines of approved and received thought, than in a general license and novelty of opinion.[2] But these critics throw out an idea of theirs, which quite possibly will not meet with universal acceptance. They say, "It is not every one who can build up a Theology for himself." The remark they add is graceful, that a modest genius does not court every

[1] Ibid.   [2] Ibid., p. 41.

kind of liberty, but that which is not divorced from virtue.

These principles explain for us the unity of educational matter, as presented to the studious world. The same marshalling and husbanding of force, which effectuates this result, operates another, akin to the former. It is the most definite coördination and subordination of courses, with a mutual understanding between Professors and faculties. Where grades exist, either in their perfect form, as in the five stages of the classical or literary course, or in a shape approximating to that, as in the three stages of the philosophical triennium, such subordination is easily secured. But, also, elsewhere the conditions of perfectly definite outlines are laid down for courses, which have any points of mutual contact.

This may be illustrated by some rules of the *Ratio*. The two Professors of Dogmatic Theology are to consider themselves dispensed from commenting on questions proper to Sacred Scripture, from treating philosophical matters, from evolving cases of Moral Theology. The Professor of Moral Theology is to despatch with the briefest definitions the matter which belongs to dogma. The Professor of Holy Scripture is desired not to go at length into points of controverted Theology. The Professor of Ecclesiastical History need not treat canons or dogma. The Professor of Canon Law will not touch Theology or Public Right, any more than his time permits, and the necessary understanding of Canon Law requires. The same reserve is practised between Theology in general, and Philosophy. Thus a Professor of Moral

Theology despatches perhaps in ten minutes the definition of Natural Law, upon which he knows two days are spent by the Professor of Moral Philosophy.

Half a century later, this question of coördination received a still fuller treatment at the hands of the General Francis Piccolomini. After requiring that philosophers and theologians alike finish conscientiously all the matter assigned for each year, he will not allow that "the example of authors who have mixed up subjects, or have followed out their questions into mere minutiæ, can be cited as of any weight with our Professors. For, whatever is to be thought of them, this method is not opportune for practical teaching in the schools." The General scouts the idea of "exploring the treasure-house of possibilities," to find out new questions; for there is reason to fear that "while folks search about for truths not ascertained, they will catch at chimeras and shadows."[1] Hence, as the *Ratio* prescribes, "opinions which are useless, obsolete, absurd, manifestly false, are not to receive treatment." The Professors are to run rapidly through questions which are easy. In Holy Scripture, difficult passages are not to be dwelt on indefinitely, nor too much time to be given to chronological computations, or topological surveys of the Holy Land.

In facing the objection, that all this entails a great expenditure of thought and matter, when Professors must despatch in such short courses what might well be treated in longer terms, the preliminary *Ratio*

[1] Ordinatio pro Stud. Sup., 1651; Monumenta Germaniæ Pædagogica, vol. ix, p. 88.

draws a sharp line of demarcation between other universities and those conducted by Jesuits. "Whatever is the custom in other universities, our method is very different from theirs, so that no less progress can be made in our schools during four years, than in others during five; because our Professors are for the most part more laborious; we have more numerous exercises; our Society, as standing in need of many workmen, requires that perfection of science which is necessary for its men, not that otiose method of others, who, having no motive of this kind to make them expeditious, divide up into many lectures what could well be treated in fewer; their vacations too are for the most part longer and more frequent."[1]

Ex ungue leonem, "You can tell a lion by his paw." Let it appear that the brevity which you study is necessitated by your limits of time; let discernment be conspicuous in your selection of matter, whether to treat summarily or to treat copiously; let the alternate courses supplement one another, so that what had to be skimmed over in one quadriennium is dilated upon more at large in your next; then, say the Fathers, the authority which the Professors enjoy with ecclesiastical dignitaries will not suffer the detriment anticipated by some, when we give condensed and accurate treatment in a shorter time of what is usually spread out through a longer.[2] The paw shows the lion.

3. We may proceed now to the typical form of Jesuit instruction. It is called *prœlectio*. This word

[1] Monumenta Germaniæ Pædagogica, vol. v, Utrum Quinquennium, etc., p. 76. [2] Ibid.

is largely the equivalent of "lecturing," in the higher faculties; of "explanation," in the lower. In either case, however, it is something specific. For this reason, and because I shall have to use the word often, I may be allowed to put it in an English dress, and speak of "prelection."

Its form, as a lecture in the higher faculties, is conceived thus: The whole proposition, which is advanced, is to be delivered consecutively, without interposing any stoppages. Then it should be repeated in the same words; and this will be taken by the students as a sign that it is to be written down; and the delivery of it should be marked by such inflections, and proceed at such a pace, especially in its obscure and finer points, that the students may readily distinguish between what is to be written and what is not. Now, while the proposition is thus being taken down, the lecturer ought not to advance new ideas, but should dally with the same, either explaining it in more phrases or clearer ones, or adducing an example or similitude, or amplifying the topic, or drawing out the same logical sequence in another order, so as to make it stand out more distinctly, or throwing out a reason or two, which, however, it is not necessary for them to note. Indeed, if the Professor brings his own papers into the school, he might have in them some select phrases, brief but not obscure, in which he sums up in few words the gist of the propositions. Longer development they will receive only in the explanation, which is then to be given.[1] In that, the Professor will endeavor to prove

---

[1] Modus Prælegendi, n. 10; Monumenta Germaniæ Pædagogica, vol. v, p. 84.

his thesis, not so much by the number of arguments, as by their weight. He should not be excessive in adducing authorities. And it belongs to his dignity, as a Master, scarcely ever to quote an author whom he has not himself read.[1] .

In the grade of Rhetoric, which is the highest of the literary or classical course, the prelection is double; one is upon the art of eloquence, wherein precepts are explained; the other is upon an author, and has for its object the development of style. Taking up an author such as Cicero, the Professor will, in the first place, make clear the sense of the passage. Secondly, the artistic structure is to be analyzed and demonstrated: the *Ratio* here details the elements of this analysis. Thirdly, other passages which are similar in thought or expression are to be adduced; other orators and poets, whether in the classics or in the vernacular, are to be cited as employing the same principles of art, in persuading or narrating. Fourthly, if the matter allows of it, the thoughts expressed by the author are to be confirmed by what wise men have said on the same subject. Fifthly, whatever else will conduce to ornamenting the passage is here in place, from history, mythology, erudition of every kind. Finally, the words are to be weighed singly; their propriety of use, their beauty, variety, rhythm to be commented upon. The whole of this treatment, however, does not come within the limits of each and every lesson.[2] The "erudition" for

---

[1] Rt. St. 1599, Reg. comm. Prof. sup. fac., nn. 7, 8; Monumenta Germaniæ Pædagogica, vol. v, p. 288.

[2] Rt. St., Reg. Prof. Rhet., n. 8; Monumenta Germaniæ Pædagogica, vol. v, p. 406.

this grade is defined to comprise "the history and manners of nations, the authority of various writers, and all learning, but sparingly, to suit the capacity of the scholars."¹

The prelection on the precepts or rules, "the power of which," says the *Ratio*, "is very great for the purposes of oratory," comprises six points. Cicero is the rhetorician who supplies the precepts; but Quintilian and Aristotle may also be used. First, the meaning of the rule is to be explained. Secondly, upon the same rule, the rhetoricians are to be collated. Thirdly, some reason for the rule is to be expounded. Fourthly, some striking passages from prose writers, and also from poets, are to be adduced in exemplification of the rule. Fifthly, if anything in the way of varied erudition makes to the purpose, it is to be added. Lastly, an indication should be given how this principle of art can be turned to use by ourselves; the style in which this is done must be marked by the most absolute choice and finish of diction possible.²

In the grade of Humanity, which is immediately below Rhetoric, the prelection is to be lightly adorned from time to time with the ornaments of erudition, as far as the passage requires. The Master should rather expatiate to the fullest extent upon the genius of the Latin tongue, on the force and etymology of words as shown by approved authors, on the use and variety of phrases, with a view to imitation. Here, as in other rules of this kind, we may notice the degree of progress made in the native tongues during two cen-

¹ Ibid., n. 1.   ² Ibid., nn. 6, 7.

turies and a half. While the *Ratio* of 1599 adds these words: "Nor let him think it out of his way to bring forward something from the vernacular, if it presents anything specially idiomatic for rendering the idea, or offers some remarkable construction;" the revised *Ratio* of 1832 substitutes these words: "Let him expatiate on a comparison between the genius of both tongues, with a view to imitation." When he is explaining a prose author, he should investigate the precepts of art, as exemplified therein. Lastly, if he thinks fit, he can give a version, but a most elegant one, of the whole passage into the mother tongue.[1] Greek has its own form of prelection.

As to the "prose writer" just mentioned, the manner of treating an historical writer in Humanity, which is otherwise called the class of Poetry, will serve by the way to illustrate the difference between what is recognized as the staple of studies in a class, and what comes in as subsidiary — a most essential distinction, characterizing this system of literary teaching. The critics of 1586 advert to it clearly. After showing the importance of including the study of historians in the course of Poetry, they say: "This will not be too onerous to the Preceptor; for the style of history is plainer and more lucid, so as not to need great study; and it would be enough to explain the course of events, as they are narrated by the author, so that he need not consult other authors who have written on the same matter. The prelection of the historian ought to be easy; after render-

[1] Reg. Prof. Hum., n. 5; ibid., p. 420.

ing a sentence of the author, the words may be lightly commented upon, and only such as have some obscurity hanging about them." The historians of whom there is question here, are Caesar, Sallust, Q. Curtius, Justin, Tacitus, Livy.[1]

"In both classes of Rhetoric and Humanities, not everything indiscriminately is to be dictated and taken down, but only certain interpretations of difficult passages, which are not readily obvious to every one, or which the Master has elaborated as the outcome of his personal study; besides, some rather striking remarks on various passages of the author under examination, such annotations as the commentators give, who edit books of various readings. This will befit the Master's dignity, and will be useful for the young men to know."[2]

The grades of Grammar have respectively their own forms of prelection, given in detail by the final *Ratio*. It will be enough for us to sketch the general form of the earlier critics.[3]

According as it is a grammar or an author that is being explained, a very different method of prelection is to be followed. In the grammar, we acquire a fund of precepts; in an author, a store of words and phrases. Wherefore, in the books of grammar, the boys must understand perfectly the things explained; they need not attend scrupulously to the words there, with a view to forming style. But, in the letters of

---

[1] Rt. St. 1856, Classis Hum.; Monumenta Germaniæ Pædagogica, vol. v, p. 195.   [2] Ibid., Class. Rhet., n. 6, p. 198.

[3] Ibid., Exercitationes lat. et græc., n. 2 ; Monumenta Germaniæ Pædagogica, vol. v, p. 166.

Cicero, and other texts of the kind, it is not so much the substance of the sentences, as the words and phrases that are of chief consequence; the significance and force of his thoughts are to be reserved for the higher classes, when the students are no longer mere boys.

In the classes of Grammar then, let the Master follow this method of explaining Cicero, or any other author. First, he will sketch, in the briefest way, the meaning of the author, and the connection between what has gone before and what is now to be explained. Then he will give a version of the period literally, preserving to the utmost the collocation of words, as they stand in the author; and also the figures employed. As to the collocation or arrangement of the words, this is of such consequence that sometimes, if a single word is put out of its place, the whole thought seems to lose its force and fall flat. Herein, too, is perceived that rhythmic flow of the style, which of itself, even if other ornaments are wanting, pleases the ear wonderfully and gratifies the mind. Thirdly, the whole period is to be resolved analytically into its structural elements, so that the boys understand distinctly what every word governs; and their attention should be directed to some useful points of good Latinity. As to this structural analysis, I may be allowed the passing remark, which is familiar to every judge of a classical education, that the disciplinary value of literary studies reaches here its highest degree of mental exercise; and that the two classical tongues, Latin and Greek, are altogether eminent as supplying materials for this exercise, in their own native structure; which, in the Latin, is an architectural build, characteristic of the reasoning Roman mind; and, in the Greek, is a subtle delicacy of conception and tracery, reflecting the art, the grace and versatility of Athens and the Ionian Isles.

After this, each word is to be examined, as to what it signifies, and to what uses it may be applied; the boy is to understand, as far as may be, the original and proper idea and force of every word, not merely its general significance, as in a shadowy outline; he should know, too, the phrases in his native tongue, which correspond with precision and propriety to the Latin. The metaphors and the figurative use of words, especially as found in Cicero, are to be explained to the boys in an extremely plain manner,[1] and by examples drawn from the plainest objects. Unless this use of words is understood, the true and genuine knowledge of the tongue is seriously obstructed. Then, picking out the more elegant turns of style, the Master will dictate them to the scholars, and afterwards require the use and imitation of these phrases in their themes. Lastly, he will go back and translate the words of the author over again, as he did at the beginning; and, if need be, do so a third and a fourth time.

As to writing, during all this, let him forbid them absolutely to take down a single letter, except when told. What he does dictate to them, he is to finish within the time of the prelection, and not prolong this time for the sake of the writing. It happens now and then that, with much labor, waste of time,

[1] Maxime rudi Minerva.

and to no good purpose whatever, the boys take down, and preserve with diligence, a set of notes which have not been thought out very judiciously nor been arranged very carefully, — notes simply trivial, common, badly patched together, sometimes worse than worthless; and these notes they commit to paper, in wretched handwriting, full of mistakes and errors. Therefore, let the dictation be only of a few points, and those extremely select.

The Masters are to be on their guard, lest private tutors at the boys' homes explain new lessons to them. These tutors have merely to repeat with the boys what has been heard in class. Otherwise, the fruit of the good explanation which is received at school is lost at home.

Repetition is now in order. Two principles govern this exercise. First, "what has often been repeated sinks deeper into the mind."[1] Secondly, "the industry of youths flags under nothing so much as satiety."[2] As soon, therefore, as the prelection is over, the Professor is to require at once an account of all that he has said, and he is to see that the whole line of his explanation is followed in the repetition. As if this seemed to imply that only the best scholars were to be called upon, the critics go on to note that not all of what has been explained should be repeated by one only, but that as many as possible should be practised every day. The Master should not follow the order in which the boys are seated, but take them here and

---

[1] Rt. St., Reg. Præf. stud. inf., n. 8, § 4; Monumenta Germaniæ Pædagogica, vol. v, p. 354.

[2] Ibid., Reg. comm. Prof. cl. inf., n. 24; ibid., p. 388.

there. However, the first to be called on are those more advanced; then the duller, or perhaps lazier ones, and these should rather be asked oftener, to be kept up to the mark.[1]

The final *Ratio* notes that the daily lesson should not exceed four lines in the lowest class of Grammar; seven in Middle Grammar. There is, as I have already observed, a prelection proper to grammatical rules; also to Greek, whether it be in the grammar or in an author. Proportion in width and depth of matter is adjusted to each grade. A careful dictation in the vernacular is to be given, which, when rendered into Latin or Greek, will exemplify the precepts explained, or the use of the phrases already dictated. And one part of the school exercises, from the lowest class up to Rhetoric, is a *concertatio* between rivals, which is a lively discussion either upon matters explained in the prelections, or upon one another's compositions. In this field of debate, as is natural, the activity of the students grows, both in the extent of the field to be covered, and in the depth of erudition required, according as the grades are mounted. And it is carried out of the class-room into select societies, called "academies," the members whereof, whether grammarians or *littérateurs*, conduct their debates, give their own prelections or repeat a choice one of their Professor's, award a place in the archives to some specially meritorious production; and they conduct all these exercises in exact keeping with their actual prelections and studies. Nor do they

[1] Exercitationes lat. et græc., Monumenta Germaniæ Pædagogica, vol. v, p. 167.

yield an inch in gravity or dignity to the great academy of theologians and philosophers.[1]

As to the native tongue, one of the earliest systems of studies in the Society, prior to the general *Ratio* by about forty years, lays down for the middle class of Grammar, that "on Mondays and Wednesdays the boys will receive the themes in Bohemian and German for their epistolary exercises."[2] This document is probably from the pen of Peter Canisius, soon after the colleges were founded at Prague, Ingolstadt and Cologne. In a directive memorial of 1602, drawn up for Mayence by Father Ferdinand Alber, a postscript is added to the effect, "Let exercise in the German tongue be furthered."[3] Jouvancy lays down the practice in this manner: "After the correction and dictation of the written exercises, the Latin author is rendered into the mother tongue, or a *concertatio* is held. These two exercises can be held on alternate days, if there is not enough of time every day for both. In rendering the author into the vernacular, you will observe three things: first, the idiom of the vernacular, and its agreement in construction with the Latin, or else its disagreement, so that the scholars learn each tongue by the other; secondly, the proper turns and elegance of the Latin style; finally, the thoughts of the author, as having a moral bearing, and as calculated to form and mould the

[1] Rt. St., Special rules of the respective classes; Monumenta Germaniæ Pædagogica, vol. v, pp. 398–448: Rules of the Academies; ibid., pp. 460–480.

[2] Monumenta Germaniæ Pædagogica, vol. ii, p. 166; Schulregeln um 1560-61.

[3] Monumenta Germaniæ Pædagogica, vol. ix, p. 145.

judgment of the boys; also the ways of men, the punishments of the wicked, the maxims of sages. Some part of an historical author should be given sometimes for their written exercise, to translate into the mother tongue; or it may be added, as an appendix, to a shorter theme. Let the boys hold a discussion among themselves upon the merits of the translation; they can write in that narrative style, to win the best places in class; as also, at the close of the year, for the premiums. However, the whole time of class is not to be taken up by such translations, as happens sometimes with negligent Masters, who shirk the labor of the prelection, and of the correction of themes. While the boys dispute among themselves on the precepts of grammar, poetry, or eloquence, one stands against many, or several against several. The subject, time, and manner of the *concertatio* is to be defined beforehand; umpires and judges are to be appointed, prizes for the victors, penalties for the vanquished. The others, who are merely listening during the contest, will show in writing what fruit they have derived from it, or will be asked questions thereupon." [1]

In the following article,[2] the same writer gives several specimens of a prelection in Cicero, Virgil, Phædrus, as adapted to the different classes. They are only passages. The whole of this system goes by passages, taken consecutively, until a whole piece has been mastered by the students. For it is in the prior perfection of detail that perfection in a larger

---

[1] Jouvancy, Ratio Docendi; c. De interpretatione vernacula, etc.
[2] Modus explicandæ prælectionis.

compass is attained. And we may also note that it is only in the original productions of perfect Masters in style, that detail can ever be adequately studied. The understanding and enjoyment of an entire masterpiece, taken as a whole, is by every law of nature and of art an easy resultant of understanding the parts. If any writers on pedagogy have thought that no student could "understand and take pleasure" in an original classic, and therefore have advocated the reading of translations as a means of receiving the "literary impressions," I fear that we need only point to the style of literary writing which seems to have resulted from doing things in this second-hand fashion — if indeed it is even second-hand. For, after all, style itself never appears in a translation; only the thoughts are translated. Thoughts are the soul of style; its expression was the body; each fitted the other in the classic original; and, in an eminent mutual fitness, an eminent style was being studied. The best translation of a classic piece has never done more than produce a bare equivalent. Wherefore, if with the striking original no thorough work has been done, it is more than probable that, in the results, nothing original and striking will ever be done.

This system of prelection, which in addition to the perfection of its *technique*, required erudition from every branch of learning,[1] made of the Professor anything but a technical pedagogue. Voltaire noticed it, speaking of his own Professor. "Nothing will efface from my heart," he wrote to Père de la Tour, Rec-

[1] Eruditio ex omni doctrina, Reg. Prof. Rhet., n. 1; ex omni eruditione, ibid., n. 8.

tor of the Collège Louis-le-Grand, "the memory of Father Porée, who is equally dear to all that studied under him. Never did man make study and virtue more amiable. The hours of his lessons were delicious hours to us. And I should have wished that it was the custom at Paris, as it used to be at Athens, that one, at any age, could listen to such lectures. I should often go to hear them. I have had the good fortune to be formed by more than one Jesuit of the character of Père Porée, and I know that he has successors worthy of him."[1]

The productions of such Professors replenished the literature of the classics, as we may see in the great editions, or *bibliothecæ classicæ*, published during the present century. Father De la Cerda of Toledo, in his three folio volumes on Virgil, in 1617, gave to literature an encyclopædia of political and moral observations, including geography, history, and the natural sciences.[2] His technical work was not inferior; for his "Grammatical Institutions" became in 1613, by an exclusive privilege, the standard of all the public schools in Spain. Father Nicholas Abram, whose "Epitome of Greek Precepts in Latin Verse" went through fifty editions in twenty-two years, published in 1632, while Professor at the College of Pont-à-Mousson, two volumes octavo on Virgil, which were then republished constantly at Rouen, Paris, Toulouse, Poitiers, Lyons, etc.[3] Undertaking the same

---

[1] Lettre 7 fevrier, 1746; Œuvres, t. viii, p. 1127; edit. 1817.

[2] De Backer, Bibliothèque des Écrivains de la Compagnie, *sub voce, Cerda*.

[3] Sommervogel, Bibliothèque de la Compagnie, *sub voce, Abram*.

labor, in behalf of Cicero, he issued two volumes folio, "by which John George Grævius profited in his edition of Cicero, Amsterdam, 1699; as well as the editor of Cambridge, whose work appeared in 1699, 1710, and 1717."[1] Father De la Rue's (Carolus Ruæus) Delphin Virgil is a familiar work in France, Holland, England; so, too, De Merouville's Delphin edition of Cicero, which was often reproduced at Cambridge, London, Dublin, etc. The same we see with regard to Sanadon on Horace, Brumoy's great work on the Greek Drama, René Rapin's various critical and poetical works; and so of the rest. Of Père Rapin's thirty-five works, there are few which were not translated into various European languages; and Oxford, London, Cambridge, have been among the most active centres of republication, or translation into English.[2]

4. This chapter, which has extended beyond the usual limits, cannot close better than with a word on books, a matter intimately connected with its subject. The Fathers of 1586 set down some principles with regard to the proper supply and use of books, as well as the expurgation of the classical standard works;[3] and accordingly the *Ratio* of 1599 ordains that "the students are neither to be without useful books, nor to abound in useless ones."[4] A multitude is considered useless, because "it oppresses the mind, and interferes with the convenient preparation of the lesson. Of books by more recent authors few are to be allowed,

---

[1] Sommervogel, ibid.   [2] De Backer, *sub voce, Rapin.*

[3] Rt. St. 1586, c. 8, De Libris; Monumenta Germaniæ Pædagogica, vol. v, p. 178.

[4] Reg. Præf. Stud., n. 29; Monumenta Germaniæ Pædagogica, p. 284.

and those very carefully selected." Yet, "a variety of authors gives a richer vein to the boys, and makes imitation easier."[1] Here the Fathers proceed to give directions for the composition of an entirely new kind of work, which would be of great use in the colleges. It is exactly the species so well known in our days under the various titles of "Precepts of Rhetoric," "Art of Composition," etc. As the development of pedagogical literature, which we took note of in a former chapter,[2] had already made some progress, the critics say: "Some one most versed in all these matters should be deputed to gather whatever is best in this line, and to compile in one treatise, written in an elegant style, all that he has selected, about the art of writing epigrams, elegies, odes, eclogues, *sylvæ* (that is, materials, "objects"), comedies, tragedies, epopœiæ, a brief method of chronology; explaining also what is the historical (or narrative) style, the poetic, the epistolary, the different kinds of speaking, and other such matters, all to be illustrated by examples."[3] Elsewhere they call for a similar work of a higher order, on the Art of Oratory. The sources which they designate for such a compilation are "the numerous publications of our Professors of Rhetoric, as well on the art itself, as on classical orations."[4] These *compendia*, or text-books, were a new idea in education.

[1] Ibid., p. 179.
[2] Ch. xi, above, p. 164 *seq*.
[3] Monumenta Germaniæ Pædagogica, vol. v, p. 180.
[4] Rt. St. 1586, Class. Rhet., pp. 197-8.

CHAPTER XVI.

THE CLASSICAL LITERATURES. SCHOOL MANAGEMENT AND CONTROL.

The subject of Literary Exercises and School Management is treated in such a manner by the critics of 1586, that justice could be done to it, only by transcribing, word for word, the several chapters of the preliminary *Ratio*. As that is impossible, within the limits of space remaining, I shall endeavor to trace the outline.

1. There is one fundamental point, however, which should be touched on, to meet a latent query in the mind. It refers to the kind of education projected throughout. It is evidently not a special training which is contemplated; not the training of specialists, or technical students. All through the system, the field of pedagogical activity is that of a general culture; and, therefore, properly an education. The result aimed at is a general one, that of developing in the young mind all fundamental qualities; of adjusting it, by the early development of all natural fitnesses, to any special work of thought and labor in the mature life of the future. It would lay a solid substructure, in the whole mind and character, for any superstructure of science, professional and special; also for the entire building up of moral life, civil and

religious. That such a general culture should go before the special seems to be obvious. To supplant it by the special, or even to abridge the process, is not only to sacrifice the general culture; it has a more serious effect than that. By a false economy, it cramps, curtails, and reduces to the smallest proportions whatever possibilities existed of general and special qualifications in the youthful mind. Without a broad, radical formation below, the amplitude of organic growth above must necessarily fall short; the roots underneath not having shot out, the development above is wanting in vigor, to ramify according to its environment, and use its opportunities. In a boy's mind, there is needed a suppleness of general powers, as only the young mind can be made supple, while at the same time it is preëminently apt to be general. It is what Seneca calls *curiosum ingenium*, "an inquisitive genius," open to everything, and prying to open everything. Memory is then at its flourishing stage, ready to be cultivated throughout the extent of a potential vastness, which will never again be experienced in life. If cultivated richly in its season, it will be capable afterwards of every kind of ready yield, according to its acquired tenacity, and according to the richness of the seed deposited in it. The imagination, too, is at the stage of impressionable and vital expansion, and is keenly sensitive to the lights and shades of objective life. These are either brought under its observation, or, better still, are pictured for it in beautiful literature; since the fine fancy of great minds paints nature, as nature herself is not found dressed at every one's door. The opening judgment also is receptive of the thoughts and wisdom, which other minds have thought out and handed down, encasing it, as they did so, in a style worthy of their own vigor, and presenting it as the heritage of the past to the present, of the wise old age of the world to its youth, which may be wiser still. And thus in each individual youth, the judgment being tenderly nursed, and learning ripening with age, what was before in the memory passes gradually into the whole character and competency of the man.

In the system which we are considering, the instrument employed for working these effects is a literature in the hands of a competent teacher; it is a great literature, and a double one. The great literatures of Rome and Greece have always been considered adequate instruments of universal culture. Under a literary aspect, the eloquence and poetry of Greece had been the mistress of Roman excellence. Under a philological aspect, the Latin tongue has been the principal basis of our modern languages, as formed in the history of Christendom. In both of them, the varied elements of richest thought are brought into contact with the undeveloped, but developing nature of the youth; glimpses of human life, individual, social, and political, favor his inquiring eyes, and lead him to feel the finest springs of human sentiment. Better still, he feels these springs as touched by the greatest masters of expression; and he conceives thought as rendered in a style worthy of the greatest thinkers; and that, in languages, one of them the most delicately organized, the other perhaps the most systematically elaborated, of all tongues living or extinct. And, besides, these two literatures come down to us, bearing in their own right what no other tongues can convey. Not as translations, which, in their best form, exhibit only a respectable degree of mendicancy, and represent other men's living thoughts in a decent misfit, these two literatures come down to us bearing in their own right all the historic memories of antiquity, as well sacred as profane; all the masterpieces of eloquence and poetry, belonging to no less than two out of the very few great epochs, those of Pericles and Augustus; all human philosophy, from Socrates, Plato, and Aristotle, down to St. Thomas Aquinas, and, further down, to Leibnitz and Newton, both of them men of classical letters; in fine, all the traditions, the Faith, and Divinity of Christendom.

To these considerations we may add one more characteristic of the classical literatures, as instruments in the class-room, and we shall have seen enough on our present topic, to understand the theory which underlies the *Ratio Studiorum*. These tongues are dead. They are not the language of common life. They are not picked up by instinct, and without reflection. Everything has to be learned by system, rule, and formula. The relations of grammar and logic must be attended to with deliberation. Thought and judgment are constantly exercised in assigning the exact equivalents of the mother tongue for every phrase of the original. The coincidence of construction is too little, the community of idiomatic thought too remote, for the boy's mind to catch at the idea, by force of that preëstablished harmony which exists among most modern tongues. Only the law of thought and logic guides him, with the assistance of a teacher to lead the way, and reassure his struggling conception.

And when, in the last instance, the boy comes to write and to speak the language so learned, and quickens it, though dead, with the very life of actual speech which makes modern languages live, we have the supreme test and proof of successful toil, that which consists in the power to reproduce. We have also the very specific advantage, in this case, that the toil has been of the most valuable kind; it has been personal labor, spent in the freshness of life on complete self-culture. For that great law of all success in life, personal labor, has been honored in the most remunerative way, by cultivating memory, exercising judgment, and acquiring in the same thoughtful, reflective manner two languages together, Latin and the mother tongue, Greek and the mother tongue, each systematically helping the others by analogy and contrast. And, withal, what is more congenial to the young than letters, language, talk?

As to the working of this Jesuit system, it is very much of a commonplace, in pedagogic history, that "a handsome style" was aimed at, and a handsome style was the outcome. The Scottish Professor, whom I quoted on a former occasion, states very exactly the value of this result. Speaking of the Structure of Sentences, he says: "Logic and Rhetoric have here, as in many cases, a strict connection; and he that is learning to arrange his sentences with order, is learning to think with accuracy and order; an observation which alone would justify all the care and attention we have bestowed on this subject."[1] And, in another connection, he quotes, with the approval which it merits, the Roman rhetorician's saying: *Curam verborum, rerum volo esse sollicitudinem,* "I would have a sufficient care be given to the diction, but the thoughts must be the object of scrupulous attention."[2] This latter principle, of diction first and matter afterwards, as translated into a process of educational development, assigns, in the *Ratio*, five grades, or seven years, more or less, to be spent on the acquirement of style, chiefly as to its body, or, if you like, its form; then two great courses of Science, natural and revealed, or Philosophy and Theology, for the acquirement of the same style, chiefly as to its soul, or, if you wish so to call it, the substratum of matter. From both together issues the thoroughly cultured man; as the well-known phrase has it: *Le style c'est l'homme,* "A style is the man himself." And, if we have just had occasion to take notice that two of the great literary epochs of the world's history, those of Pericles and Augustus, are made present to us by the classical literatures, it is a subject of historical verification that a third great literary epoch, the age of Louis XIV, was created under the influence of this system.

The manner in which the critics of 1586 discuss the question of Greek shows the practical eye they kept

---

[1] Blair's Lectures on Rhetoric and Belles-Lettres; lecture XII, at the end.

[2] Ibid., lecture XIX, On Forming Style, at the end.

on the requirements of actual life, and the conditions of concrete surroundings.[1] Their conclusions are embodied in a rule of the Director or Prefect of Studies: "He should not grant an immunity, particularly for any length of time, from either versification or Greek, except for a grave reason."[2]

Upon this theme there is a facetious touch in the report of the Upper German Province, which was sent to Father Aquaviva some three years after the final *Ratio* was published. The deputies say: "Some ask for an exemption from Greek and versification, in behalf of the older monks and nobles. But as the rule itself insinuates that an exception can be made, for a sufficiently grave cause, there is no need of a change. If we are facile in the matter, whether with monks or nobles, we shall end by eliminating Greek altogether. But, if one is seen to be altogether inept and incapable, the impossibility of the thing exempts him; for, if God himself does not enjoin impossibilities, why, neither should we impose Greek on such disciples." Father Aquaviva replies, "That is correct."[3]

2. Under the head of Exercises, the preliminary *Ratio* treats elaborately and minutely the literary direction of a class. The subjects are orthography, and all that pertains to it; the prelection, as explained before; the repetitions, daily themes, and the method of daily correction; the recitation of lessons by heart;

---

[1] Rt. St. 1586; Monumenta Germaniæ Pædagogica, vol. v, pp. 160–4.

[2] Reg. Præf. stud. inf., n. 31; Monumenta Germaniæ Pædagogica, vol. v, p. 364.

[3] Monumenta Germaniæ Pædagogica, vol. v, p. 491.

parsing; and the speaking of Latin. Jouvancy gives the order of the daily class exercises. And he makes this reflection: Few things are to be taught in each class, but accurately, so that they remain in the minds of the boys; the teacher is to remember that these young intellects are like vases with a narrow orifice, which waste the liquid, if it is poured in copiously, but take it all, if it comes in by drops.[1]

There are, besides, a number of aids to School Management. These are the division of the class into parties of ten apiece, or *decuriæ*; the exposition, once or twice a month, of some passage by a student, in the presence of invited friends; contests between rivals or parties; the delivery of an original piece or else an oratorical contest, every week; the exhibition or delivery of original poems; the annual distribution of premiums; the use of the stage, when "the boys can produce some specimen of their studies, their delivery and powers of memory." The composition of the tragedy and minor drama devolves, as we saw before, upon the Professors of Rhetoric and Poetry.

A general condition in the management of a class is absolute silence and attention. Besides, it belongs to the college programme to insure application, not only in school to class exercises, but out of school to private study, especially when holidays intervene. The usual weekly relaxations scarcely rise to the rank of "holidays." For the amount of time to be assigned in private study to composition and other work is part of the daily order, whether the students be *alumni*, day-scholars, or *convictores*, boarders. All

[1] Ratio Docendi, c. ii, De discipulorum eruditione, art. 3.

must have enough to occupy them, "that the boys be deterred from roaming about to their hurt." The same applies to the ordinary intervals between school hours, "particularly," say the Fathers, "on the days in summer, when there is much time in the early afternoon, before classes are resumed; and we hear the court-yard resounding with cries and noisy pastimes, hour after hour."[1]

Boys were the same genus then as now. It took all the efficacy of a benign firmness to control that element which tries the experience of every age. The German Fathers draw a graphic picture of these sixteenth century boys. They are commenting on the rule which requires the Prefect of Studies at the end of school to be on the ground and supervise. They write thus to Father Aquaviva: "Many object to this; but it seems reasonable. For, if somebody is not on hand, some one whom the scholars revere, then like a herd,[2] all in a heap, they will fill the whole place with their yells and uproar, their tussling, laughter, and jostling. Now, it is necessary to require the observance of decorum on the part of our scholars; since, if we leave room anywhere for unmannerliness, it will get at once into the school-rooms and ruin everything."[3] In this sense, a certain small number of rules in the *Ratio*, only fifteen in number, and very short, are directly presented to the students for their observance. "None of our students shall come to college with arms, poniards,

---

[1] Monumenta Germaniæ Pædagogica, vol. v, Exercit. lat. et græc., n. 8, p. 170. [2] Sicut porcelli inter se commixti.

[3] Monumenta Germaniæ Pædagogica, vol. v, p. 493.

knives, or anything else that is prohibited, according to the circumstances of time or place." Swords and daggers were part of a gentleman's personal equipment in those times. "They must abstain entirely from swearing, injurious language or actions, detraction, lies, forbidden games, from places, too, that are dangerous, or are forbidden by the Prefect of Schools; in fine, from everything which is adverse to purity of morals." Other rules follow, equally radical for those times, and reconstructive of education for the future.[1]

For, in these days of ours, we are not accustomed to see students walk in and out of a lecture room as they choose. And many other inconveniences of the sixteenth century are not usual with us. But the reason is, that we come three hundred years later than those times, and are enjoying the fruits of other people's labors.

An ascendency of personal tact and address, conspicuous in the Jesuit teachers, is usually commented upon and referred to some cause or other, in themselves or in the general organization of the Society. Omitting that, I prefer to designate one secret of control, which is full of significance, though not so likely to arrest attention. It is an insensible method of organization, making its way among the youths themselves, and subserving the purpose of general collegiate control. There were, in all, four classes of auditors, mingled together, and intermingling their influences. That of the strongest of course prepon-

[1] Reg. Externorum Auditorum Soc.; Monumenta Germaniæ Pædagogica, vol. v, p. 458.

derated. There were Jesuits themselves in the higher courses. There were boarders, *convictores*, who remained for ten, or rather eleven months of the year, entirely under the control and direction of the Fathers. Among these were whole houses of Religious or Ecclesiastics. Besides, there were *alumni*, day scholars, that great body of students originally contemplated in the Constitution of Ignatius. These, however, owing to their divided life, partly at school, partly at home, were not found to represent, as a rule, the fullest effects of the education. Finally, there were *externi*, external students, such as not being entered on the books, still attended lectures; and to this category we must refer such general gatherings as those several thousand hearers, who were in attendance for hours, before the time, at Father Maldonado's lectures in Paris, and made him go out into the open air to satisfy all. Now, besides the bond of affection which attached scholars to the Professors, there was another bond, that of their character as Sodalists. This character denoted membership in the Sodality of the Blessed Virgin Mary, a religious association which is most highly commended in the *Ratio Studiorum*, and which gathered into itself all that was excellent in the body of students. The literary and scientific "academies" were recruited only from the Sodality. Thus, by a double process, an aristocracy of virtue and talent was created among the students themselves, tending not only to the maintenance of order, but to the active development of all those qualities which an educational system most desires.

CHAPTER XVII.

EXAMINATIONS AND GRADUATION. SCHEDULE OF GRADES AND COURSES.

1. All examinations, as projected by the *Ratio Studiorum*, are conducted by word of mouth. Writing enters the examinations, only when the written word itself is the subject of investigation. Thus, in the grades of the literary course, the composition of the student, from its elementary qualities of spelling, punctuation, grammar, up to the most varied forms and species of style, comes under examination for advancing to the next grade. But even then, after each of the three examiners has inspected carefully the written composition, and consulted the Master's reports of the individual's progress during the year, they call in the writer, submit his paper to him, and subject him to an oral investigation upon it. After that, they proceed to the other branches, all by word of mouth.

In the higher courses, where style is no longer a matter of study, writing never appears in examinations. Written dissertations, special lectures, literary pieces of all kinds, composed for certain occasions, are merely a part thenceforth of the exercises incident to those courses.

To speak here only of Grammar and the Humanities, each new-comer, on presentation of the credentials required, is examined by the Director or Prefect of Studies, who "places him in the class, and with the Professor, adapted to the boy's qualifications; in such a manner, however, that the young person be rather worthy of the class above, than unworthy of the class in which he is placed."[1] It is the remark of the earlier critics, that "severity must be practised in examinations, since it is more injurious for boys to ascend a grade, when not fit, than, if really fit, to be kept where they are; and, in addition to that, if they are advanced when not qualified, they create no slight disturbance in the upper class."[2]

Into the lowest grade, neither youths advanced in age, nor boys of very tender years, are to be admitted. The plea that parents merely want the children to be in good hands is not a sufficient reason for taking them; the only exception is for young boys who are really far advanced for their years.

These conditions of age, and sufficient preparation for entering the classical course, illustrate very distinctly several features of the policy which the Society pursued. Father Joseph Calasanzio, a priest of great zeal, petitioned the Rector of the Roman College, which was flourishing with more than two thousand students, to open some schools for the unprovided children of Rome. There is a Latin word coined from the first four letters of the alphabet,

---

[1] Rt. St., Reg. Præf. stud. inf., 11; Monumenta Germaniæ Pædagogica, vol. v, p. 358.

[2] Rt. St. 1586, Ratio promovendi, etc.; Monumenta Germaniæ Pædagogica, vol. v, p. 177.

for designating this elementary class of scholars, who are not yet qualified for literature. The word is *abecedarii*. The term is employed both in the Constitution of Loyola and in the *Ratio*. The Rector declined. Father Joseph applied to the General Claudius Aquaviva. He too declined; he referred to the Constitution of the Society, which had been distinctly and in all its parts approved by the Popes. Unable to have his idea carried out by the Jesuits, Father Joseph opened his first "Pious School" in Rome, which was soon frequented by 1200 little boys, *abecedarii*. After the founder's death in 1648, his work spread into the vast system of *Scuole Pie*. In our times, the revised *Ratio* of 1832 recognizes the element of Preparatory Departments. It merely requires that they be entirely under the same jurisdiction as the College proper.[1]

Another feature of the policy which these conditions illustrate and which they also further, is that of their tending to discriminate between the right kind of scholars and others, whose circumstances will debar them from ever reaching the ultimate end of higher culture. Where circumstances are not propitious, neither is the culture altogether desirable. For what is more injurious to society at large than to have young people hurt in two ways, positively and negatively; positively, by placing them in a false environment of culture, which cannot be theirs in future life; negatively, by taking up with such culture all the time and labor which might usefully be spent in receiving a plainer education, and reach its term in any

[1] Reg. Præf. stud. inf., n. 8, § 12.

commonest walk of life? Besides, the liberal education itself suffers prejudice; for it is misinterpreted; since it comes to be estimated then by results and by circumstances which do not appertain to it. Every system should be set on its own basis, and be built up subject to its own conditions. The absoluteness of Loyola's Constitution throughout, and of the *Ratio Studiorum* in particular, throws this policy into relief at every turn.

After the boy's admission into a class, he advances thenceforward, either with the whole class, at the general and solemn promotion every year, or, if he excels, as the reports and the Master will determine, he is not to be detained in that grade, but may ascend, at any time of the year, after a fitting examination. A number of conditions, hard to realize, make this special promotion barely possible from the grade of First Grammar to Humanity, or from Humanity to Rhetoric.[1] On the other hand, "if any one is found to be utterly incapable of entering the next grade, no account is to be taken of any petitions."

2. In the philosophical and theological courses, both of which terminate in the conferring of degrees, the system of examinations for all students, who are not members of the Society, refers only to those degrees, at the time when application is made for them. For the philosophical degree, the first preliminary is an hour's disputation with three examiners, on the matter of the whole course, and that in presence of the other students. The result being satis-

---

[1] Rt. St., Reg. Præf. stud. inf., n. 13; Monumenta Germaniæ Pædagogica, vol. v, p. 360.

factory, permission will then be granted to prepare for a public defence of all Philosophy. This is the method for the solemn form of graduation, which, in the old style, confers upon the successful student, after three years of Natural Sciences, or Philosophy, the title of Master of Arts.

At this point start the three professional lines of Medicine, Jurisprudence, Theology. The last-named faculty ends in much the same manner as that of Philosophy, but with a much greater amplitude of public acts or defence, and then finally with a defence of all Philosophy and Theology together. This entitles the defendant to the degree of Doctor of Divinity, which is conferred in the most solemn manner.

There is a pedagogical history connected with the present subject, which it may be well to sketch in two stages, first, that of the sixteenth century, and secondly, that of the nineteenth.

Ignatius of Loyola had legislated in his Constitution to this effect: "In the study of Arts, courses shall be arranged in which the Natural Sciences shall be taught; and, for these, less than three years will not suffice; besides which, another half-year shall be assigned the students, for repeating the matters they have heard, for holding public acts of defence, and for receiving the degree of Master. The whole course, therefore, shall be three years and a half, up to the reception of the degree."[1] Again, Ignatius had legislated for Divinity: "The course of Theology shall be six years in length; all the matters that have

[1] Constitutiones, pars iv, c. 15, n. 2; Monumenta Germaniæ Pædagogica, vol. ii, p. 60.

to be read will be treated in the first four; in the other two, besides making a repetition, those who are to be promoted to the degree of Doctor will make the usual acts of defence."[1]

Having this legislation before them, with the experience of forty years to illustrate its working, the critics of 1586 are confronted, at the same time, with a set of historical facts, which seem not to be in harmony with the legislation. While Loyola's system was obviously the organization of education, the facts, which they notice, show a concomitant process going on, in an inverse sense, towards the dissolution of system. This, no doubt, was owing to the disturbed condition of the sixteenth century. Making an effort to bring the *Ratio* and the facts more into harmony, the critics reason in this manner: —

"It is hard to expect everywhere that external students will be content to hold their acts of public defence, only after their course of Philosophy or Theology; and that, during the half-year, or the two years specified beyond. For, in Italy, scarcely any are promoted to the degrees by our faculties, except our own alumni, or *convictores,* who cannot wait so long as that in expectancy, and who will readily slip away to Medicine or Jurisprudence; nay, they are alienated from us, and are offended at this severity, seeing that, in the other universities of Italy, they can most easily obtain the degree if they want it. In Germany, too, such intervals of protracted waiting are scarcely tolerated; and they rather think they have done something, if they have gone through a

[1] Ibid., n. 3.

four-year course in Theology. And it would seem proper to grant them a relaxation there; otherwise, the men are deterred from seeking the Doctorate; so that Germany will have but few Catholic Doctors in the future; whereas, it abounds in non-catholic Doctors, whose promotion is to be had any day. In France, too, the philosophers do not wait beyond the close of the triennium to be made Masters of Arts; they could not put up with delay, for they are hurrying on to Law. The same is the condition of things with the German philosophers, for other reasons. Therefore the Reverend Father General might consider whether he will dispense with the observance of the Constitution in the Italian and Transalpine Provinces; the more so, as the Constitution itself says that it is to be observed, as far as may be."[1]

In accordance with this, the *Ratio Studiorum* is not absolute in its general legislation, and leaves room for the special conditions of different countries. A most distinct conception of the meaning and process of conferring degrees may be had, by consulting the typical constitution of an exclusively Jesuit university, as exhibited in the *Monumenta Germaniæ Pædagogica*.[2] The third part of this document treats exclusively of the "Variety of Academic Degrees and the Conditions for Each." And it begins by saying: "As it is expedient to confer Academic degrees on those who are found worthy of the same, so the utmost caution is to be practised, lest, at any time, they be conferred on

---

[1] Rt. St. 1586, De Gradibus, etc.; Monumenta Germaniæ Pædagogica, vol. v, p. 110.   [2] Vol. ix, pp. 359–387.

such as would only bring the name of the Academy into discredit, and the degrees themselves into contempt. Wherefore no degree is ever to be conferred upon any one, who has not undergone all the tests which the customs of universities require."

Passing on from the sixteenth century to our time, an important gap has to be crossed in the educational history of the Order. It is that of the Suppression, during about forty years at the end of the last century and the beginning of the present. These blank pages signify the total loss of property and position, with a severance in many places of the educational traditions for almost sixty years, and the entire destruction of them in many other parts. Besides, like "goods derelict," the whole system of education which, by means of the Society, had passed out of a limited number of mediæval universities, and had been accommodated with a home gratuitously in over seven hundred cities and towns of a dozen nationalities, was found by the Order, at its resurrection, to be largely in the hands of State authorities, or, at least, not independent of State control. Restored, but having had to struggle into existence, under altered and unfavorable circumstances, this pedagogical system may be viewed with interest, as it stands towards the close of the nineteenth century. For this purpose I may be allowed to glance at it, in several parts of the world, under the precise aspect which I have just been regarding, that of endeavoring to complete its work of education with Academic degrees.

In the United States, it has the same freedom of action as any other system of higher education, with none of the special support which is given to organizations endowed by the State.

In many parts of the continent of Europe, the property of the Order is in an habitual or chronic state of confiscation, and the members, as educators, are legally outlawed. Education can scarcely thrive when on the wing.

In Austria, where the Society is fully recognized, its teachers are, by a cross-move, practically debarred from State recognition. To pass on their students for State degrees, it is required that they themselves be certified State teachers. To become such teachers, they must have followed in actual attendance, and during four years, the special course of Grammar, History, etc., in which their certificate afterwards will be recognized. Meanwhile, as Jesuits, they have gone through the courses which I have sketched in the pages of this essay; and they are certainly, by this time, not to be confounded with young persons, who are merely prospecting some limited field of pedagogic activity, as the scope of their lives. Hence, at this most energetic and ripe period of their lives, they must waste four years, as if they were young normal scholars, in following out some one or two lines of pedagogical formation; and that, merely to have their word admitted when they pass their students on for the State degrees.

In Great Britain and the dependencies of the British Empire there are no such harassing restrictions. The conditions for matriculation, and for the subsequent series of examinations, in such universities as those of London, Calcutta, or Laval, are quite in keeping with the American ideas of social liberality; however high and exacting otherwise may be the standard requisite for success, either in the pass-examinations or in the Honors. Nor, if special matriculation is again required in certain English universities, before entering their courses of Medicine, does that impose any special hardship. Hence, St. Francis Xavier's, Calcutta, ranks among the highest of what are called the "Christian schools" of India. To make matters clearer, I shall take two instances, one from Great Britain itself, the other from the Dominion of Canada.

Stonyhurst will illustrate the working of the State system, as coming in contact with the *Ratio Studiorum*. The matriculation examinations at the London University create no special difficulty, although the higher classes of the literary curriculum may be regarded as under a strain, in the double effort to satisfy the *Ratio*, and to matriculate at that university. After matriculation, the process is considerably smoother. To take the classical or mathematical Honors, in the B. A. or M. A. examinations, is altogether in harmony with the usual course of the Jesuit system. At once, after the B. A. Honors, a good place on the Indian Civil Service list is within easy reach. And, in general, changes made by the Civil Service Commissioners have all been in the direction of adapting their competitive examinations to the ordinary school curriculum. In preparation for the military academies of Woolwich and Sandhurst, students follow the regular school course at Stonyhurst, to within two years or so of the time for entrance; and then they merely take up their special course, designed for the military cadetship. The same is now possible with regard to the navy, since the age for entering that service has been somewhat raised. And, to mention one of the courses which are altogether proper to the Jesuit system, that of Philosophy, the usual lectures of the two years' philosophical curriculum have only to be supplemented with a few special lectures, and the students are ready for the philosophical papers of the B. A. examination, in the London University.

Montreal exhibits the relations of Jesuit and State systems in a Catholic country. The University of Laval is at the same time chartered by the State and by the Pope. The Jesuit Professors in the College at Montreal conduct their own studies, examine their students, and merely send them with certificates to receive degrees at the University.

From this history it appears, that, though the curriculum of Divinity in the Jesuit system need have undergone no great change during three centuries, beyond the usual self-accommodation of the courses to new and pressing questions, its curriculum of Philosophy has been materially affected, with reference to the general world of students. This, as foreseen in the *Ratio Studiorum* of 1586, and as referred to again in the revised *Ratio* of 1832, causes a double arrangement to be made. First, wherever members of the Order are pursuing their studies, the philosophical triennium is, as a matter of course, in full operation, and is prolonged with individuals into a fourth year, for reviewing the subjects and prosecuting them further; and this seminary course, if connected with a public college, remains open as ever to the outside world. Secondly, to meet the requirements of external students, who do not desire the full triennium, the Provincial "will see that a course of Philosophy be established according to the customs and necessities of the country."[1] Hence a biennium, or two-year course, is commonly established; and, according to the needs or desires of the locality, it is conducted either in Latin or in the vernacular.

3. Now we may review succinctly the different courses as conducted by the year, and as distributed through the week.

THE LITERARY CURRICULUM.

The grading is based upon the principles of a classical education. Other branches enter a classical course, as completing the staple studies. But, on their own merits, they receive a special distribution of their own. The Prefect of the lower studies is instructed to "distribute History, Geography, the elements of Mathematics, and whatever else is usually treated in these classes, in such a manner that each Master can satisfactorily and conveniently finish the matter assigned to him." This is to be done "after consulting the Provincial authority," which assures stability in the manner of organizing these branches.[2] As to the mother tongue, the study of which is bound up intimately with the classic literatures, a general

---

[1] Rt. St., Reg. Prov., 17, § 2.
[2] Rt. St. 1832, Reg. Præf. stud. inf., n. 8, § 11.

direction is given once for all to the Professors of these grades: "In learning the mother tongue, very much the same method will be followed as in the study of Latin." And, in the form of prelection to be used, they are to adopt the method specified as peculiar to the historian and the poet, which is more summary than the prelection of the central prose author: "Much the same method will be followed in giving the prelection on classic authors in the vernacular."[1]

LOWER GRAMMAR. The grade of this class is the perfect knowledge of the rudiments, and an incipient knowledge of syntax. In Greek: reading, writing, and a certain portion of the grammar. The authors used for prelection will be some easy selections from Cicero, besides fables of Phædrus and lives of Nepos.

MIDDLE GRAMMAR. The grade is the knowledge, though not entire, of all grammar; another portion of the Greek grammar; and, for the prelection, only the select epistles, narrations, descriptions, and the like from Cicero, with the Commentaries of Cæsar, and some of the easiest poems of Ovid. In Greek: the fables of Æsop, select and expurgated dialogues of Lucian, the Table of Cebes.

UPPER GRAMMAR. The grade is the complete knowledge of grammar, including all the exceptions and idioms in syntax, figures of rhetoric, and the art of versification. In Greek: the eight parts of speech, or all the rudiments. For the lessons: in prose, the most difficult epistles of Cicero, the books De Amicitia, De Senectute, and others of the kind, or even some of

[1] Ibid., nn. 12, § 2; 28, § 2.

the easier orations; in poetry, some select elegies and epistles of Ovid, also selections from Catullus, Tibullus, Propertius, and the eclogues of Virgil, or some of Virgil's easier books. In Greek: St. Chrysostom, Xenophon, and the like.

HUMANITY. The grade is to prepare, as it were, the ground for eloquence, which is done in three ways, by a knowledge of the language, some erudition, and a sketch of the precepts pertaining to Rhetoric. For a command of the language, which consists chiefly in acquiring propriety of expression and fluency, the one prose author employed in daily prelections is Cicero; as historical writers, Cæsar, Sallust, Livy, Curtius, and others of the kind; the poets used are, first of all, Virgil; also select odes of Horace, with the elegies, epigrams, and other productions of illustrious poets, expurgated; in like manner, orators, historians, and poets, in the vernacular. The erudition conveyed should be slight, and only to stimulate and recreate the mind, not to impede progress in learning the tongue. The precepts will be the general rules of expression and style, and the special rules on the minor kinds of composition, epistles, narrations, descriptions, both in verse and prose. In Greek: the art of versification, and some notions of the dialects; also a clear understanding of authors, and some composition in Greek. The Greek prose authors will be Saints Chrysostom and Basil, epistles of Plato and Synesius, some selections from Plutarch; the poets, Homer, Phocylides, Theognis, St. Gregory Nazianzen, Synesius, and others like them.

RHETORIC. The grade of this class cannot easily be defined. For it trains to perfect eloquence, which comprises two great faculties, the oratorical and poetical, the former chiefly being the object of culture; nor does it regard only the practical, but the beautiful also. For the precepts, Cicero may be supplemented with Quintilian and Aristotle. The style, which may be assisted by drawing on the most approved historians and poets, is to be formed on Cicero; all of his works are most fitted for this purpose, but only his speeches should be made the subject of prelection, that the precepts of the art may be seen in practice. As to the vernacular, the style should be formed on the best authors. The erudition will be derived from the history and manners of nations, from the authority of writers and all learning; but moderately, as befits the capacity of the students. In Greek, the fuller knowledge of authors and of dialects is to be acquired. The Greek authors, whether orators, historians, or poets, are to be ancient and classic: Demosthenes, Plato, Thucydides, Homer, Hesiod, Pindar, and others of the kind, including Saints Nazianzen, Basil, and Chrysostom.

The compilers of the preliminary *Ratio* throw out some very useful hints, relative to the work and scope of this class. They say, for instance, that the students of Rhetoric "are to be assisted with almost a daily exposition of some poet, to derive thence the variety and richness of poetic imitation and diction." Again, "nothing dialectic is to be made the subject of prelection in this class, since rhetoricians are to be kept as far away as possible from the style, invention, and spirit of dialectics." "Two or three years" are spoken of as spent in this grade.[1] At any rate, "all our day-scholars or boarders[2] should spend one year in Rhetoric before they enter on Philosophy; this should be brought home to their parents. The others, who attend our courses from outside,[3] should be persuaded to do the same."[4] If they still insist upon entering the philosophical curriculum at too early an age, special means are suggested to discountenance such a practice.

All these five grades are evidently so connected as not to overlap one another. Neither are they to be multiplied, except in the sense of allowing more than a single division, when scholars are very numerous. If all the grades cannot be maintained in any place, "the higher ones, as far as possible, are to be kept, the lower being dispensed with."[5]

THE PHILOSOPHICAL CURRICULUM.

With the side branches sufficiently learned, with the boy's native talents "stimulated" or "cultivated," as the *Ratio* frequently expresses itself,[6] and his memory enriched with the fullest materials for style in two languages, Latin and the vernacular, while Greek has subsidized his culture, the student enters on the study of Philosophy, using scholastic Latin as the vehicle of expression.

---

[1] Ibid.
[2] Alumni sive convictores.
[3] Externi.
[4] Reg. Rect., n. 12.
[5] Reg. Prov., n. 21, § 4.
[6] Excitetur ingenium; excolatur ingenium.

This instrument for the expression of philosophical thought possesses the qualities of subtlety, keenness, and precision, which the dialectic practice of all universities had tended to develop in it, from the twelfth century onwards. With the addition of Cicero's fulness and richness, which the colleges cultivated with so much ardor, the scholastic Latin of men like Molina, Ripalda, Liberatore, Franzelin, and so many others, has flourished to a degree of literary excellence.

Mathematics runs parallel with the course of Philosophy, and upon that branch of science there is a rather eloquent passage in the *Ratio* of 1586.[1] Physics was always included in the Aristotelian philosophy. The career of Modern Physics was then in the future. But, as in Mathematics pure and applied, the courses were always advanced to the foremost rank, and in Arithmetic and Geometry we notice that, as early as 1667, a single public course, under the direction of Jesuits at Caen, numbered four hundred students,[2] so, in the middle of the next century, the eighteenth, we find physical cabinets in regular use, and experimental lectures given to the classes by the Professors of Physics.[3] The basis of the study is thus laid down in the rules of the revised *Ratio:* "The Professor is to expose theories, systems, and hypotheses, so as to make it clear what degree of certitude or probability belongs to each. Since this

---

[1] De Mathematicis; Monumenta Germaniæ Pædagogica, vol. v, p. 141.

[2] Crétineau-Joly, Histoire de la Compagnie, tom. iv, ch. 3, p. 202.

[3] Compare the ordinance for the upper German Province, 1763, n. 7; Monumenta Germaniæ Pædagogica, vol. ix, p. 441.

faculty makes new progress every day, the Professor must consider it part of his duty to know the more recent discoveries, so that in his prelections he may advance with the science itself."[1] The general assemblies had legislated on this subject, as I indicated before; assigning its proper place in Philosophy to what they called "the more pleasant" or the "lighter" form of Physics. Indeed, Philosophy itself in the course of three centuries came to feel many new needs and submitted to new lines of treatment.

First Year. LOGIC AND GENERAL METAPHYSICS. *One Professor: eight hours a week.* Introductory sketch of Philosophy. Dialectics or Minor Logic: ideas, judgment, reasoning. Logic Proper: The criteria of truth; species of knowledge, and general rules of criticism and hermeneutics. General Metaphysics or Ontology: The notions of being and the categories. MATHEMATICS. *One Professor: six hours a week.* All that prepares for the Physics of the following year, viz., algebra, geometry, plane and spherical trigonometry, and conic sections. This rapid course, in so short a time, supposes that the matter is not entirely new, but has been studied already in the literary course.

Second Year and part of the Third. SPECIAL METAPHYSICS. *One Professor: four hours a week.* First, Cosmology: The origin of the world, the elements of bodies, the perfection of the world, its nature and laws, supernatural effects and their criteria, as examined by philosophical principles. Secondly, Psychology: The essence of the human soul, and its

[1] Rt. St. 1832, Pro Physica, nn. 34–5.

faculties: sensation, imagination, memory, the nature of intelligence and reason, appetite, will, freedom; the essential difference between soul and body; the simplicity, spirituality, and immortality of the soul; the union of soul and body, the nature and origin of ideas; the vital principle of brutes. Thirdly, Natural Theology: God, His existence and attributes, etc., as viewed by the light of human reason. PHYSICS. *One Professor: nine hours a week.* Mechanics, dynamics; the properties of bodies, hydrostatics, hydraulics, aerostatics, pneumatics; the elements of astronomy; light, caloric, electricity, magnetism, meteorology. What is not completed in this year is continued in the next, with the elements of natural history. Much of this course may have been seen in the literary curriculum. "The matters are not to be treated so exclusively from a rational standpoint, as to leave barely any time for experiments; nor are experiments so to occupy the time, that it looks like a merely experimental science." CHEMISTRY. *One Professor: three hours a week.* Inorganic and organic.

Third Year. METAPHYSICS. *One Professor: four hours a week.* What remains of the course just described, under the second year. MORAL PHILOSOPHY. *One Professor: four hours a week.* The end of man, the morality of human actions, natural law, natural rights and duties; the principles of public right. PHYSICS. *One Professor: two hours a week.* Geology, astronomy, physiology. Part of the course above can be reserved for this year. MATHEMATICS. *One Professor: three hours a week.* Analytical geometry and differential calculus.

In these courses of Natural Science, if the matter is not altogether new, as having been studied in the lower faculties, the philosophical attitude of theoretic criticism is quite specific throughout this curriculum.

THE THEOLOGICAL CURRICULUM.

As the Jesuit theologians of Cologne announced in their programme of 1578 that, while they followed St. Thomas, yet "neither all the matters, nor those alone which he treated," were to be handled by them; so, in every age, the standard adopted has been adhered to, with the same practical eye to the needs of the times. The reason is the same as those theologians assigned; because, they said, "Every age has definite fields of conflict, which render it necessary that Theology be enlarged with a variety of newly disputed questions, and, in fact, that it assume a new form."[1] In the arrangement of Scholastic Theology the *Ratio* suggests the following form: —

Scholastic Theology. FOUR YEARS. *Two Professors: each four hours a week. One course.* Religion and the Church; God in Unity and Trinity; His attributes, predestination: God as Creator; the Angels; the creation of Man and his fall; the Incarnation; Three of the Seven Sacraments. *The other course.* Human acts, virtues, and vices; the theological virtues; the cardinal virtues; right and justice; religion; grace; the Sacraments in general; the rest of the Seven Sacraments.

[1] Monumenta Germaniæ Pædagogica, vol. ii, p. 245.

Moral Theology. TWO YEARS. *One Professor: five and a half hours a week.* The scope of this course is to form Ministers of the Sacraments. *One year.* Human acts, conscience, laws, sins, the Commandments, excepting the seventh. *The other year.* The seventh Commandment, which includes contracts; the Sacraments, censures, the states and duties of life.

Ecclesiastical History. TWO YEARS. *One Professor: two hours a week.* The questions, necessary and opportune, in the history of each century.

Canon Law. TWO YEARS. *One Professor: two hours a week. One year.* Persons, judgments, penalties. *The other year.* Things.

Sacred Scripture. TWO YEARS. *One Professor: four hours a week.* General prolegomena. A book from the Old and New Testament alternately.

Hebrew. ONE YEAR. *One Professor: two hours a week.* Supplemented with one hour a week on Syriac, Arabic, Chaldaic, during four years.

GENERAL DISTRIBUTION OF TIME.

The compilers of the preliminary *Ratio* made an effort to draw up a uniform system for the distribution of time in the various countries. But the final *Ratio* preferred to leave the matter thus: "Since the variety of countries, times, and persons is apt to introduce variety in the order to be observed, and in the distribution of hours for study, repetitions, disputations, and other exercises, as also in vacations, the proper authority will report to the General whatever he thinks more expedient in his Province, for the better advancement of studies, that a definite arrangement may be come to, which will meet all exigencies; keeping, however, as near as possible to the common order of our studies."[1] Accordingly, a rule of the General Prefect of Studies prescribes that "he lay down not only an order of studies, repetitions, disputations to be observed by members of the Society, by our scholars, and by external students at large, under the direction of their Professors; but also that he distribute all their time, to the effect that they spend the hours of private study well."[2]

I shall give three sketches of actual arrangements for the conduct of the literary or secondary curriculum; and one normal arrangement for the two departments of superior education in Philosophy and Theology. The three schedules for the secondary course are taken from the English speaking world. That numbered (I), if presented in full, would read very much like the usual arrangement of an American college. It is the method more or less adopted by the Jesuit colleges which centre around the St. Louis University in the Western States. The schedule numbered (II) represents the system of Georgetown College, and of others in the Eastern States; it looks like a close adaptation of the system as presented in these pages. Number (III) is the method of Stonyhurst College, England; and to it may be referred the Canadian system, and that of Hindustan. The hours indicated in this schedule include the set

---

[1] Rt. St., Reg. Prov., n. 39.
[2] Reg. Præf. Stud., n. 27.

time for studies, besides the hours of class. The set study time, in a boarding college, may be taken to average four and a half hours a day; other hours may be added thereto, from free study time, or hours of superfluous recreation. The Stonyhurst arrangement is interesting, as being that of a faculty two hundred and ninety-nine years old, without any intermission in its career. Its original home was St. Omer's, France, where Father Parsons founded the college in 1592. At the suppression of the Order in France, 1762, the college moved to Bruges in Belgium; thence, in 1773, to Liége; whence, under the stress of the French Revolution, it took refuge in England, and opened its courses at Stonyhurst, Lancashire, in 1794.

The schedule for the philosophical triennium (Superior Instruction, B) is taken from Woodstock College and St. Louis University; that of the theological course (Superior Instruction, C) from Woodstock. In these schedules, as well as in that not exhibited here for the seminary course of Literature (Superior Instruction, A), no material difference would be found to exist between one house of studies and another in the Society.

DISTRIBUTION OF HOURS PER WEEK.

Secondary Instruction. — *Literary.*

	I.			II.		
Grades	I.-IV.	V.-VI.	VII.	I.-IV.	V.-VI.	VII.
	Four Years.	Two Years.	One Year.	Four Years.	Two Years.	One Year.
Age of Student	13–16.	17–18.	19.	13–16.	17–18.	19.
SUBJECTS.						
Classics	9.	9.	..	13½.	13½.	..
Mathematics	4.	4.	4.	5½.	5½.	..
English and Accessories	12.	9.	6.	8.	5.	..
Natural Sciences	..	3.	..	..	3.	10.
Philosophy	..	..	10.	..	..	12.

III.

Grades	I.-IV.	V.-VII.	Philosophical curriculum.
	Four Years.	Three Years.	
Age of Student	11–15.	16–18.	..
SUBJECTS.			
Classics	18.	18.	..
Mathematics	8½.	8½.	..
English	6.	6.	..
French	5.	..	..
History and Geography,	3.	..	..
Natural Sciences	..	3–6.	..
Philosophy	..	..	Two Year Course, as below (*b*).

SUPERIOR INSTRUCTION. — (A) *Literary.*

SEMINARY COURSE.

Literature........ Two Years .... For Members of the Order.

SUPERIOR INSTRUCTION. — (B) *Philosophical.*

TRIENNIAL COURSE.

Years .... I.   II.   III.

SUBJECTS OF COURSES.

Philosophy:
- Logic, Ontology. } .... $8+5$ (Disputation).
- Cosmology, Psychology. } .... $4+3$ (Disputation).
- Psychology, Natural Theology. } .... $4+3$ (Disputation)
- Moral Philosophy................................ $4+3$ "

Mathematics:
- Algebra, Geometry, Trigonometry. } ..6.
- Analytical Geometry, Calculus. } .... 3.
- Mechanics .... 9 (Three Months).

Physics............................. 9 (Seven Months).
Chemistry .... 3 (Ten Months).
Geology, Astronomy, Physiology. } .... 2.
Specialties............Outside of this Triennium.

BIENNIAL COURSE.

(*a*) Two Year Curriculum, included in the Triennium.
(*b*) Similar Curriculum, conducted separately in English.

SUPERIOR INSTRUCTION. — (C) *Theological.*

SEXENNIAL COURSE.

Years	I.	II.	III.	IV.	V.	VI.
SUBJECTS OF COURSES.						
Scholastic Theology.	8+5 (Disp.).	8+5 (Disp.).	8+5 (Disp.).	8+5 (Disp.)	Biennium of General Repetition, Philosophical and Theological; and Special Seminary Work.	
Moral Theology,	5½	5½	½	½		
Ecclesiastical History.	2	2	..	..		
Canon Law....	..	..	2	2		
Sacred Scripture.	..	..	4	4		
Hebrew	2	..	..	..		
Syriac, Arabic, Chald.	..	1	1	1		

Specialties.....Outside of this Sexennium.

SUPERIOR INSTRUCTION. — (D) *Law.*

Conducted by a Faculty not of the Order.

SUPERIOR INSTRUCTION. — (E) *Medicine.*

Conducted by a Faculty not of the Order.

CHAPTER XVIII.

CONCLUSION.

It will not have escaped the attentive reader, that almost all the history, pedagogic or otherwise, which has been sketched in this essay, falls within the lines of what has been called the Counter-Reformation; and some portion of it belongs to what is styled, in the present century, the Counter-Revolution. For this reason, if the facts recorded seem at all new, he will discern the reason. They have lain outside of one of the beaten paths in history.

Beyond the facts of evolution, as they may have appeared in these pages, I do not pretend to have found a place for this system in any plan of pedagogic development. Nor do I lay claim to the far-sightedness which may discern any posthumous development, as the legacy of this system to the world of education. Politically, its place has often been assigned to it summarily by main force. But, pedagogically, too, the day may come, when gathered to the other remains which moulder in the past, it can look down from a grade and place of its own in evolution, and look out, like others, on a progeny more favored than itself, the fair mother of fairer children; even as the old university system of mediæval Europe, particularly that of the great University of Paris, can look down from its silent and solemn place in history, as the direct progenitor of the *Ratio Studiorum*. "We, too, have been taught by others," said Possevino in 1592. Indeed, as is evident, the last thing which the system ever seems to dream of, which never, in fact, crosses the path of its intellectual vision, is that it is playing the rôle, perchance, of a pedagogic adventurer, or courting notice by some new and striking departure. No doubt, in its integrity, it is singularly the system of the Jesuits, and, in a multitude of practical elements, it embodies the elaborate experience of one practical organization of men. But, none the less, if we look down for its foundations, we pass through the Renaissance of Letters, and find the traditions of scholastic Europe; and further down still, in the stratification of history, we come to the principles of education as defined by Aristotle, Plato, and Socrates.

As to its ulterior evolution, I may designate two forms which the system has been invited to assume. Rather, I may point to an epoch in its history, at which general and universal education divided off into two lines; and, by one or other way, almost all the secondary and superior education, which prevails amongst us, reaches our present time. The principles adopted on one side, however extravagant they may have been at their first adoption and in all the glow and fervor of a new departure, will certainly recommend themselves to some. The other was practically, if it has not as yet been formally, adopted by the Order as a continuation of its old method, and as a revision in the nineteenth century of what itself had laid down in the fifteenth. I will quote, to explain one of the movements, a writer, M. Drevon, whom I cited once before,[1] chiefly because he is quite recent, and also because he is entirely out of sympathy with the system of the Jesuits. For the other, I will quote one of the latest Generals of the Society of Jesus, Father John Roothaan.

When the Jesuit colleges, more than ninety in number, were abruptly closed in France, then, says the first writer, "the departure of the Jesuits was the occasion of a noisy demonstration against the instruction which had been imparted in the colleges. A multitude of books[2] were at once seen pouring into the market, presenting plans for a new system of education, which should be more in keeping with the progress of Science and Philosophy. Men of the gravest authority, like the President Roland, did not disdain to occupy themselves with these matters, and to enter into details: 'The moment was come,' cried one of them, 'to set up furnaces, to add bellows thereto, and initiate scholars into the doctrine of gases.'[3] The reaction was so much the more violent, as spirits had been the longer suppressed. It went even beyond the just measure, as happens almost always in such circumstances; so that, says a contemporary writer,[4] children, properly instructed, ought to have become, at the age of fifteen, agriculturists sufficiently well qualified, intelligent naturalists, prudent economists, shrewd business men, enlightened politicians, profound metaphysicians, prodigious geom-

---

[1] Chapter vi, above, p. 96.
[2] By M. D'Alembert, M. L'Abbé de Condillac, and others.
[3] L'Abbé Proyart, De L'Éducation Publique. [4] Id., ibid.

etricians, without prejudice to writing and drawing, to universal geography, and ancient as well as modern history; without prejudice to the French language, English also and German and a little Latin; and again without prejudice to music and heraldry, to dancing and fencing, to horsemanship, and, above all, to swimming. But people had not long to wait before deploring such excess. All this agitation proved unfortunately sterile; and as I have just said, on the eve of the French Revolution, secondary education had not taken a step forward during fifty years. . . .

"It came to a new birth in 1808, and found itself very much where it had been, before this long sleep. Napoleon declared that the new method of the University was very like that of the ancient University of Paris; only that the courses 'left something to desire with regard to drawing, modern languages, geography, history, and especially mathematical and physical sciences.' This was progress, no doubt, and it is well to grant it. But Napoleon is mistaken, when he pretends that the new University is a child of the ancient one. It is preëminently a child of the Jesuits. For, as we have remarked, the Jesuits, at the beginning, took great care to make no innovations. They accepted, as they found them, the old methods, introduced little by little their own mode of procedure, an alteration most calculated to assure their influence and their success. The grand old University which went down to the second rank, so to say, in public education, submitted to the influence of its detested and triumphant rivals, and, in spite of itself, it allowed itself to be permeated by their methods. Hence, in 1808, at the moment when Napoleon dreams that he is reëstablishing the University, the ideal of public instruction was a mixture of the old university traditions and the empiric methods of the Jesuits."[1]

It does not come within the scope of this writer to indicate how, from this historical point of divergence, the modern practical method of instruction came to be fully organized. Each system went its own way. I pass on to the other line, or rather back to the Jesuit *Ratio;* and I will merely point out what process of adjustment it then underwent.

In 1832, Father Roothaan, General of the Society, addressed an encyclical letter to the Order. To give an abstract of it, he says: "In the very first assembly after the restoration of the Society, a petition had been received from the Provinces, and daily experience since then has shown it to be more and more necessary, that the System of Studies should be accommodated to the exigencies of the times. After a consultation, involving much labor and accurate study, a form of revised *Ratio* has been drawn up, which is now offered for use and practice, in order that after being amended again if necessary, or else enlarged, it may receive the sanction of a universal law. The undertaking was approached with the greatest reverence for a System which had been approved by two centuries of successful operation, and which had been extolled, not unfrequently, by the very enemies of the Order.

[1] Histoire d'un Collège Municipal, etc., Bayonne; par J. M. Drevon, 1889; last chapter, Réforme et conclusion, pp. 443 *seq.*

"Of the novelties which had been introduced into the method of educating youth, during the last fifty years or more, was it forsooth possible that all could be approved and adopted in our schools? New methods and new forms invented day after day, a new arrangement of matter and of time, often self-contradictory and mutually repugnant — how could all this be taken as a rule for our studies?

"In the higher schools or in the treatment of the graver studies, it is a subject of lamentation with prudent men that there is no solidity but much show,— an ill-arranged mass of superfluous knowledge, very little exact reasoning—; that the sciences, if you except Physics and Mathematics, have not made any true progress, but are in general confusion, so that where the final results of truth are to be found scarcely appears. The study of Logic and severe Dialectics is almost in contempt, whence errors come to be deeply rooted in the minds of men who are not otherwise illiterate; and these errors, by some fatality or other, are made much of, as if they were ascertained truths, and they are lauded to the skies, because nothing is treated with strictness and accuracy, no account is made of definitions and distinctness of reasoning. Thus, tasting lightly of philosophical matters, young men go forth utterly defenceless against sophistry, since they cannot even see the difference between a sophism and an argument.

"In the lower schools, the object kept in view is to have boys learn as many things as possible, and learn them in the shortest time, and with the least exertion possible. Excellent! But that variety of so many things and so many courses, all lightly sipped of by youth, enables them to conceive a high opinion of how much they know, and sometimes swells the crowd of the half-instructed, the most pernicious of all classes to the Sciences and the State alike. As to knowing anything truly and solidly, there is none of it. Something of everything: nothing in the end.[1] Running through the courses of letters in no time, tender in age, with minds as yet untrained, they take up the gravest studies of Philosophy and the Higher Sciences; and, possessing themselves therein of scarcely any real fruit, they are only captivated by the enjoyment of greater liberty; they run headlong into vice, and are soon to become teachers themselves of a type, which, to put it as gently as possible, I will call immature.

"As to the methods, ever easier and easier, which are being excogitated, whatever convenience may be found in them, there is this grave inconvenience; first, that what is acquired without labor adheres but lightly to the mind, and what is summarily gathered in is summarily forgotten; secondly, and this, though not adverted to by many, is a much more serious injury, almost the principal fruit of a boy's training is sacrificed, which is, accustoming himself from an early age to serious application of mind, and to that deliberate exertion which is required for hard work.

"In some points, however, which do not concern the substance of education, the necessities of our times require us to modify the practice of our predecessors.

[1] **Ex omnibus aliquid: in toto nihil.**

And to consult the requirements of such necessities, far from being alien to our principles, is altogether in keeping with the Institute.

"In the superior courses, how many questions are there which formerly never entered into controversy, which now are vehemently assaulted, and must be established by solid arguments, lest the very foundations of truth be sapped! Therefore the questions which are alive call for special discussion, solution, refutation.

"In Physics and Mathematics we must not prove false to the traditions of the Society, by neglecting these courses which have now mounted to a rank of the highest honor. If many have abused these sciences to the detriment of religion, we should be so much the farther from relinquishing them on that account. Rather, on that account, should the members of the Order apply themselves with the more ardor to these pursuits and snatch the weapons from the hands of the foe, and with the same arms, which they abuse to attack the truth, come forward in its defence. For truth is always consistent with itself, and in all the sciences it stands erect, ever one and the same; nor is it possible that what is true in Physics and Mathematics should contradict truth of a higher order.

"Finally, in the method of conducting the lower studies, some accessory branches should have time provided for them, especially the vernacular tongues and literatures. But the study of Latin and Greek letters must always remain intact and be the chief object of attention. As they have always been the principal sources, exhibiting the most perfect models of literary beauty in precept and style, so are they still. And, if they were kept more before the eyes and mind, we should not see issuing from the press, day after day, so many productions of talented men, with a diction and style no less novel and singular, than are the thoughts and opinions to which they give expression. The commonalty regard them with admiring awe and stupor; but men of knowledge and correct taste look with commiseration and grief on these unmistakable signs of an eloquence, no less depraved than the morals of the times.

"The adaptation of the *Ratio Studiorum*, therefore, means that we consult the necessities of the age so far as not in the least to sacrifice the solid and correct education of youth."[1]

This is the substance of a document not unworthy of the letters and ordinances in behalf of education, issued by a long line of experienced and learned judges in the art of training youth. The modifications made in the old *Ratio* have been few; and I have taken note of them in the preceding analysis.

So then the edifice of the past stands, with the latest modifications introduced into its façade by the spirit of the present. As the monumental structures which stud the soil of Europe, and are set amid royal parks or rich fields of waving grain, have been tributes of devotion from princes of the church or princes of the land, and are not only the memorials of kings or peoples, but are especially the architec-

---

[1] Epistola P. Roothaan, 1832; Monumenta Germaniæ Pædagogica, vol. v, p. 228 *seq.*

tural record of centuries; so a system recognized in history as great, elevated in the order of highest human achievement, that of educating humanity, and resting on the basis of oldest traditions and the wisdom of the remotest past, has not been the work of an ordinary individual, nor of a day. Masters in their art, and centuries in their duration, have combined to build it up, a monument of the practice and theory of generations. With devoted zeal and prudence, secular communities, and even pagans in times far gone by, had brought the stones, and contributed tithes to the erection of the fabric. But it is only too well known that Ecclesiastics and Religious men have been the architects of the monument as it stands. And they did not build better than they knew; for their structure is precisely one of knowledge, chiefly of divine knowledge, raised into a consistent theory, and honored by the most practical use. So the very first sentence in the *Ratio Studiorum,* speaking of the "abundant practical fruit to be gathered from this manifold labor of the schools," mentions that fruit as being "the knowledge and love of the Creator."

I may be permitted then to close this work by quoting their own poetry, which is inscribed on a statue of Christ. The statue overlooks a park in front of it, and the fields hard by, and the rich garden of studious youth, within the college walls alongside. Thus one inscription reads: —

TIBI · HAEC · ARVA · RIDENT · ATQUE · AGGERE
COMPLANATO · HAE · FLORIBUS · NITENT · AREOLAE · ET
PUBES · UNDIQUE · ACCITA · VIRTUTIBUS
SCIENTIIS · QUE · ADOLESCIT.[1]

And again the granite reads: —

QUAS · CIRCUM · CERNIS · CHRISTO
URNAE · FLORIBUS · HALANT · NE · CARPE
INCESTO · POLLICE · QUISQUE · FUAS.[2]

---

[1] For Thee these meadows smile, and, on the hill-top smoothed away, these beds bedeck themselves with flowers; and the youth from every clime unfolds, in virtue and in science, the hopes of Christian manhood.

[2] The urns thou see'st around breathe the fragrance of their flowers to Christ. Pluck them not, with hand unhallowed, whosoe'er thou be.

BIBLIOGRAPHICAL APPENDIX,

INDICATING SOME OF THE SOURCES AND OTHER WORKS, MORE EASY OF ACCESS.

PACHTLER, G. M., S. J.: Ratio atque Institutio Studiorum, 1586; Ratio Studiorum, 1599, 1832; and other pedagogical documents: — Comprised in MONUMENTA GERMANIÆ PÆDAGOGICA, vols. ii, v, ix (to be followed by others); Berlin, A. Hofmann & Co., 1887.

JOUVANCY, JOS., S. J.: Ratio Discendi et Docendi pro Magistris Scholarum Inferiorum, 1 vol. 12mo; Avignon, Fr. Seguin, 1825.

SACCHINI, FRANC., S. J.: Paraenesis ad Magistros Scholarum Inferiorum Soc. Jes.; Protrepticon ad Magistros Scholarum Inferiorum Soc. Jes. —— JUDDE, CLAUDE, S. J.: Instruction pour les Jeunes Professeurs qui enseignent les Humanités: — Comprised in MANUEL DES JEUNES PROFESSEURS, 1 vol. 18mo; Paris, Poussielgue-Rusand, 1842.

CRÉTINEAU-JOLY, MONSIEUR M. J.: Histoire Religieuse, Politique et Littéraire de la Compagnie de Jésus, 6 vols. 12mo; 3d edit.; Paris, V. Poussielgue-Rusand, 1851.

MAYNARD, MONSIEUR L'ABBÉ: The Studies and Teaching of the Society of Jesus, 1 vol. 8vo; Baltimore, John Murphy & Co., 1855.

THE JESUITS: Their Foundation and History, by B. N., 2 vols. 8vo; Benziger Bros., New York, 1879.

GENELLI, CHRISTOPHER, S. J.: Life of St. Ignatius of Loyola, 1 vol. 8vo; Benziger Bros., New York.

DE ROCHEMONTEIX, CAMILLE, S. J.: Un Collège de Jésuites aux XVIIe. et XVIIIe. siècles, Le Collège Henri IV. de la Flèche, 4 vols. in 8vo; Le Mans, Leguicheux, 1889.

DANIEL, CHARLES, S. J.: Les Jésuites Instituteurs de la Jeunesse Française, au XVIIe. et au XVIIIe. siècle, 1 vol. 12mo; Paris, Victor Palmé, 1880.

DE BACKER, AUGUSTIN, S. J.: Bibliothèque des Écrivains de la Compagnie de Jésus, ou Notices Bibliographiques 1° de Tous les Ouvrages Publiés par les Membres &c., 2° des Apologies, des Controverses Religieuses, des Critiques Littéraires et Scientifiques Suscitées à leur sujet; 3 large folios (see above, page 134); Liége, chez l'Auteur, A. De Backer; Paris, chez l'Auteur, C. Sommervogel, 1869. Only 200 copies were struck off; it is embodied and amplified in the following, now in process of publication: —

SOMMERVOGEL, CARLOS, S. J.: Bibliothèque de la Compagnie de Jésus: — Première partie, Bibliographie; seconde partie, Histoire. Bibliographie, tom. i, Abad-Boujart, in 4to, à double colonne, 1928 col.; Bruxelles, Oscar Schepens, 16, rue Treurenberg; Paris, Alphonse Picard, 82, rue Bonaparte, 1890.

WETZER UND WELTE'S KIRCHENLEXICON: 2d edit., by Cardinal Hergenroether and Dr. F. Kaulen; vol. vi, "Jesuiten," col. 1374-1424; Freiburg, Benjamin Herder, 1889.

INDEX.

ABRAM, FATHER NICHOLAS, 245
Academies of the Jesuits, 76
Alber, Father Ferdinand, 242
Allen, Cardinal, 57
Alvarez, Grammar of, 167
Anderledy, Father Anthony, 128
Aquaviva, Father Claudius, 52, 59, 70, 82; the fifth General of the Order, 126; creates a commission to draw up a method of studies, 144; provisional rules of, 148
Aquinas, St. Thomas, 11, 45; the standard in theology, 148
Argento, Father John, 71, 76
Aristotle, use of, 166
Astronomical observations of the Jesuits, 172
Augustine, 9
Azor, John, 144

BACON, LORD, 46, 93; his debt to Possevino, 94
Bader, Father George, 104, 107
Bayonne, the College of, 96
Beckx, Father, 128
Bellarmine, literary productiveness of, 135
Belles-lettres, 82; the Jesuits preeminent in the study of, 189
Berchmans, John, 113
Blair's "Rhetoric," 132, 252
Boarding colleges, 100
Bobadilla, Nicholas, 33, 43
Bonald, Viscount de, 7
Bonaventure, St., 11
Borgia, Francis, 24; succeeds Laynez, 66, 110; founds the Roman college, 111; the third General of the Order, 124
Borromeo, St. Charles, 73
Bossuet, 66
Bourdaloue, 106, 165

Broeckaert, Father, 167
Brouet, Pasquier, 33
Buffer, Father, "Practical History" of, 168
Buys, Father, 73, 144

CALASANZIO, FATHER JOSEPH, his "Pious School," 260
Calcutta, Jesuit school at, 268
Campano, Father, 66
Campian, Edmund, 57, 212
Canisius, Father Peter, 90; the Catechism of, 134, 242
Caraffa, General Vincent, 81, 128
Catharine II., 129
Centurione, Father Aloysius, 128
Cerda, De la, Father, 245
Chalotais, La, 44
Christian schools, 3
Cicero used as a text-book, 166
Class hours, 196
Classical literature in the scheme of Jesuit education, 250
Clavius, Father Christopher, 170
Clement of Alexandria, 43
Clement XIV. dissolves the Order, 129
Coduri, John, 33, 53
Coimbra, university at, 109
Colleges, Jesuit, number of, 70 et seq.; rise of, in Spain, 110
Confessional, the, in educational institutions, 102
Coton, Father, 66
Cretineau-Joly, M., 39

D'ALEMBERT, 4
Daniel, Father Charles, 46, 93
Daniel, G., 169
De Backers, 67, 69; his dictionary of Jesuit authors, 134
Descartes, 92
Dictation, how practised in the

INDEX.

Jesuit seminaries, 217 et seq.; objections to, by Possevino, 223
Disputation, the place of, in the Jesuit system, 198, 209 et seq.; syllogistic or discursive, 212; numerous attendance upon required, 213; superintendence of, 215
Divinity, courses in, 191 et seq.
Doctrine, uniformity of, among the Jesuits, 142
Domench, Father Jerome, 110
Drevon, M., 287
Dupanloup, 99

EDUCATIONAL system of the Jesuits, the tributes of Ranke and D'Alembert to, 4; the Revolution the sequel of the overthrow of, 6; explanation of its rise, 14; kinship between it and the Paris university, 32; defined, 43; development of, 52; as formulated in the Constitution, 56 et seq.; Laynez's rule concerning the system of colleges, 59; no tuition fees, 66, 117; system and method of, 67; number of colleges, 70; number of students, 71 et seq.; ramifications of, 74 et seq.; scope and method of, 82 et seq.; classification of, 87; grades in, 89; subordinate elements in, 89 et seq.; moral scope of, 98 et seq.; vacations, 104; ascendency of the masters, 107; law and medicine in, 116; the study of mathematics in, 127; the development of geography, history, and physics, 127; the *Ratio Studiorum*, 143 et seq.; the practice and order of studies, 152; result of, the formation of professors, 156; the literary curriculum, 158; proficiency in belles-lettres, 159; the study of history, 168; of geography, 169; of mathematics, 170; manner of instruction, 176; philosophy studied after the literary courses, 178; masters advance with their scholars, 180; the rectors, 186; the study of divinity, 191 et seq.; courses in divinity, 197; thoroughness of, 205; the use of disputation, 208 et seq.; the place of dictation in, 217 et seq.; co-ordination of the courses in, 227; the prelection, 233; study of the classical literatures, 250 et seq.; school management, 255 et seq.; the lowest grade, 260; system of examinations, 262 et seq.; academic degrees, 265; literary curriculum, 270; philosophical curriculum, 274; theological curriculum, 278; distribution of time, 279; origin and evolution of the system, 286
Expurgating authors, 108

FRIBOURG, Jesuit university suppressed at, 130
Frederick the Great, letter of, to Voltaire, 79, 129

GENERALS of the Order, 124 et seq.
Geography, method of teaching, 169
Germany, Loyola, the founder of the Jesuit order in, 114
German college in Rome, 117
Goa, seminary at, 74, 109
Gonzaga, Aloysius, 113
Gonzales, Gaspar, 144
Grammar, 179; prelection in the grade of, 237; method of teaching the classical languages in, 238; the daily lesson in, 241
Gregory XIII., papal seminaries founded by, 73
Grotius, 79
Guisani, Anthony, 144

HUEBNER, BARON VON, 7
Humanity, the course in, 83 et seq., 158, 188; the prelection in the grade of, 237

INGOLSTADT, university at, 115

JANSSEN, 118
Jesus, Society of, birthday of, 33, 34; receives its bull of confirmation, 51; constitution of, 54 et seq.; not admitted to Germany at the present day, 123

INDEX. 301

Jouvancy, 29, 127; his *Ratio Discendi et Docendi*, 162, 242

KESSEL, FATHER, 60
Kleutgen, Father, *Ars Docendi* of, 167
Knox, John, 144
Kostka, Stanislaus, 113

LATIN composition, elegant command of, by the Jesuits, 188
Laval, university of, 269
Law and medicine studied in the Jesuit universities, 116
Laynez, James, 28, 33, 54; elected successor to Loyola, 55, 59, 124
Le Jay, Claude, 33
Lefèvre, Peter, 33, 110 *et seq.*
Lenormant, Charles, 100
Literary productiveness of the Jesuits, 134
Literary curriculum of the Jesuits at present, 270 *et seq.*
Loyola, St. Ignatius of, 8; begins his education, 15; story of his life, 19 *et seq.*; becomes a master of arts, 33; his self-discipline, 36; at Rome, 40, 53; promulgates the constitution of his Order, 55; death of, 55, 119; his educational system, 56; his care for Germany, 114; founds a German college in Rome, 117; his educational policy successful, 118

MAISTRE, COUNT DE, 6
Maldonado, a double-headed disputant, 212
Moriana, 112, 168
Mathematics in the Jesuit system of education, 170 *et seq.*
Mercurian, Father Everhard, the fourth General of the Order, 126
Montague, college of, Loyola at, 31
Montmorency, Father, 65
Monumenta Germania Pædagogica, the, 75
Moral education, the, prescribed by Loyola, 102

NADAL, JEROME, 120
Netherlands, Jesuit schools in, 5
Nickel, Father Goswin, 128

OLAVE, MARTIN, 120
Oliva, General Paul, 73, 128

PACHTLER, FATHER, 63, 76
Papal Seminaries founded by Gregory XIII., 73
Parma, Duke of, 69
Paris University, the, 13; Loyola at, 25
Parsons, Robert, 57
Pascual, John Sacrista, 21
Pedagogics in the *Ratio Studiorum*, 147
Peltier, Father John, 111
Perry, 67
Petau, Father Denis, 167
Philosophy, course of, what it includes, 173
Philosophical Curriculum, the, at the present time, 275 *et seq.*
Piccolomini, Father Francis, 128, 231
Polanco, John, 115, 120
Porée, Père, Voltaire's preceptor, 132, 245
Plafer, Dr., 94
Plato, 98
Possevino, Father Anthony, Bacon's forerunner, 94, 103, 107
Prælectio, the typical form of Jesuit instruction, 232 *et seq.*
Professors formed by the Jesuit system, 156 *et seq.*; literary productions expected from, 188; in the Jesuit Seminaries, co-ordination between, 230
"Provincial Letters" of Pascal, 105

QUINTILIAN, use of, 166

RANKE, VON LEOPOLD, 4, 114, 118
Rapin, Père, 132; works of, 246
Ratio Studiorum, the, 8, 32, 52, 56, 86, 89; 143, formation of, by Aquaviva, 144 *et seq.*, 151, 152, final form of, 154, 183, 230, 235
Rectors of colleges, duties of, 186
Repetition, in the scheme of Jesuit education, 198; in the Grammar Grade, 240
Revolution, the French, 6

Rhetoric, instruction in, 89, 178 *et seq.;* double prelection in, 234
Ribadeneira, 29, 54, 87, 89, 102
Riccioli, Father, 169
Robertson, 79
Rochemonteix, Father, 80, 88
Rodriguez, Simon, 33
Roman College, the, 103 ; founded by Lèfevre, 111 ; other colleges following its course, 112
Roothaan, Father, 289
Rossignol, 135
Rue, Father de la, author of the Delphin Virgil, 246

SACCHINI, 54, 177
Saint-Yves, college of, 80
Salmeron, Alphonsus, 33
Secchi, Father, 67
Schall, Adam, 169
Scheiner, Father, 169
Scholastics, Jesuit, expected to teach, 176
Schools, the cathedral, 9 ; of study, of the Jesuits, 127
School management, 255 *et seq.*
Sirmond, James, 167
Sodalities, the, 103, 258
Sommervogel, 67, 134
Southwell, Father Nathaniel, 133
Sorbon, Robert of, 208, 211
"Spiritual Exercises," the, 27
Stonyhurst, 268
Strada, Damian, 168
Strada, Father Francis, 191
Strassmeyer, 67
Studies, Practice and Order of, in Jesuit seminaries, 152
Suarez, Francis, 112, 203

TEXT-BOOKS of the Jesuits, 131
Theological instruction, method of, 202 *et seq.*
Theological curriculum at the present time, 278 *et seq.*
Theology, scholastic, Jesuit authors in, 203
Tiraboschi, 165
Toffia, Vittoria, 112
Tucci, Stephen, 144
Tyre, James, 144

UNIVERSITY system, rise of the, 10
Urban VIII., 42

VACATIONS in the Jesuit system, 104
Verbiest, Ferdinand, 169
Vernacular, the study of, 164, 242
Vienna and Ingolstadt, the Jesuits first centres in Germany, 115
Villanova, Francis, 24, 110
Visconti, Ignatius, 3, 128
Vitelleschi, Mutius, 70, 108 ; the sixth general of the order, 126, 131
Voltaire, tribute of, to the morality of the Jesuits, 105, 132 ; and Père Porée, 244

XAVIER, FRANCIS, 33, 37, 69, 109

ZACCARIA, literary productiveness of, 134
Ziegler, Father, 170

www.ingramcontent.com/pod-product-compliance
Lightning Source LLC
Chambersburg PA
CBHW030812230426
43667CB00008B/1177